The Biggest Holiday Book Ever

Janet Dellosa
Patti Carson

This book contains favorite pages from the "Stick Out Your Neck" Series. The pages have been compiled from activity and fun books, learning activity books, blank reproducible workbooks, an egg carton book and duplicating master books.

"Stick Our Your Neck" Series
Carson-Dellosa Publishing Company, Inc.
P.O. Drawer 16327/Greensboro, NC 27416

Table of Contents

Months, Days, Seasons	3-38
Fall/Back to School	39-72
Halloween	73-106
Thanksgiving	107-144
Christmas	145-179
New Year's Day	180-181
Winter/Groundhog Day	182-221
St. Valentine's Day	222-246
Presidents' Day	247-252
March	253-259
St. Patrick's Day	260-272
Spring	273-309
Easter	310-335
Mother's Day/Father's Day	336-337
Summer	338-356
July Fourth	357-359
Birthdays	360-384

This book provides children, Kindergarten through Grade 5, with stimulating and fun activities centered around seasonal themes. The projects reinforce following-direction skills and vary in difficulty, ranging from relatively simple activities to those requiring greater concentration. Self-explanatory activities include unscrambling words, cut and paste, color codes, hidden words, mazes and secret messages. In addition, there are worksheets which can be used as fill-in activities or to reinforce color skills. Color, cut and paste worksheets are provided for the teachers to fill in directions to match appropriate skills. Lined, decorative border pages are excellent for use in thank-you notes and letters, handwriting and storywriting activities and in final spelling tests. Also included are award certificate pages for holidays and special occasions.

Copyright © 1987, Carson-Dellosa Publishing Company, Inc., Greensboro, North Carolina 27416, publishers of the "Stick Out Your Neck" and "Let's Learn" Series. All rights reserved. Permission is hereby granted, with the purchase of one copy of **The Biggest Holiday Book Ever**, to reproduce the activities in this book for use with children in the classroom. No parts of this publication may be stored in a retrieval system, or transmitted, in any form, or by any means-electronic, mechanical, photocopying, recording or otherwise- without the prior written permission of the copyright owner.

Name _____   **Calendar Cover-ups**

Color and cut out the calendar cover-ups. Glue each cover-up to an appropriate calendar date on the calendar pages in this book. Fill in the dates on the calendar pages. Mark the special holidays.

© Carson-Dellosa Publ. CD-0946

Name _____

Draw lines to connect the snowflakes in this picture that look the same. Color the picture.

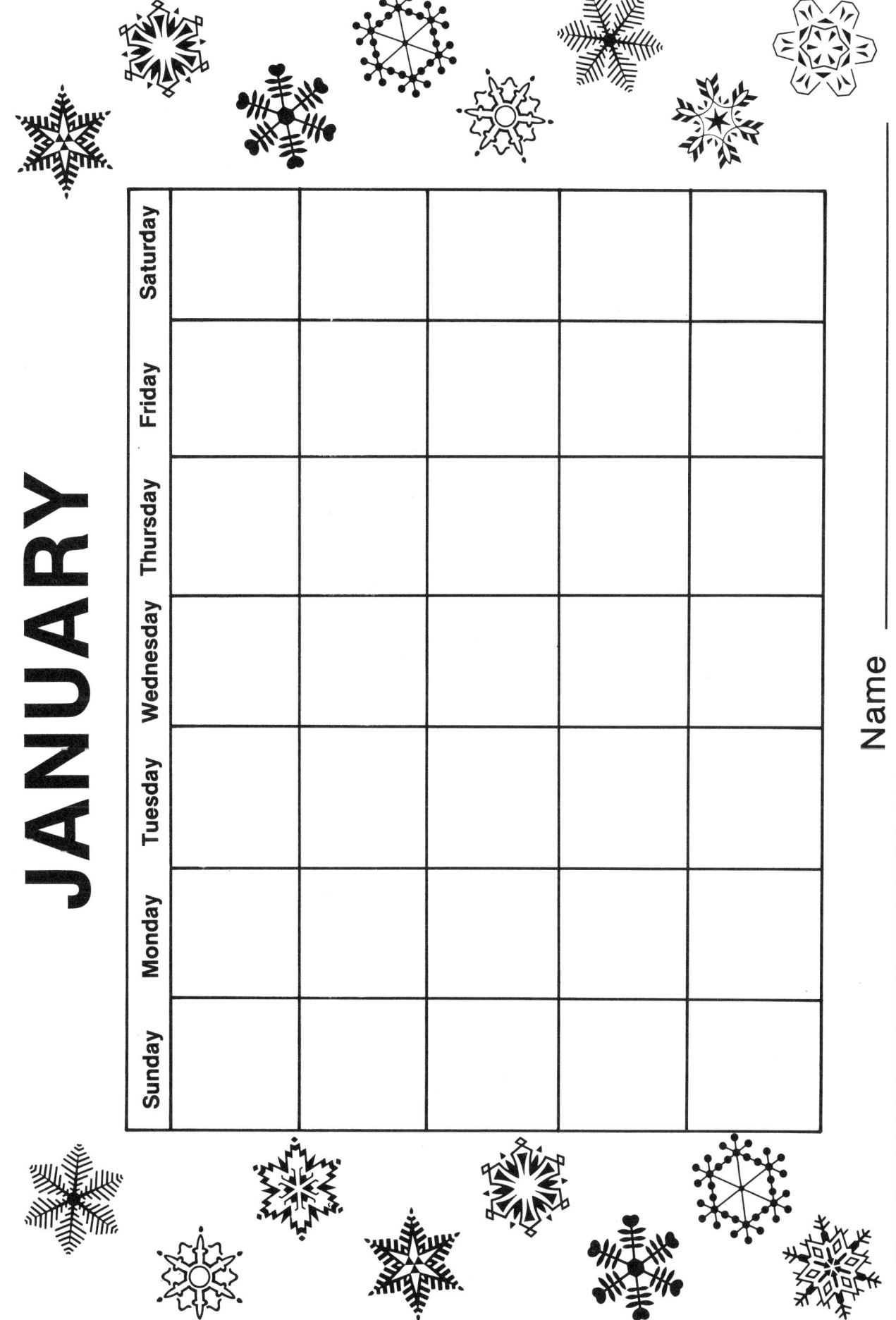

Name _____

Read the words in both word lists. Circle them in the heart below. Color the picture.

Word List
lace
arrow
friend
sweets
ribbon
roses
party
mail
gift

Word List
valentines
flower
cupid
candy
kisses
bow
red
treats
cards
love

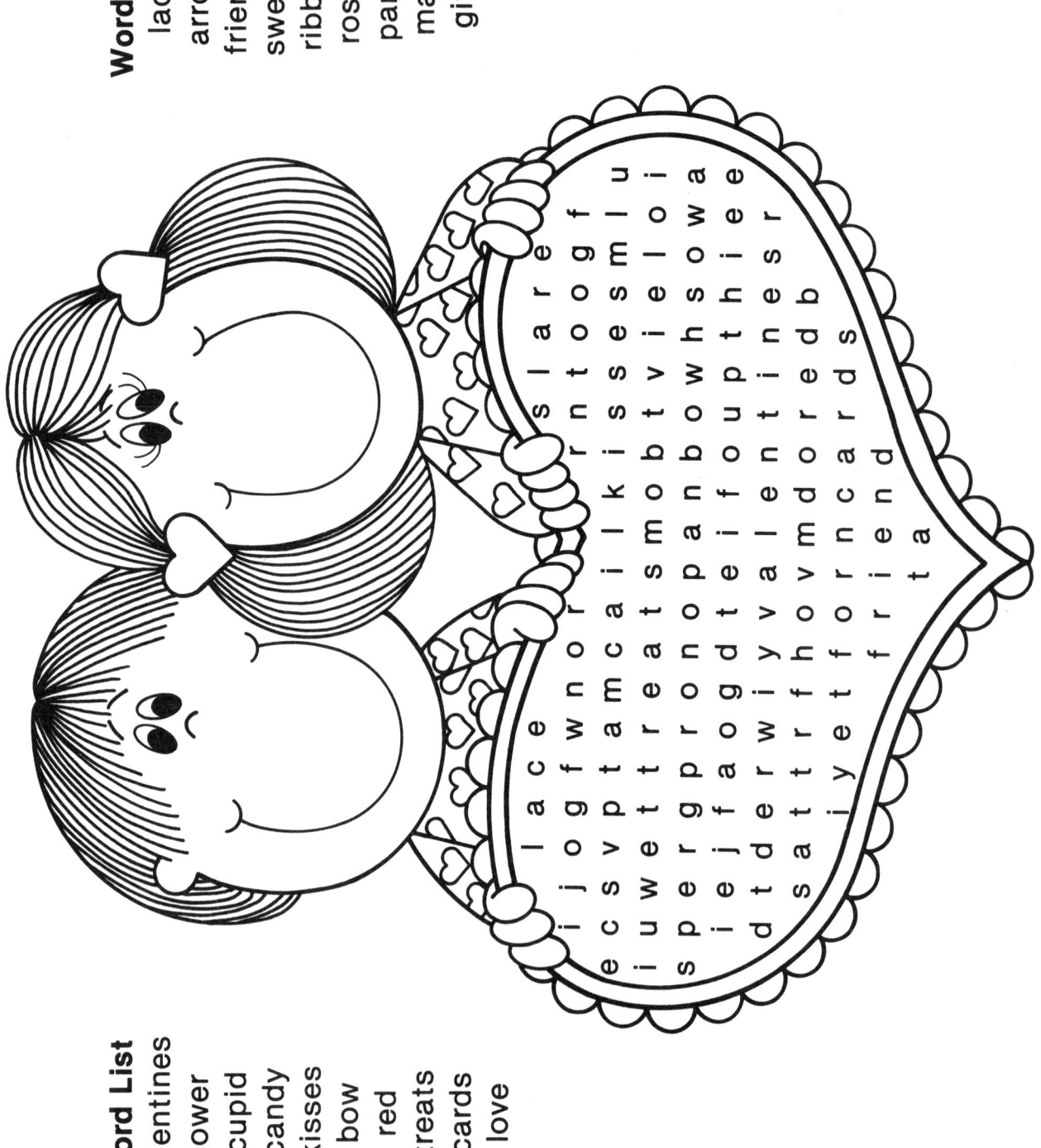

6

© Carson-Dellosa Publ. CD-0946

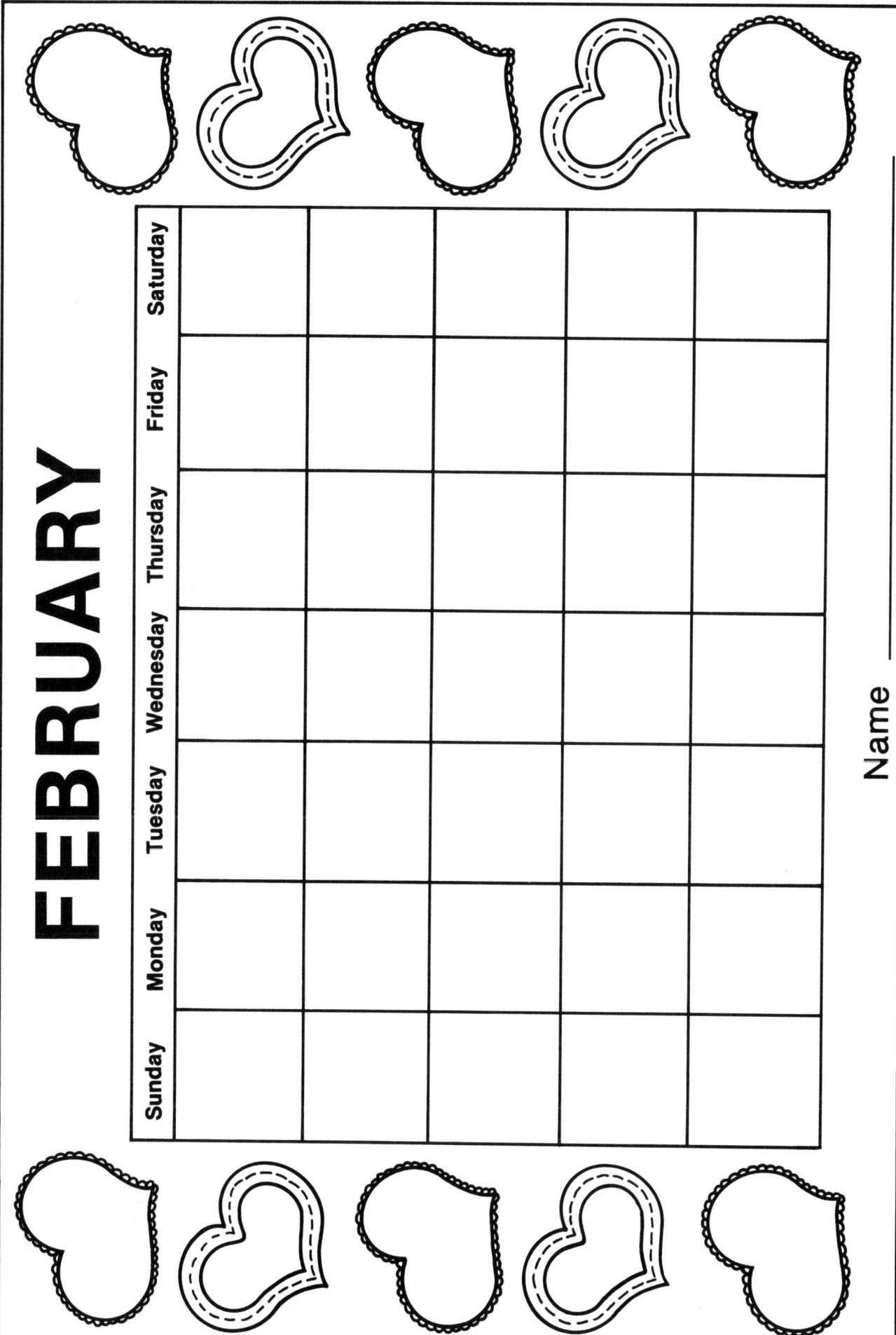

Name

Solve the problems to find the message in the secret code. Match the letters beside the answers to the matching numbers below. Color the picture.

8	4	6	7	4	16
+11	+5	+8	−4	+9	−9
M	F	O	A	K	U

10	7	13	19	3	6
−4	−6	+3	−8	+5	+6
D	T	N	I	S	H

9	8	13	12	3
+9	−6	−8	−2	+1
E	R	L	P	C

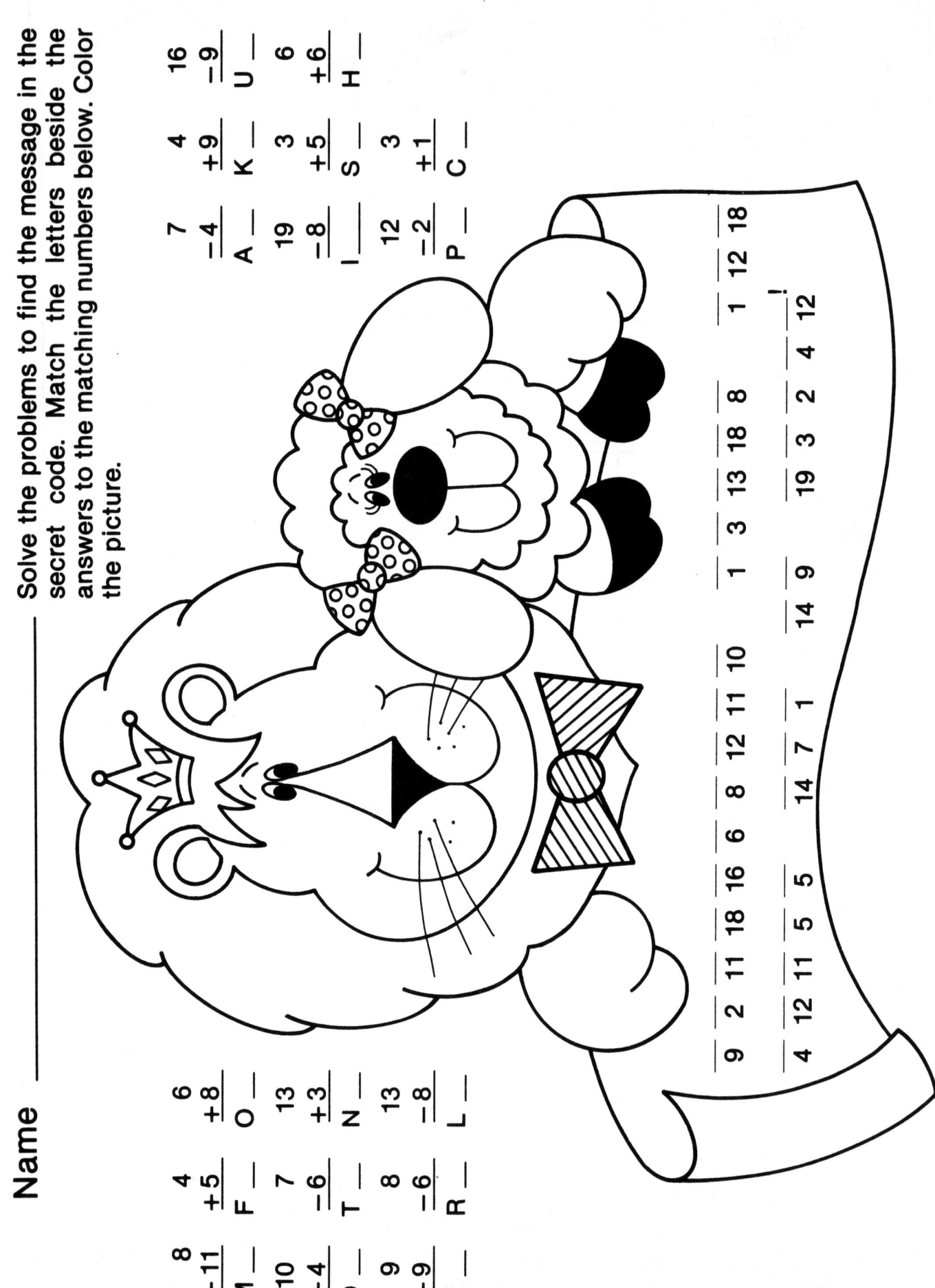

$\overline{9}$ $\overline{2}$ $\overline{11}$ $\overline{18}$ $\overline{16}$ $\overline{6}$ $\overline{8}$ $\overline{12}$ $\overline{11}$ $\overline{10}$ $\overline{1}$ $\overline{3}$ $\overline{13}$ $\overline{18}$ $\overline{8}$ $\overline{1}$ $\overline{12}$ $\overline{18}$

$\overline{4}$ $\overline{12}$ $\overline{11}$ $\overline{5}$ $\overline{5}$ $\overline{14}$ $\overline{7}$ $\overline{1}$ $\overline{14}$ $\overline{9}$ $\overline{1}$ $\overline{3}$ $\overline{19}$ $\overline{3}$ $\overline{2}$ $\overline{4}$ $\overline{12}$!

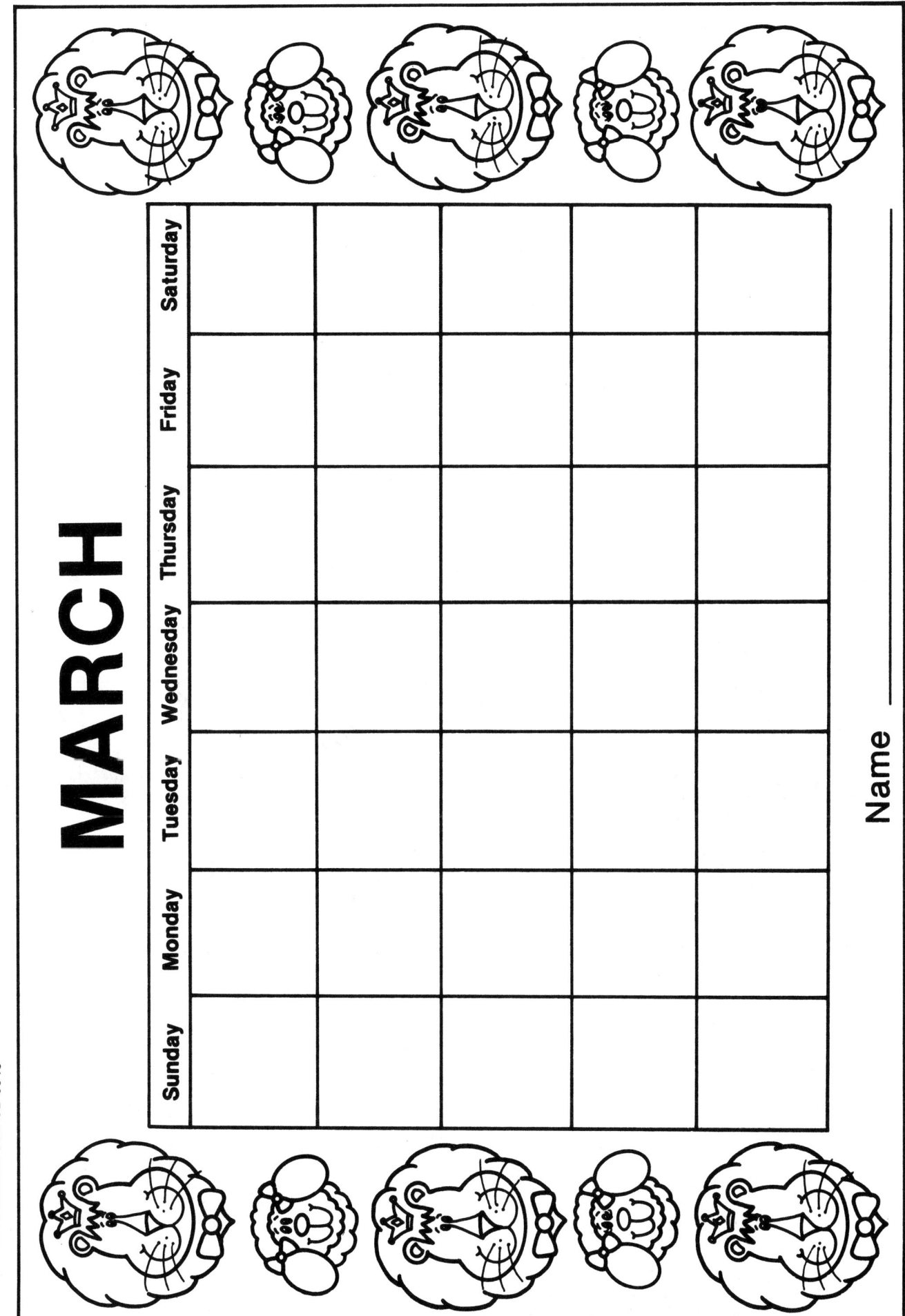

Name _____

Connect the dots.
Color the picture.

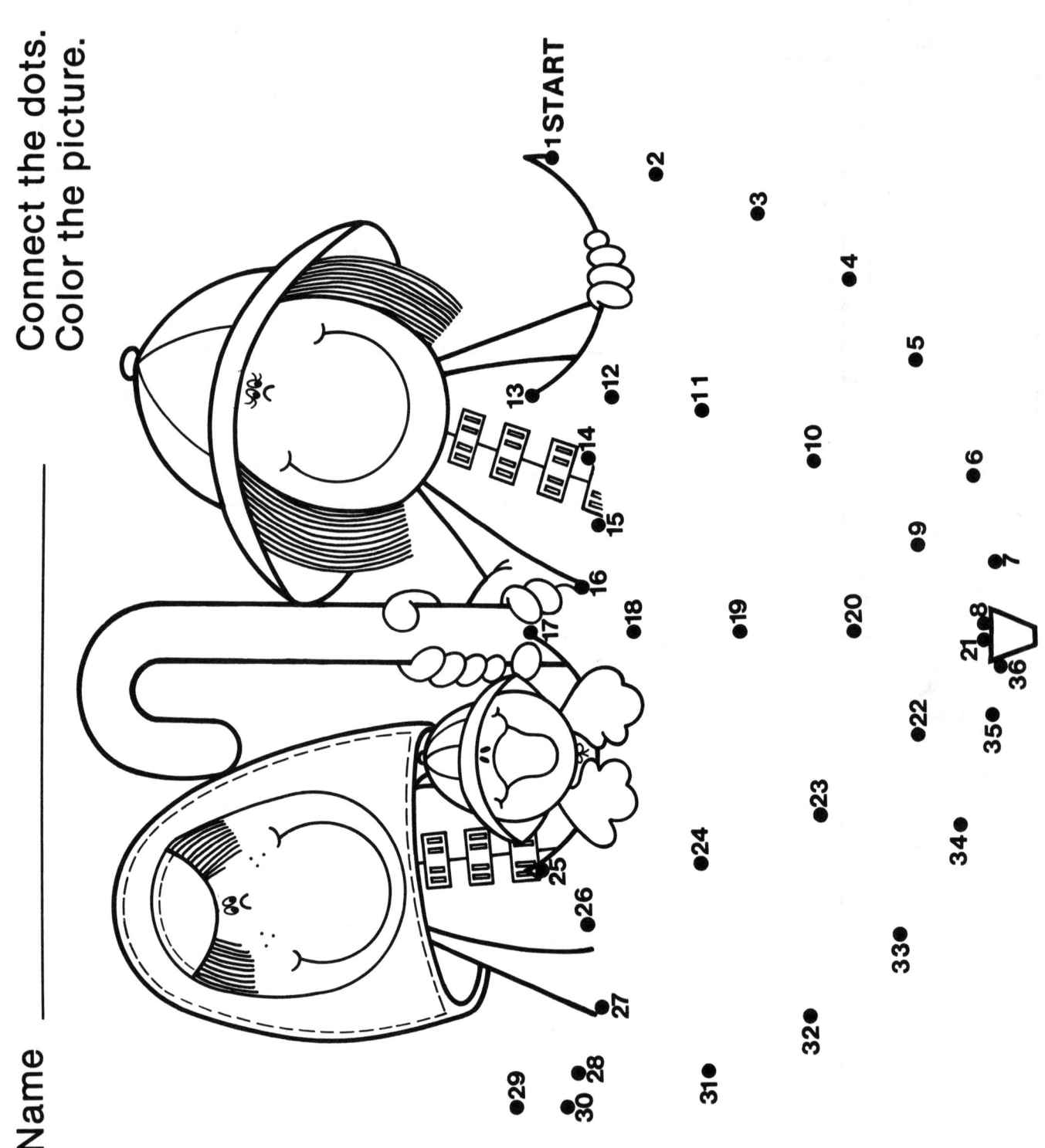

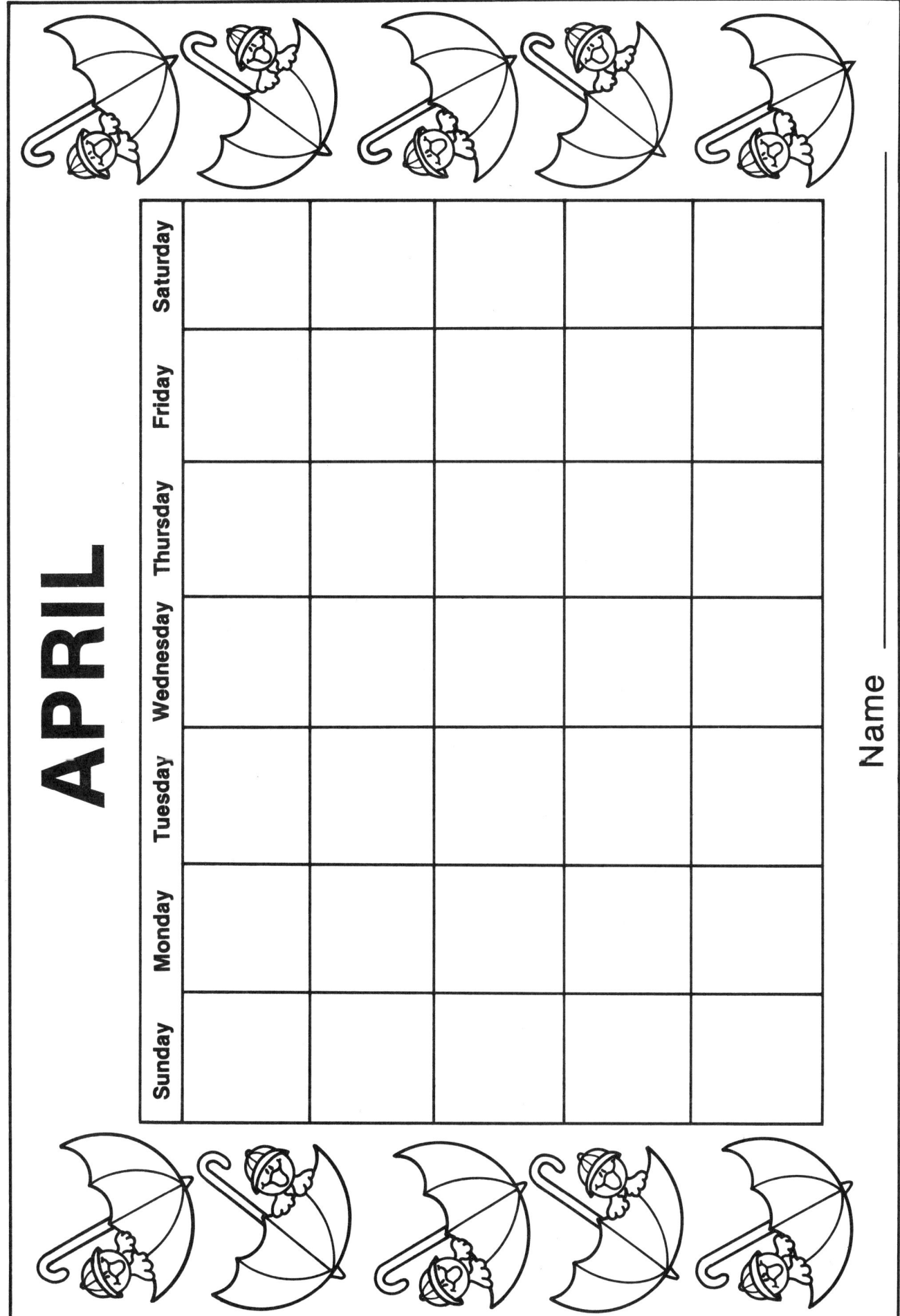

Name

Solve the problems in the lists. Use +, −, and = to find the same problems hidden in the puzzle. Circle each hidden problem. An example has been done for you. Color the picture.

Problem List

- 5 − 4 = ___
- 7 + 9 = ___
- 6 − 4 = ___
- 4 + 5 = ___
- 10 − 9 = ___
- 13 + 4 = ___
- 5 − 2 = ___
- 3 + 8 = ___

Problem List

- 1 + 7 = 8
- 12 − 6 = ___
- 15 + 3 = ___
- 12 − 4 = ___
- 15 − 7 = ___
- 11 + 6 = ___
- 7 + 2 = ___
- 9 + 2 = ___

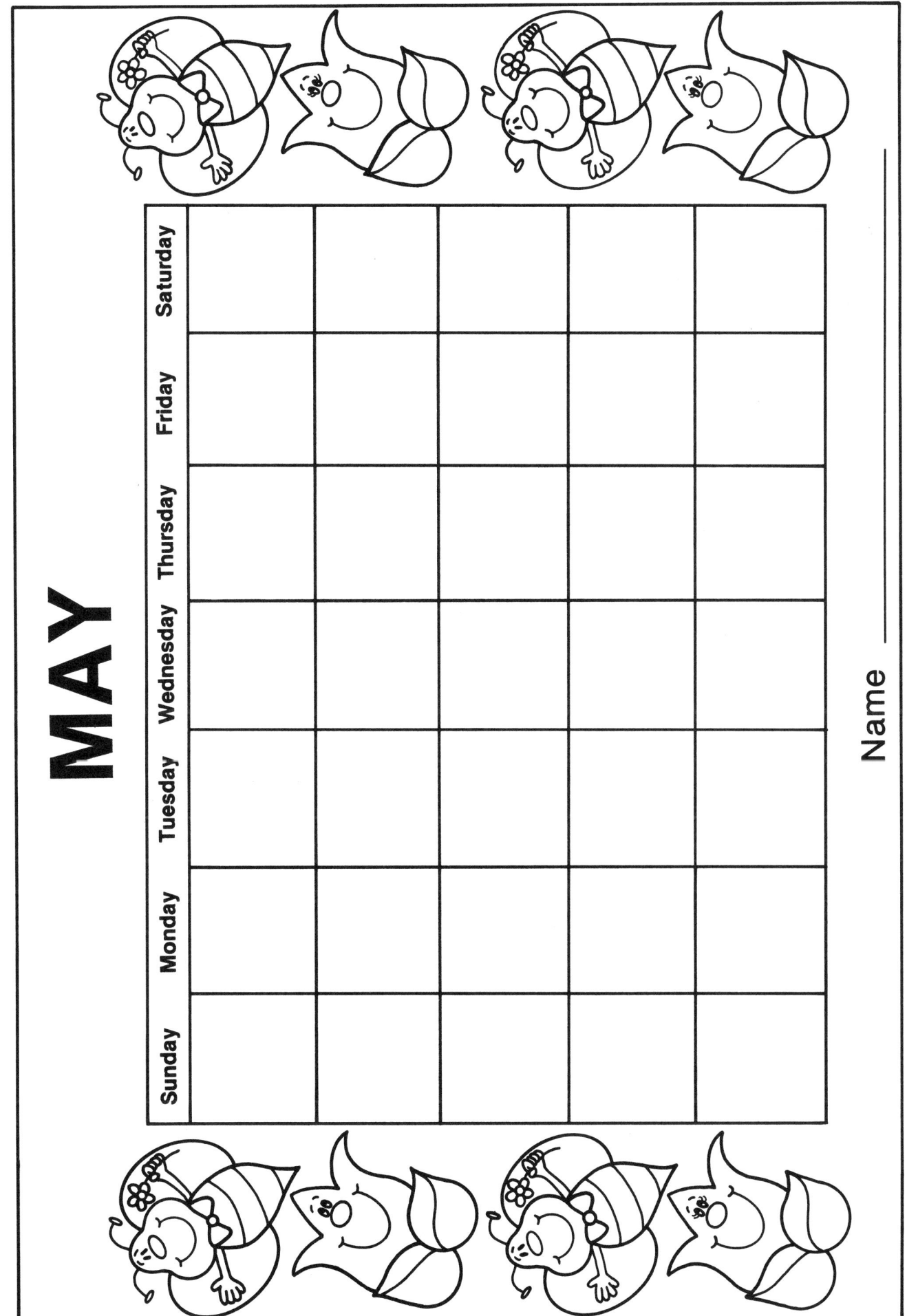

Name _____

Use the word list to help you unscramble the words below. Color the picture.

Word List
inning
catch
game
base
slide
park
bleacher
mitt
wiener
glove
score
cheer
umpire
coach
player
pitcher
swing

1. egvol _____
2. hacoc _____
3. arkp _____
4. desil _____
5. hatcc _____
6. nginni _____
7. aecblehr _____
8. timt _____
9. rumpie _____
10. yelpar _____
11. chirpet _____
12. aemg _____
13. newrie _____
14. roesc _____
15. herec _____
16. ginsw _____
17. seba _____

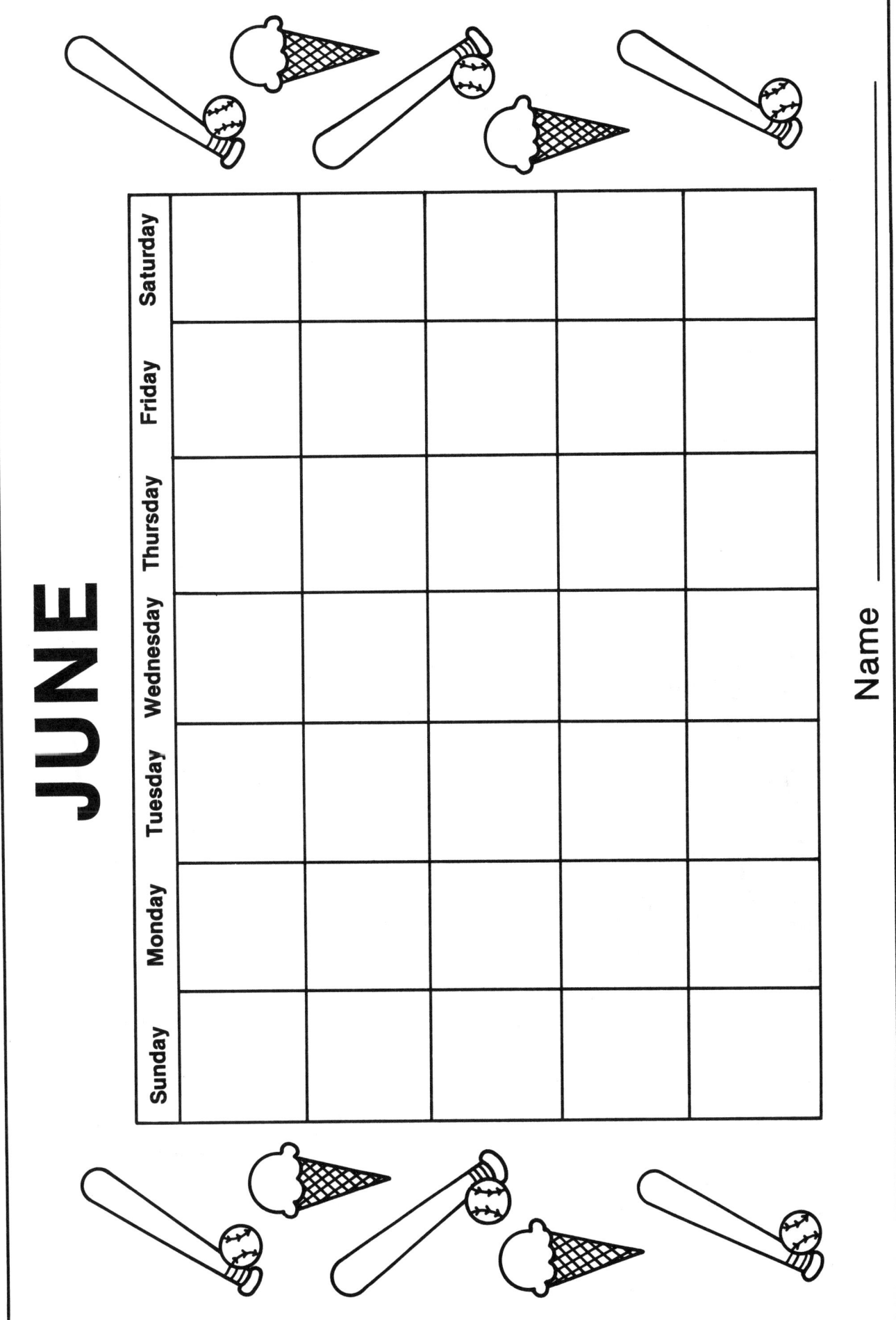

Name

Match the letters to the numbers. Use the code to help you find the secret message below. Color the picture.

Code

P = 18 B = 12 I = 1
A = 3   H = 13 U = 4
T = 5   D = 16 O = 6
S = 14 R = 8   Y = 11
N = 17

_ _ , _ _ _ _
1 5 14   6 4 8   17 3 5   1 6 17 14

_ _ _ _ _ _ _ _ _ _ _ ,
12 1 8 5 13 16 3 11   14 13 6 4 5

_ _ _ _ _ _ _ _ _ _ !
13 1 18   13 1 18   13 6 6 8 3 11

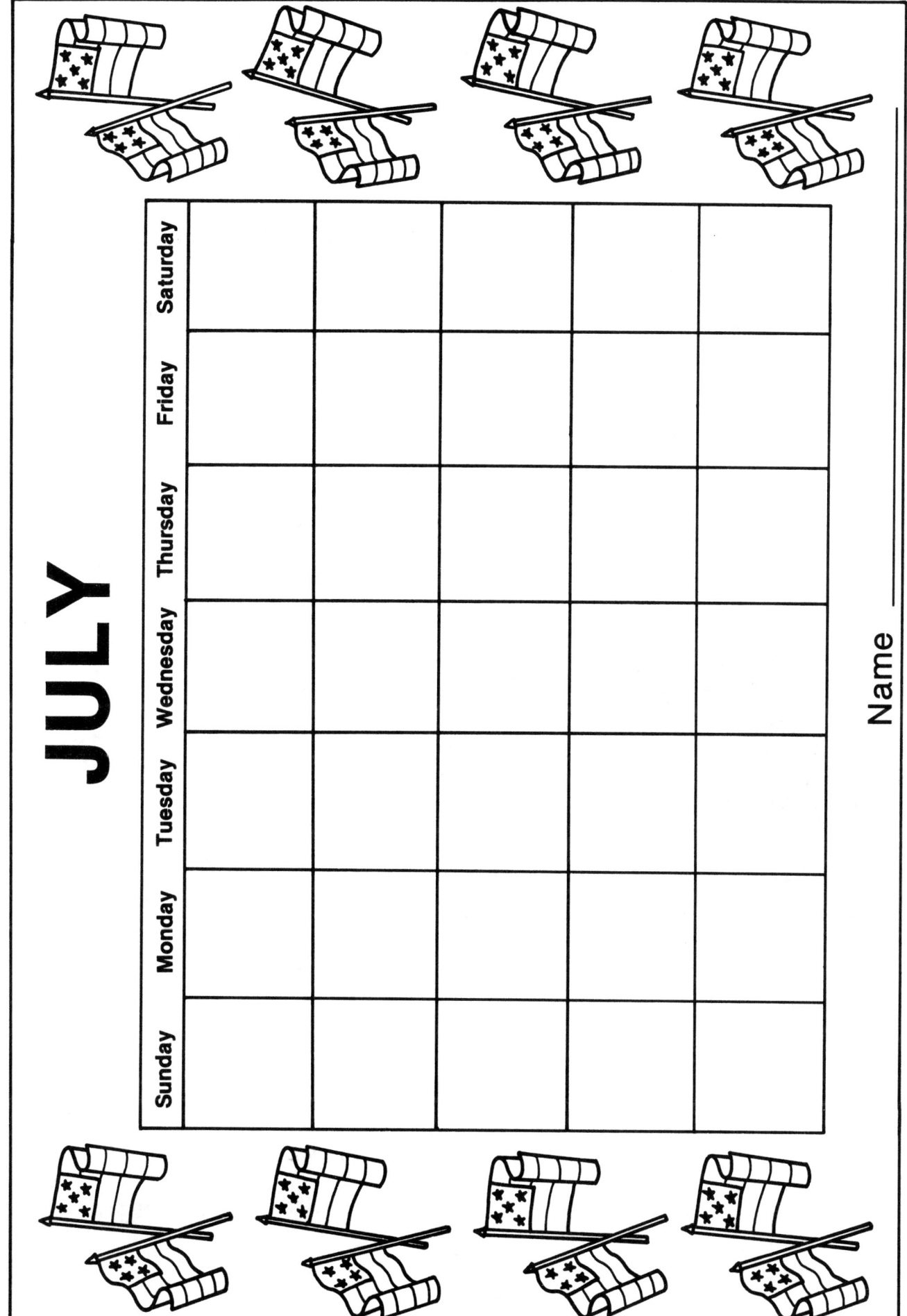

Name _____

Name _____

Follow the path through the maze to help Sandy Beach find his friend Shelley Shore. Color the picture.

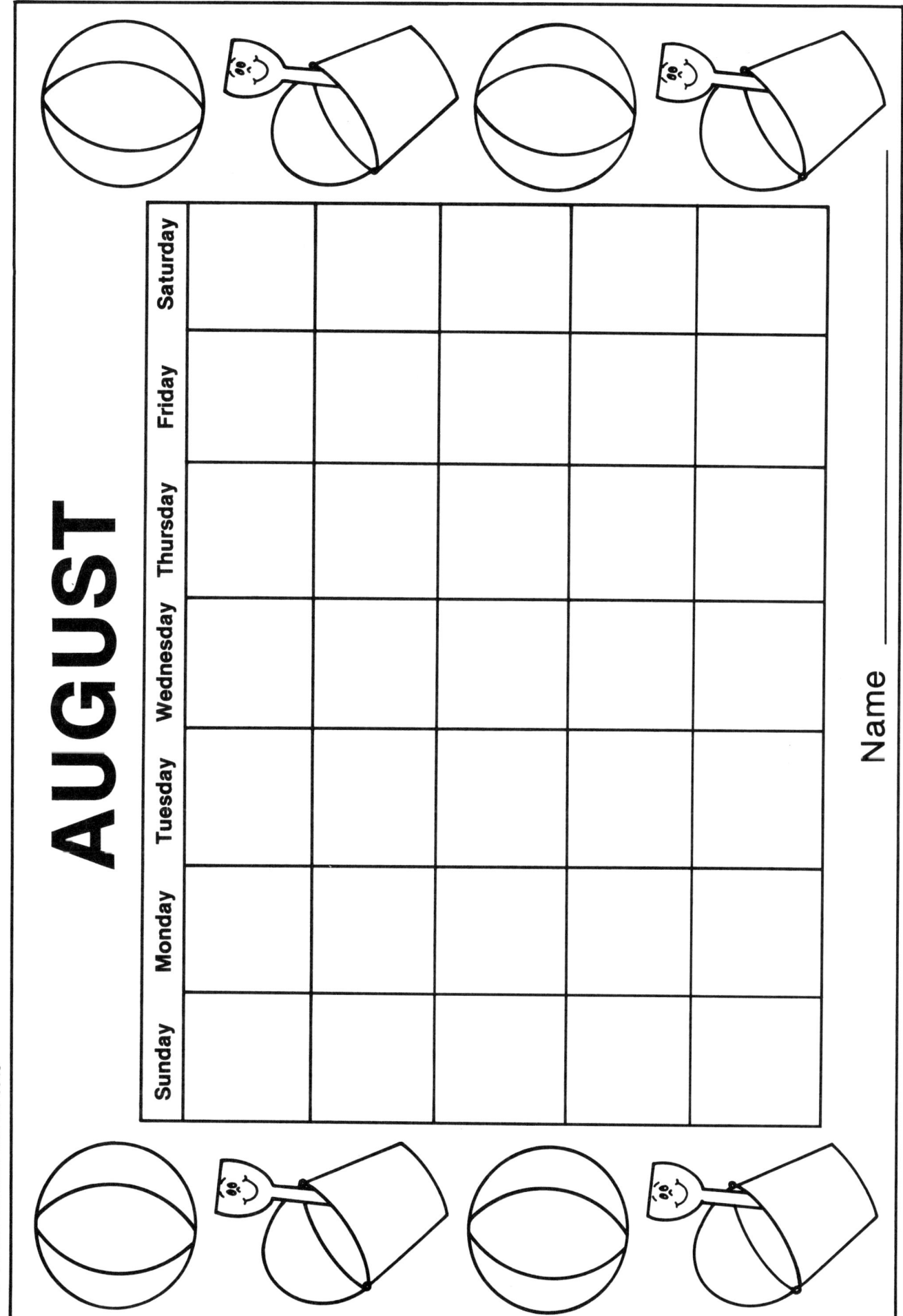

Name _____

Your Word List

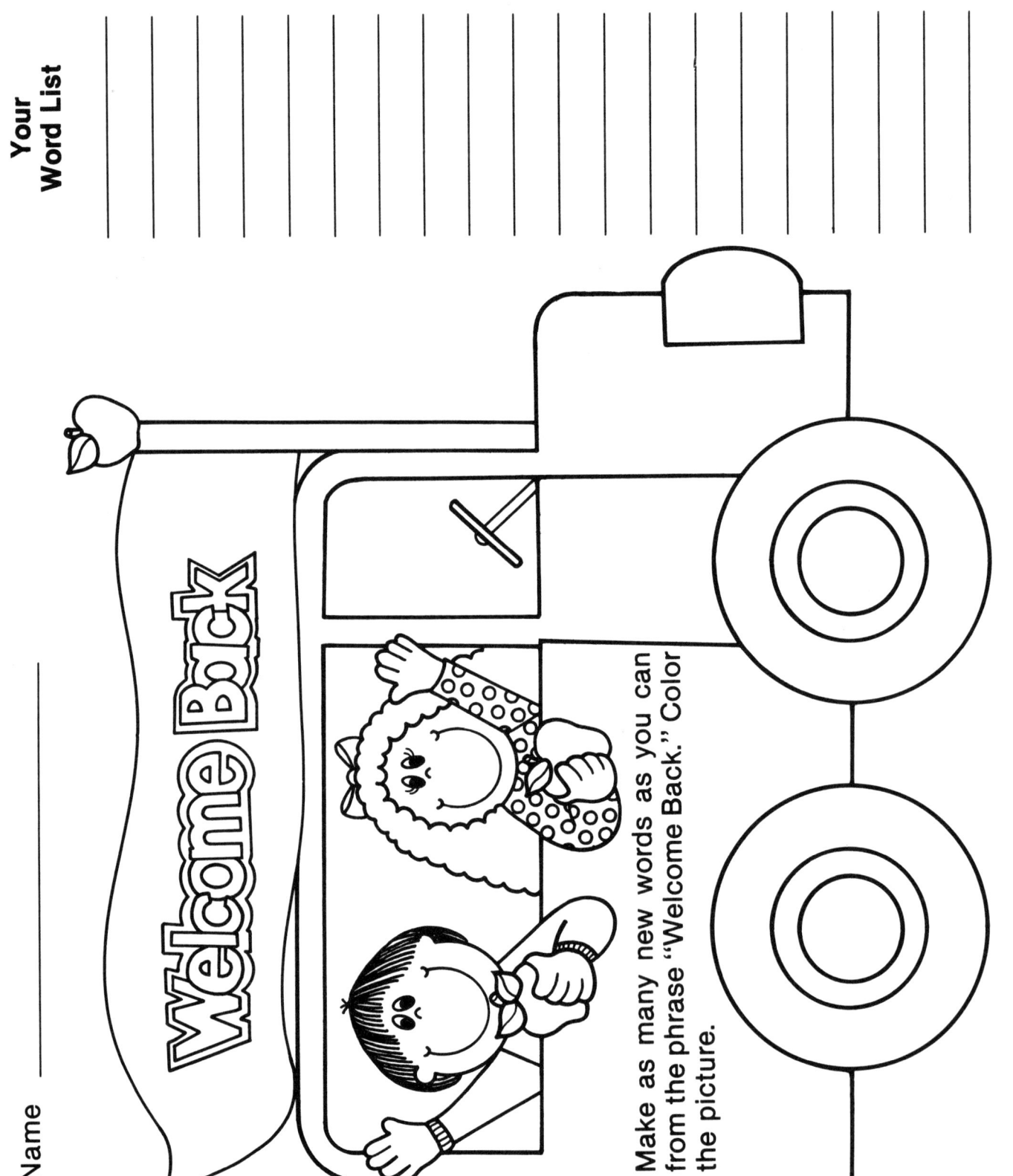

Make as many new words as you can from the phrase "Welcome Back." Color the picture.

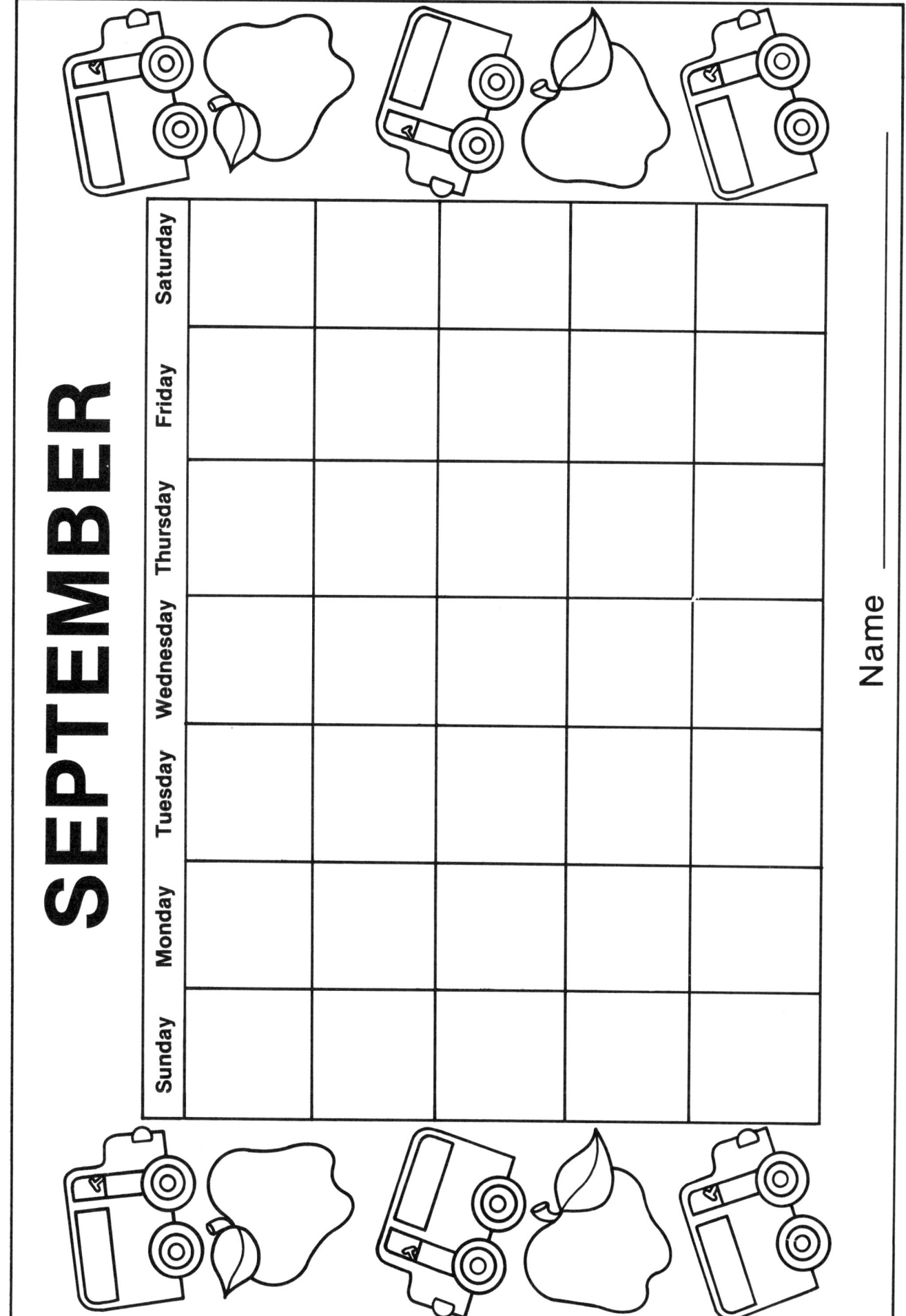

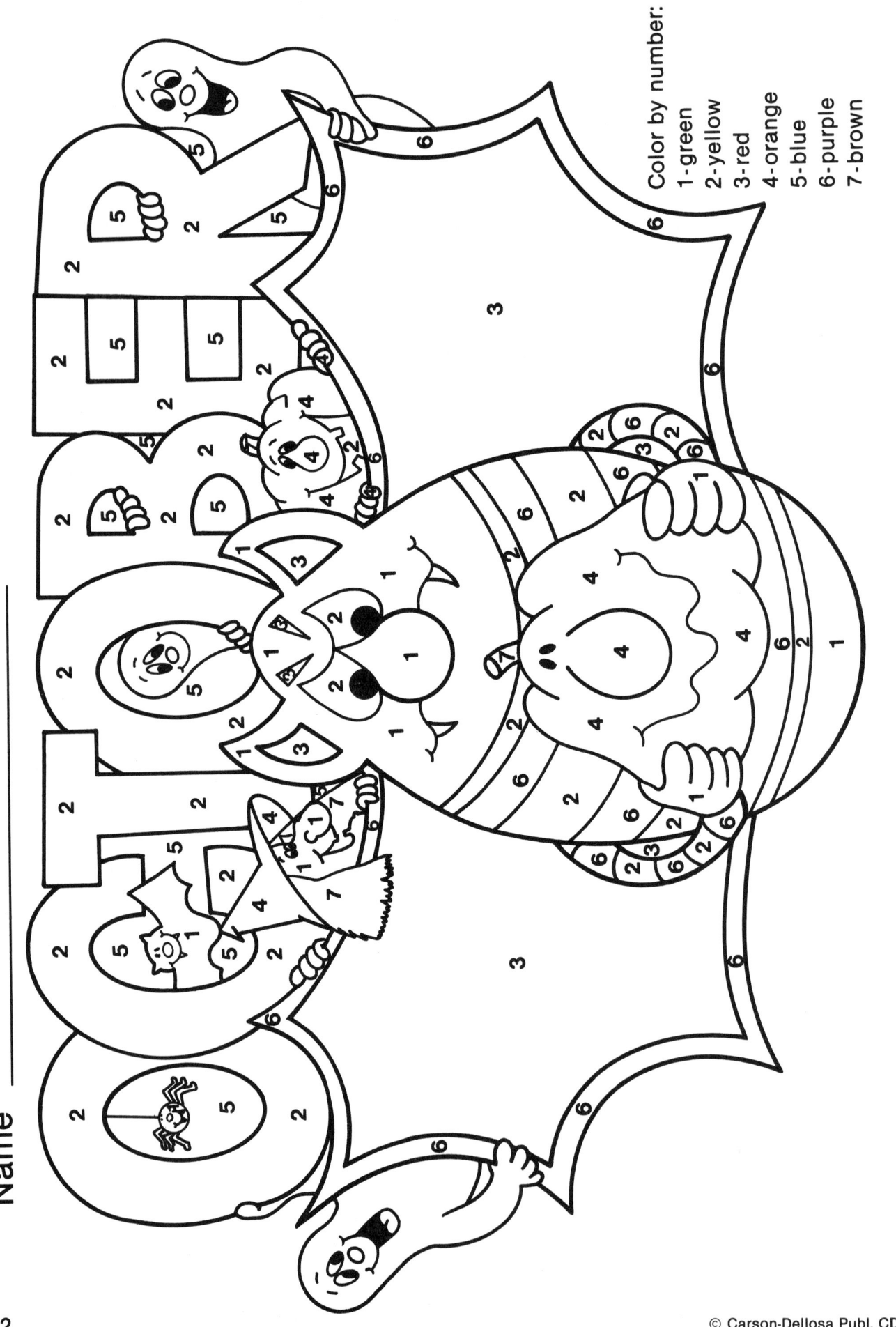

OCTOBER

Sunday	Monday	Tuesday	Wednesday	Thursday	Friday	Saturday

Name _____

Name _____

Use the chart to help you identify the tracks below. Answer the following question and color the picture.

| Turkey | Raccoon | Cottontail | Sparrow |

How many tracks did you find?

___ turkey tracks

___ raccoon tracks

___ cottontail tracks

___ sparrow tracks

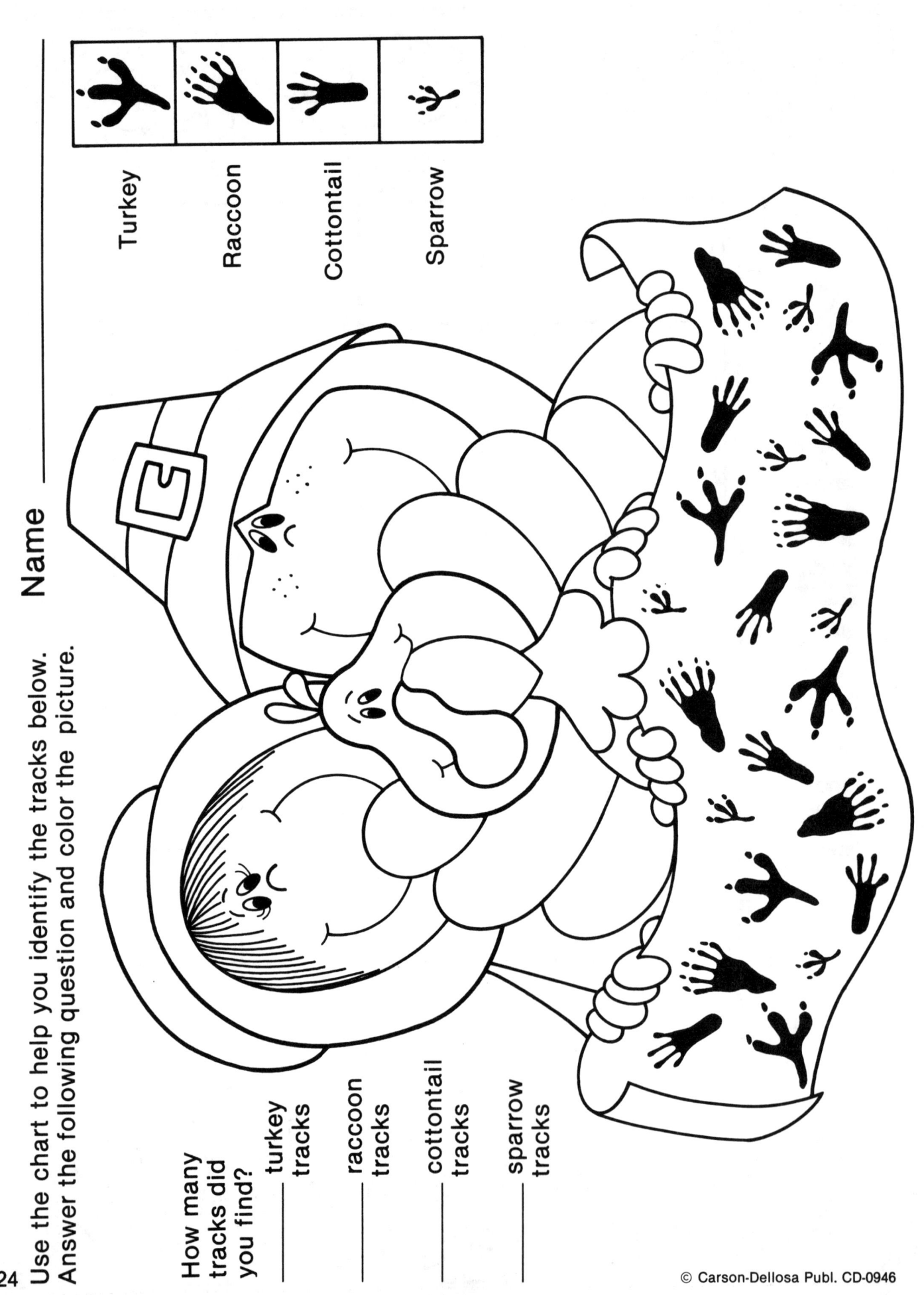

© Carson-Dellosa Publ. CD-0946

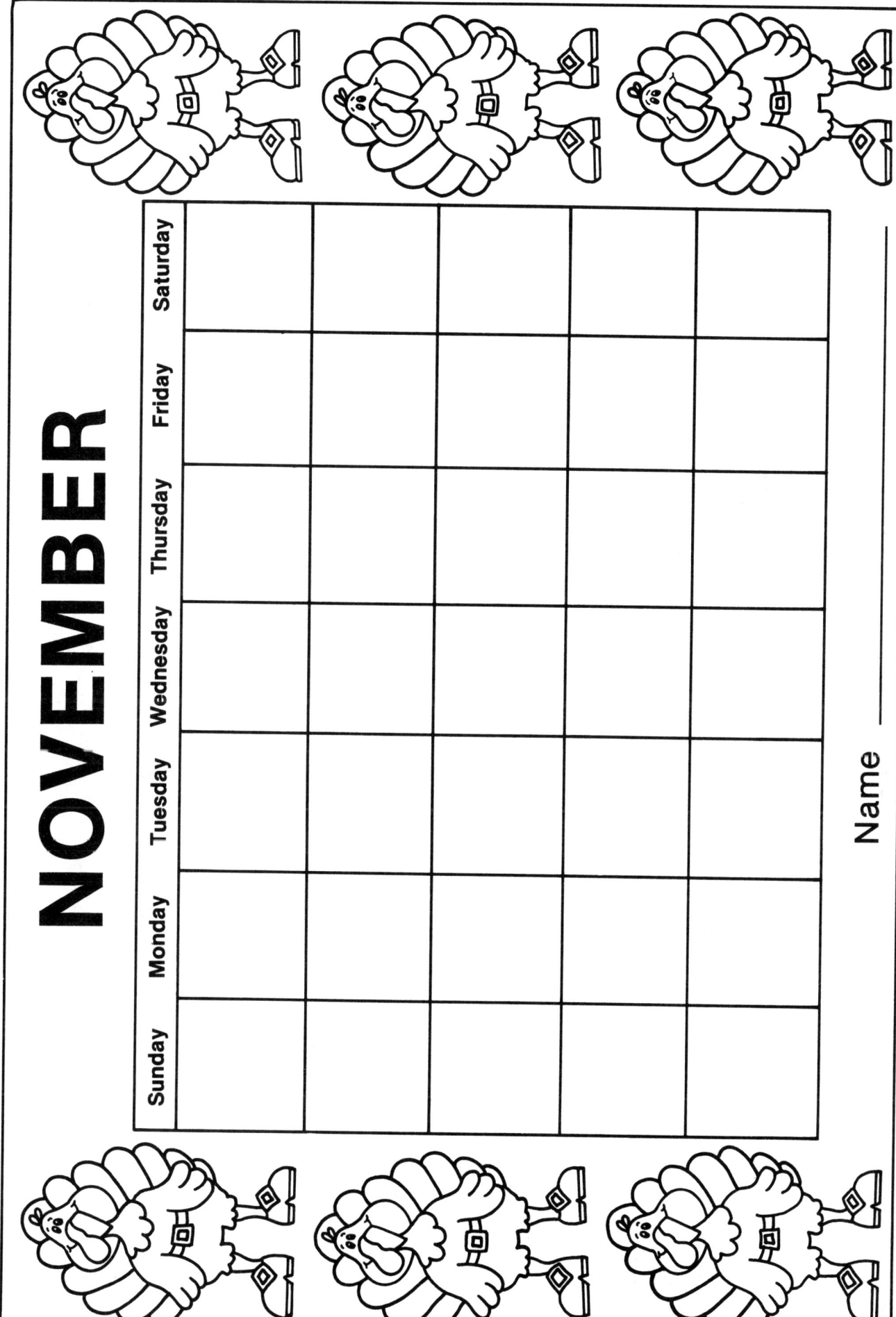

Name _____

Word List

angel	ribbons
presents	paper
star	candles
bow	candy
cards	family
tree	snow

Read the words in both word lists. Circle them in the banner below. Color the picture.

Word List

treats	snowman
tinsel	shovel
snowball	gloves
holly	wreath
scarves	ornament
stockings	chimney

```
Q U   S S S D
S N O W I K   O T C N D
R I B B O N S F A N G E L T G N I M I E A G M K
G L O V E S C A R D S G T Y H S J E N S N J I D
S H O V E L A P R E S E N T S E F N G H O L L Y
T R E A T S N F D S N O W B A L L T S H G F Y L
A T R E E D D C H I M N E Y J
R L O P I K Y G F D E W S
    X C A N D L E S K O
      S C F E I
```

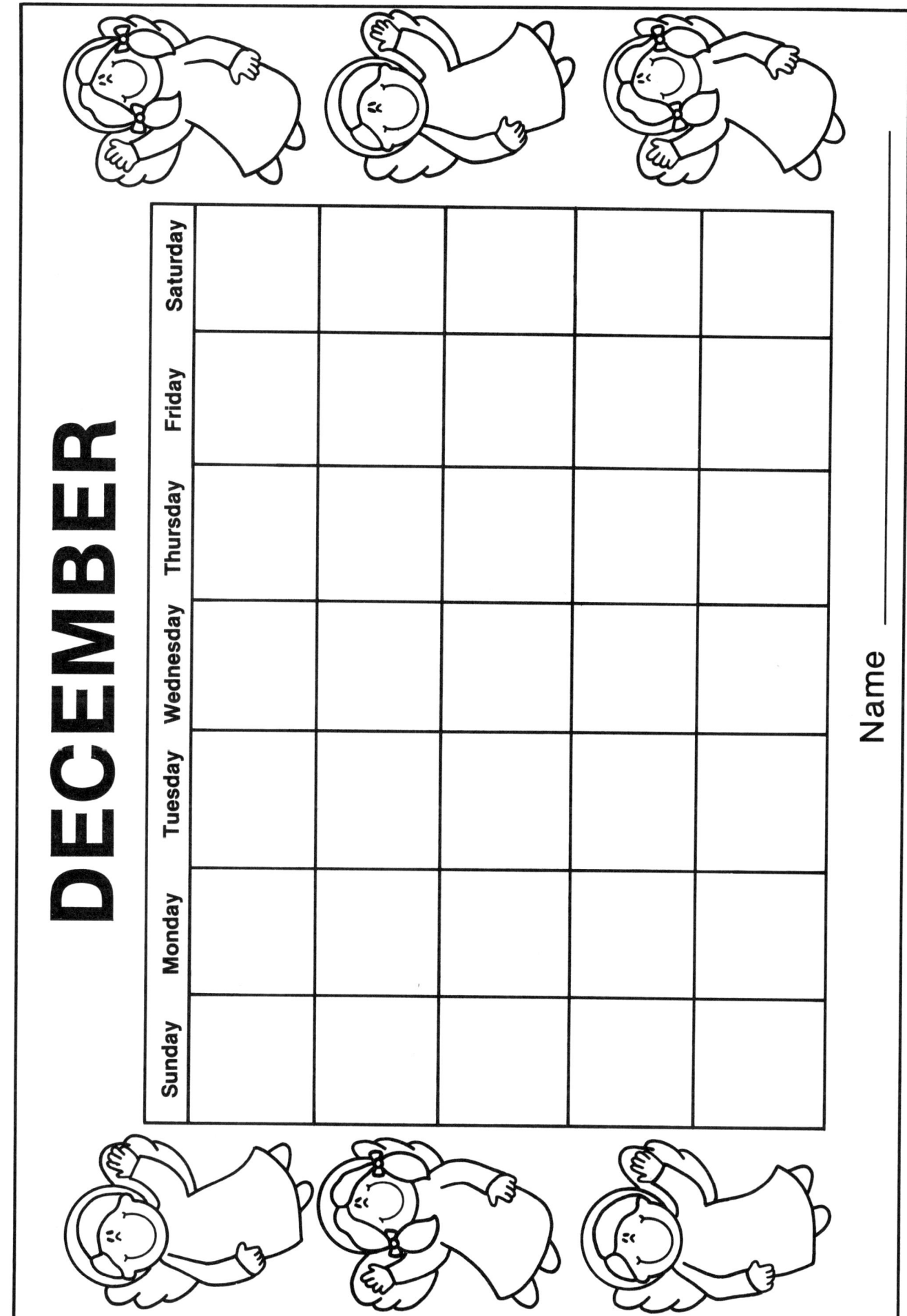

Name _____   **Months and Days of the Week**

Fill in the letter of the correct abbreviation for each month.

____ 1. January		a. Mar.
____ 2. February		b. Sept.
____ 3. March		c. Jan.
____ 4. April		d. Oct.
____ 5. August		e. Feb.
____ 6. September		f. Nov.
____ 7. October		g. Dec.
____ 8. November		h. Apr.
____ 9. December		i. Aug.

Fill in the letter of the correct abbreviation for each day.

____ 1. Sunday		a. Mon.
____ 2. Monday		b. Wed.
____ 3. Tuesday		c. Sun.
____ 4. Wednesday		d. Fri.
____ 5. Thursday		e. Sat.
____ 6. Friday		f. Tues.
____ 7. Saturday		g. Thurs.

© Carson-Dellosa Publ. CD-0946

Name _____

Months

The twelve months located on the pictures are not in the correct order. List the months in the correct order on the lines below.

1. _____
2. _____
3. _____
4. _____
5. _____
6. _____
7. _____
8. _____
9. _____
10. _____
11. _____
12. _____

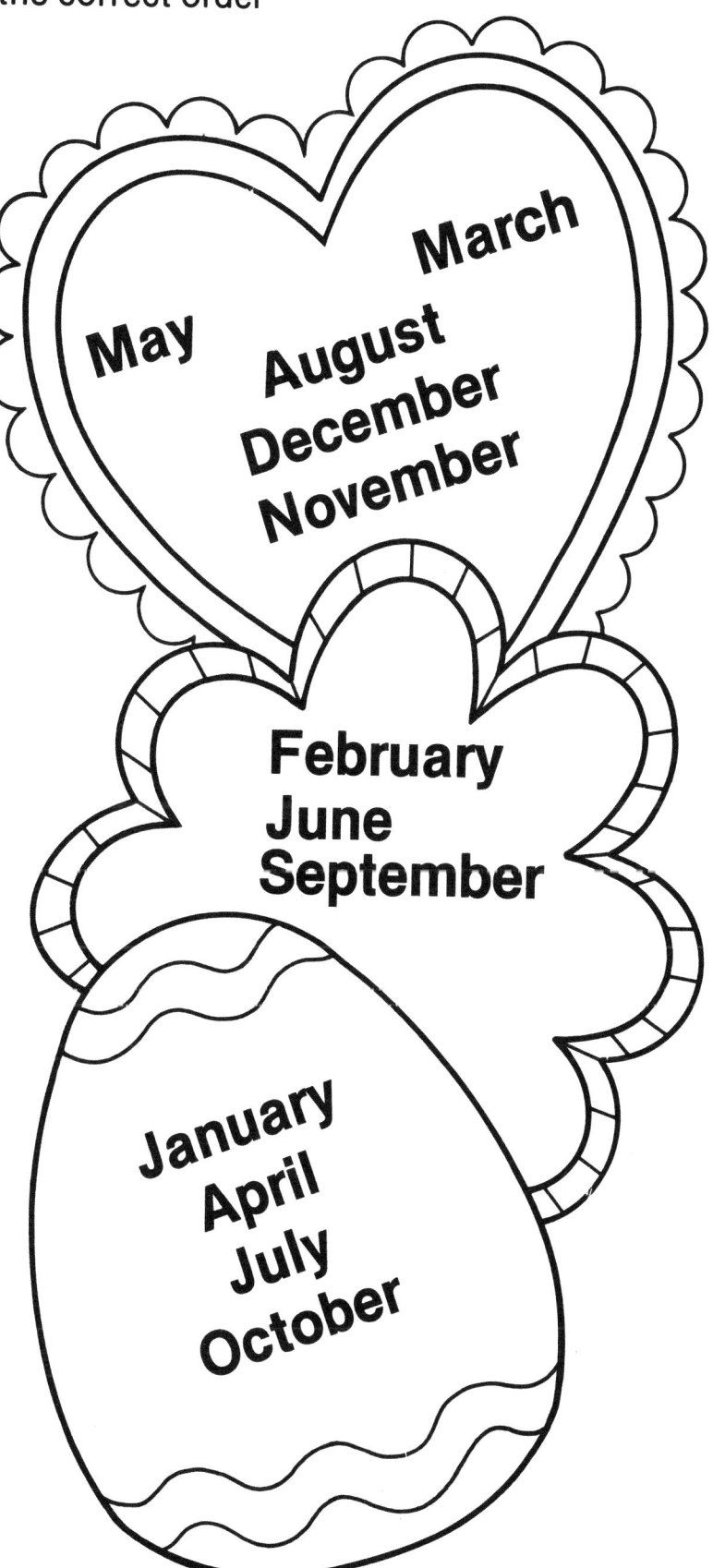

© Carson-Dellosa Publ. CD-0946

Name _____   **Months**

Write the name of the missing month on each line.

1. Christmas is celebrated during the month of _____.
2. Valentine's Day is celebrated during the month of _____.
3. The month with the shortest name is _____.
4. Halloween is celebrated in the month of _____.
5. The month just before October is _____.
6. The month just after July is _____.
7. The last day of the year comes in _____.
8. St. Patrick's Day is celebrated in the month of _____.
9. Independence Day is celebrated in the month of _____.
10. Thanksgiving is celebrated in the month of _____.
11. The month that comes just before July is _____.
12. The month just after March is _____.
13. New Year's Day is celebrated in the month of _____.

30

© Carson-Dellosa Publ. CD-0946

Name _____   **Days - Months**

Unscramble the words in the scrambled word list. (Hint: The scrambled words are names of days and months.) Circle the same answers hidden in the puzzle. The words are printed across and down, and some words share a letter. An example has been done for you.

Scrambled Word List

1. TSUDHRYA THURSDAY
2. EJNU _____
3. COTROBE _____
4. ECDMERBE _____
5. HRAMC _____
6. UTASGU _____
7. ODMNYA _____
8. AJUNRAY _____
9. TSRAAUDY _____
10. DEDWNSEYA _____
11. AMY _____
12. ESTMPEEBR _____
13. YBFUERRA _____
14. FDYIRA _____
15. PIARL _____
16. EDTUASY _____
17. VNMBOERE _____
18. YJLU _____
19. ASNDUY _____

```
A S M A R C H
J H K P C D E
D K J R I M O
E F A I L O C
C J U L Y N T
E T G N J D O
M U U J F A B
B E S H R Y E
E S T J I K R
R D G H D F M
J A F V A E M
D Y J B Y B A
J A N U A R Y
U J H G F U I
N N S S W A T
E O A E E R H
J V T P D Y U
G E U T N K R
H M R E E D S
M B D M S D D
J E A B D H A
U R Y E A M Y
P O L R Y M Z
S U N D A Y W
```

© Carson-Dellosa Publ. CD-0946   31

Months

Name _____

Read the clues. Fill in the months to complete the puzzle.

Down
1. The month after August
2. The first month of the year
4. The first month of summer
5. The month we carve jack-o'-lanterns.
7. A spring month
9. The month before May

Across
3. The month we celebrate Christmas
6. The last month of summer
7. The first month of spring
8. The month we send valentines
10. The month we carve turkeys
11. The month we shoot fireworks

Word List
September
March
May
June
October
December
July
January
April
August
February
November

Name _____ **Months**

Unscramble the letters in each box to spell a month of the year. Write the month on the line below the box.

Now write the months in correct order on the lines below.

| USUTAG |
_____

1. _____

| UJEN |
_____

2. _____

| RBOCTOE |
_____

3. _____

| YRAUJNA |
_____

4. _____

| EMVONEBR |
_____

5. _____

| YAM |
_____

6. _____

| RBEPESTME |
_____

7. _____

| IRALP |
_____

8. _____

| RBUFREAY |
_____

9. _____

| LJYU |
_____

10. _____

| EBEMDCER |
_____

11. _____

| AMRHC |
_____

12. _____

© Carson-Dellosa Publ. CD-0946

33

Name _____   **Seasons**

Read each riddle. Cut out the names of the four seasons at the bottom of the page. Paste the name of the season in the box under the riddle that tells about it. Cut out the four pictures. Paste the one that you think goes with each season in the box above the riddle. Write the names of the months in that season on the lines beside each box.

1) [ ] Months
   1. _____
   2. _____
   3. _____

   New things start to grow -
   You say, "Good-bye" to snow.
   Kites fly in the breeze -
   Buds burst out on trees.

   (Paste Season Here)

2) [ ] Months
   1. _____
   2. _____
   3. _____

   Throw off your coats,
   Swim, fish, sail in boats.
   Hot weather's the reason,
   Most remember my season.

   (Paste Season Here)

3) [ ] Months
   1. _____
   2. _____
   3. _____

   Days begin to get cool,
   You go back to school.
   My holidays are great fun -
   What's your favorite one?

   (Paste Season Here)

4) [ ] Months
   1. _____
   2. _____
   3. _____

   To many places I bring
   Wind, snow, sleet and ice,
   But in some parts of the country,
   The weather is still warm and nice.

   (Paste Season Here)

| Fall | Spring | Summer | Winter |

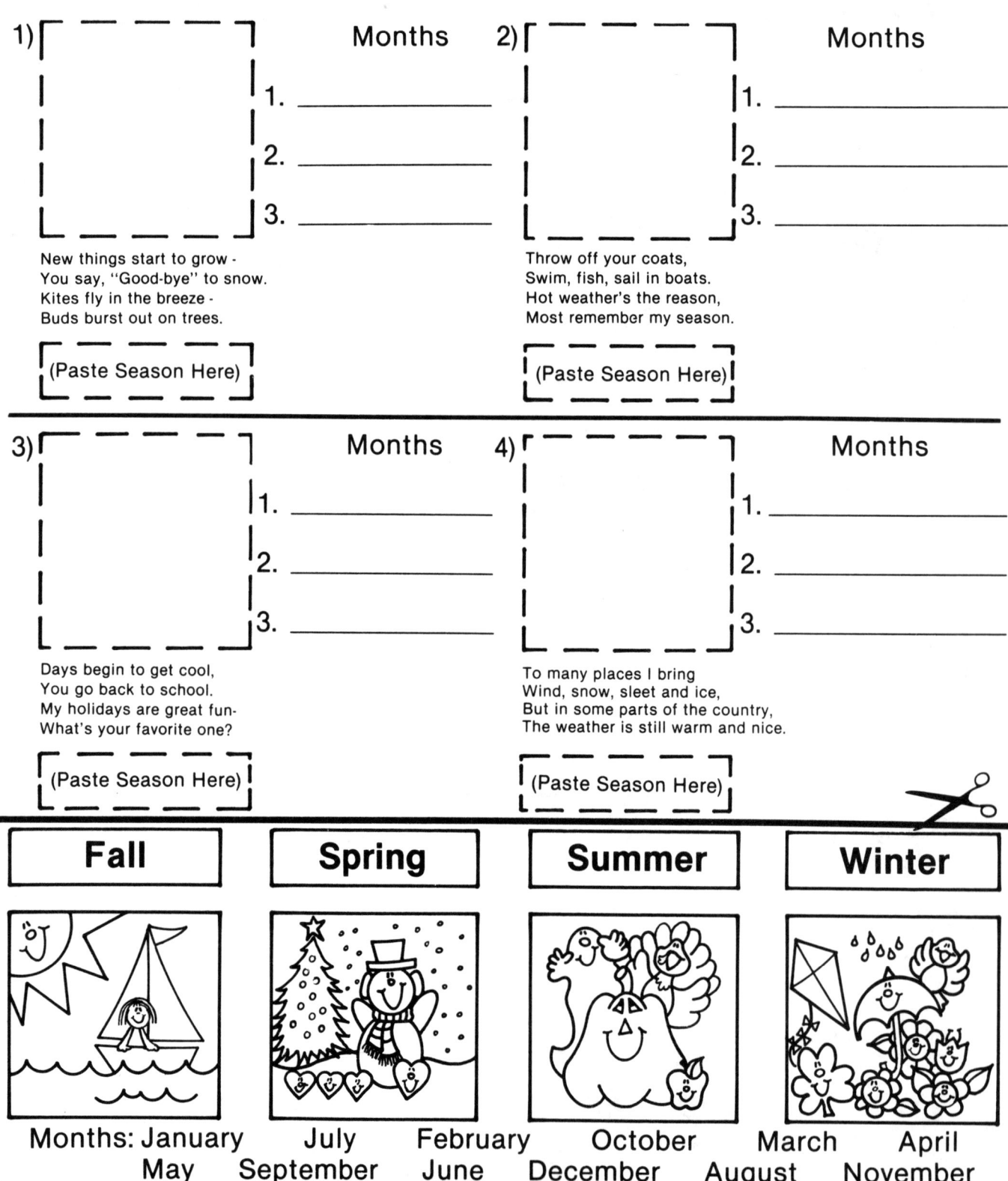

Months: January   July   February   October   March   April
        May   September   June   December   August   November

© Carson-Dellosa Publ. CD-0946

Name _____   **Months - Seasons**

Check up time!

Write the correct answer on each line.

1. There are _____ months in each year.

2. The months of the year in correct order are:

   1. _____ 2. _____ 3. _____
   4. _____ 5. _____ 6. _____
   7. _____ 8. _____ 9. _____
   10. _____ 11. _____ 12. _____

3. Nine months of the year can be abbreviated. The abbreviations for these months are:

   _____ , _____ , _____ , _____ , _____ ,
   _____ , _____ , _____ , and _____ .

4. Three months of the year are not abbreviated.
   They are _____ , _____ , and _____ .

5. During each year there are four seasons.
   They are _____ , _____ , _____ , and _____ .

6. The three fall months are: _____ , _____ , and _____ .

7. The three winter months are: _____ , _____ , and _____ .

8. The three spring months are: _____ , _____ , and _____ .

9. The three summer months are: _____ , _____ , and _____ .

© Carson-Dellosa Publ. CD-0946

Name _____   **Days of the Week**

Read each sentence and fill in the correct day of the week.

1. If today is Monday, yesterday was _____.

2. If yesterday was Tuesday, today is _____.

3. If tomorrow will be Friday, today is _____.

4. If today is Sunday, yesterday was_____.

5. If yesterday was Wednesday, today is_____.

6. If tomorrow will be Tuesday, today is _____.

7. If today is Thursday, tomorrow will be _____.

8. If yesterday was Saturday, today is _____.

9. If tomorrow will be Wednesday, today is _____.

10. If today is Friday, tomorrow will be _____.

We enjoy every day of the week.

Name _____   Seasons

Each of the seasons has three months. Find and circle the three months in each season's word search. Then write the months in that season in order on the lines.

Fall Months

```
        H G
    K X A S G Y F I O
    J W H E I Z E N F
    L V N J P B K O D G
    M U O C T O B E R B
    J T M F E C D L C H
    N O V E M B E R V I
    C Z X A B E B P W
    B A Y U E R Q S D
        S A T R S R J
```

1. _____
2. _____
3. _____

Winter Months

```
        B D A C D E
    K A E D I C B M
    N L J C E H G D F Q C
    T R O E P S U E V K B
    W X Z M J A N U A R Y
        F E B R U A R Y
        P O E G H R J L
          S R M N Y Q
```

1. _____
2. _____
3. _____

Spring Months

```
    A R C G Q X D H
    B S H M F C P G
    I B I A P R I L
    W T L J R E Y Z F
    M A Y K C D A E L
    V U M N H O J K Q
        M N O P R S
```

1. _____
2. _____
3. _____

Summer Months

```
        A T U C
      G R O C B H
    Q A U G U S T D
    H G P B N I D M J
    Y F A V Z F E L U K
    X J U L Y E J L N
    W L J I M O N E
    V U W S X Q P
```

1. _____
2. _____
3. _____

© Carson-Dellosa Publ. CD-0946

Name _____

WRITING HOLIDAY THANK YOU NOTES

Good writing manners during the holidays are EASY - as you will see.

In this book you will see samples of holiday and special occasion thank you notes for you to copy. You will also find decorated stationery that you can use to write your own letters and notes. (pp. 144, 174, 181, 241, 314, 384). You might wish to write thank you notes on the following special occasions:

VALENTINE'S DAY - You received a special valentine (or gift) and you wish to say "Thank you". (pp. 240-241)

EASTER - You were given all kinds of goodies and you want to say "Thank you". (pp.313-314)

MOTHER'S DAY - What a perfect time to let your mother know how much you think of her by writing her a note. (pp.336-337)

FATHER'S DAY - You appreciate so many things Dad does for you. Tell him so in a note. (pp. 336-337)

THANKSGIVING - It's nice to enjoy a big Thanksgiving dinner! Send a note to the person who made the dinner. Tell the cook how much you enjoyed it! (pp. 142-144)

CHRISTMAS or HANUKKAH - The gifts you received made you very happy. The people who were good to you will be glad to receive a thank you note. (pp. 172-174)

FRIENDSHIP - You have some friends you like very much. You would like to write and say, "Thank you for being my friend!" (pp. 383-384)

NEW YEAR'S DAY - You would like to wish someone "the very best" for the coming year. (p. 181)

Name _____   Apple for the Teacher Art Project

1. Color and cut out all of the pieces.
2. Glue a hand and pencil to the right side of the apple. (See example.)
3. Glue a hand and pencil to the left side of the apple. (See example.)
4. Glue a leaf to each side of the stem. (See example.)

Example

Welcome Back to School!

© Carson-Dellosa Publ. CD-0946

39

Name _____
Directions:

Name _____

School Story Starter
Use some of the words on the apple to write about school.

school, teacher, test, classroom, bell, fire drill, learn, pencil, recess, hopscotch, finish, principal, cook, nurse, student, flag, spelling, reading, sandwich, janitor, fun, apple, lunch, eraser, swing set, clock, books, chalk, blackboard, practice, study, clay, desk, gym, quiz, jump rope, carton, sing, exercise, sneakers, line up, project, leader, hallway, math, quiet, office, milk, crayons, library, whistle, listen, pictures, friend, play, rules, papers, kickball, classmate, story

Name _____

Name _____

Name_____

Directions:

Name _____   **Fall Finger Play Poem**

Read the finger poem. Perform the finger movements as you read the poem again.

SIX FOOTBALL PLAYERS
by Gail Aemmer

Six football players, huddled all together.
   (Hold up 6 fingers)

The first one says, "This is football weather!"
   (Hold up 1 finger)

The second one says, "I'm a kicker, you know!"
   (Hold up 2 fingers)

The third one says, "I can really throw!"
   (Hold up 3 fingers)

The fourth one says, "I'm a runner, you see."
   (Hold up four fingers)

The fifth one said, "I'm strong as can be!"
   (Hold up 5 fingers)

The sixth one says, "I can tackle quite well."
   (Hold up 6 fingers)

It's time for the game; now everyone yell!
        Yeah!
   (Wave all ten fingers)

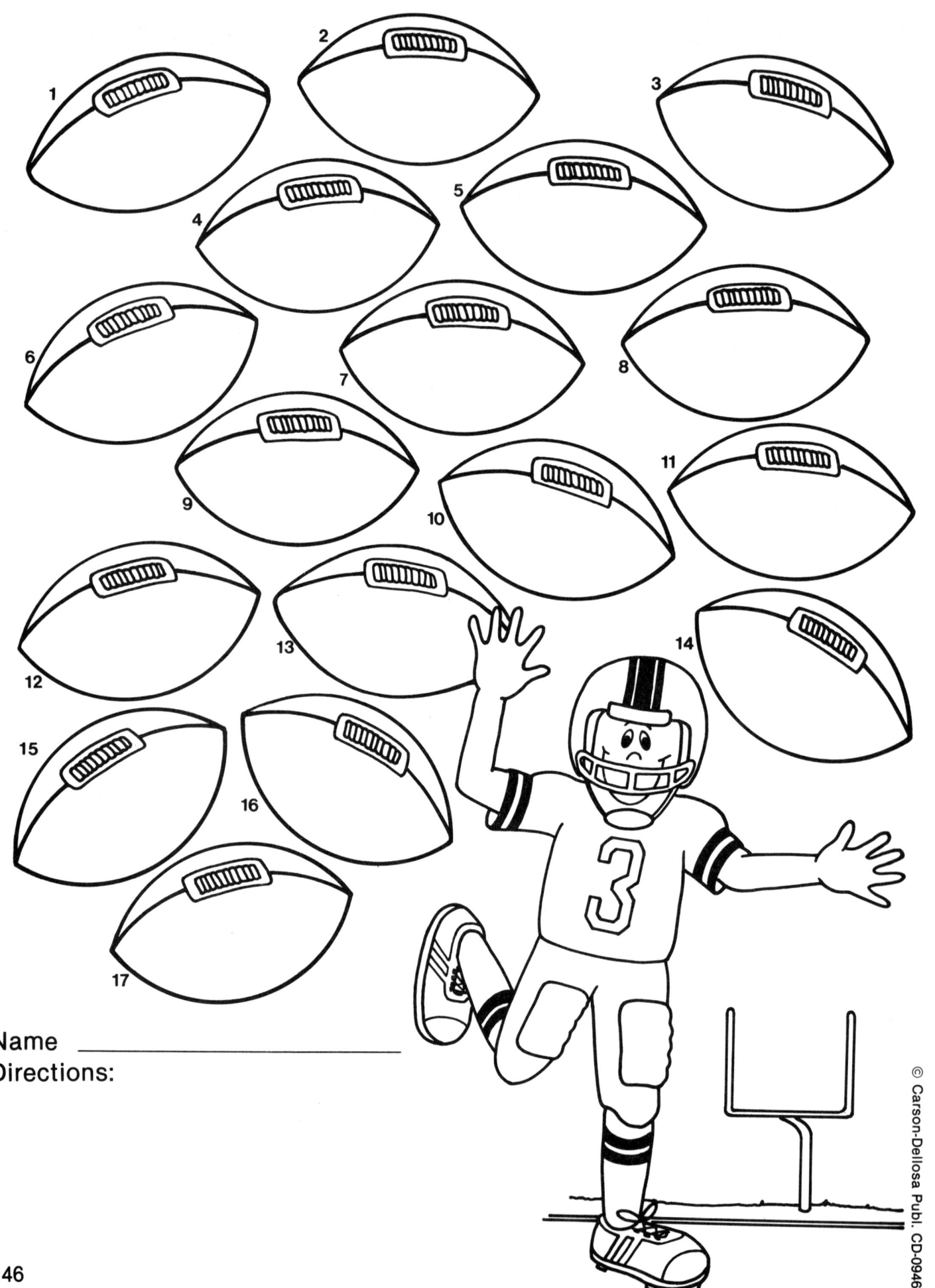

Name _____
Directions:

Name _____ Seasons - Fall

Read the clues. Find the correct word in the word list and write it in the puzzle.

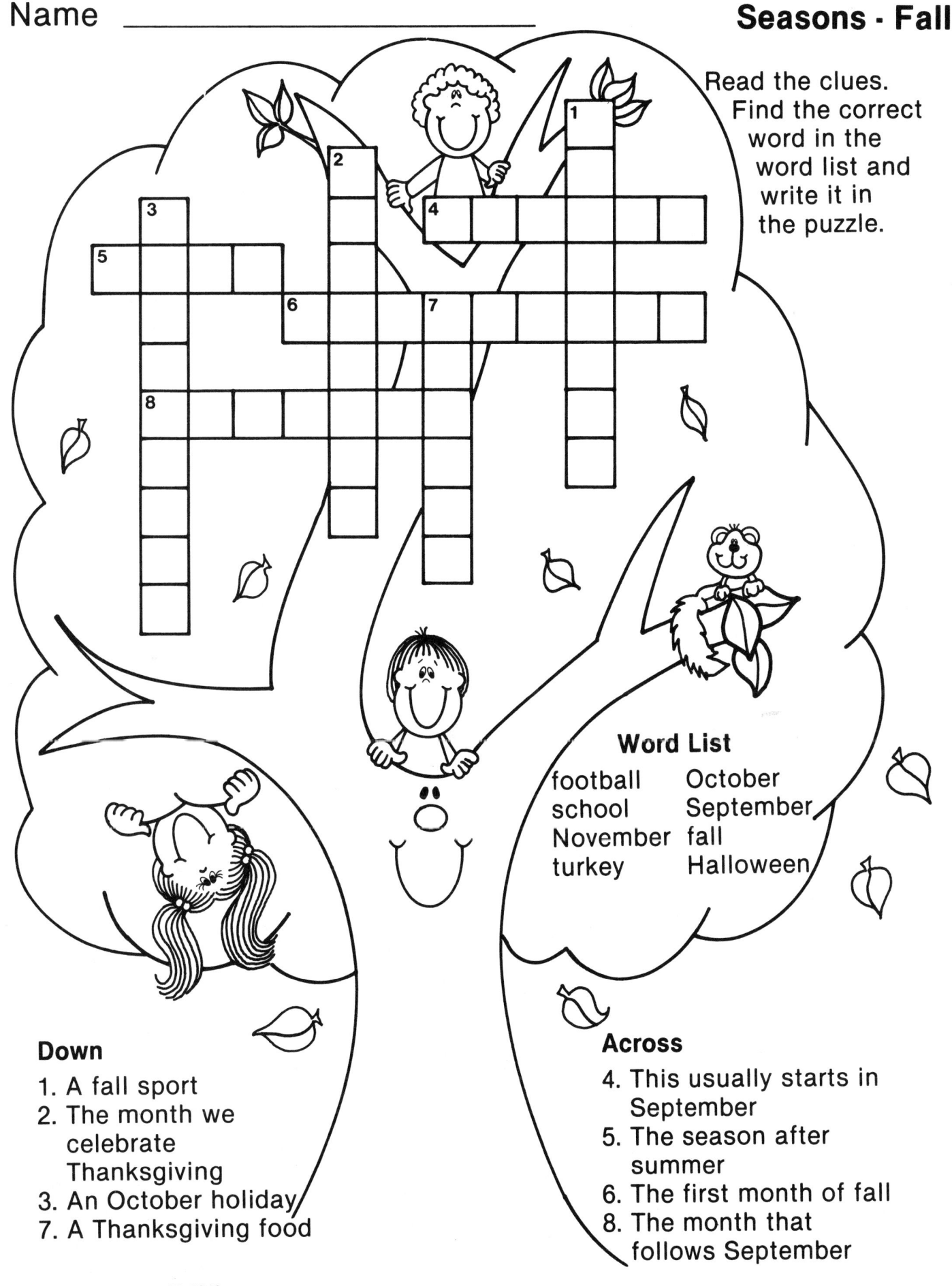

Word List

football   October
school   September
November   fall
turkey   Halloween

Down
1. A fall sport
2. The month we celebrate Thanksgiving
3. An October holiday
7. A Thanksgiving food

Across
4. This usually starts in September
5. The season after summer
6. The first month of fall
8. The month that follows September

Name _____
Directions:

Name _____
Directions:

49
© Carson-Dellosa Publ. CD-0946

Name _____

TIME OF YEAR: fall

MATERIALS: white paper, crayons and pencils

DIRECTIONS: Overlap leaf patterns to trace an allover design on a piece of white paper. Color shapes using fall colors. Color some shapes solidly and make a design on others. This project makes a very colorful bulletin board or chalkboard border.

sample of completed project

leaves

Name _____

Name _____   **Fall Finger Play Poem**

SQUIRRELS AND ACORNS
by Gail Aemmer

Read the finger play poem. Perform the finger movements as you read the poem again. You may wish to repeat the poem several times.

Color the picture.

Five little squirrels with acorns to store.
  (Hold up 5 fingers)

One went to sleep and now there are four!
  (Put 1 down)

Four little squirrels hunting acorns in a tree.
  (Hold up 4 fingers)

One fell down, and now there are three!
  (Put 1 down)

Three little squirrels wondering what to do.
  (Hold up 3 fingers)

One got lost, and now there are two!
  (Put 1 down)

Two little squirrels tossing acorns for fun.
  (Hold up 2 fingers)

One got tired, and now there is one!
  (Put 1 down)

One little squirrel playing in the sun.
  (Hold up 1 finger)

He ran away, and now there are none!
  (Put last finger down)

Name _____

Use some of the words below to help you write a fall story.

wind, apples, jumping, harvest, school, garden, frost, squirrel, hiking, colors, gather, acorns, rake, cider, nuts, sunset, store, leaves, pile, chipmunk

Name _____

Name _____

Use some of the words below to help you write a fall story.

Fall

How to Use

Related Poems
 Enlarge any of the patterns to use as the center of a bulletin board. Direct students to copy a related poem. Display the papers on the bulletin board.

Award Sayings
 Use an award saying with its related pattern to create student awards.

Related Poems

Acorns are proud of the
 caps that they wear,
'Cause without them their heads
 would be totally bare.

Award Sayings

I'm "Oak"-kay!
My teacher is "nuts" about me!

My color's usually gray or brown.
I'm known for acting like a clown.
But all agree, I never fail
To have a beautiful, bushy tail.

I'm nuts about school!
I'm storing my knowledge.

Leaves can be big;
Leaves can be small;
But in the autumn
They're brightest of all!

Unbe"leaf"able student!
"Leaf" it to me!

Pass-kick-punt and run.
Touchdown! One by one.
People scream, "More, more!"
As players fight to raise the score!

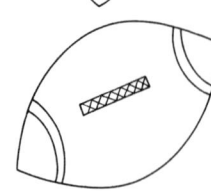

I'm a pro!
I made my goal!
I'm a kickin' good student!

Name _____

Fall
(Instructions on previous page)

© Carson-Dellosa Publ. CD-0946

Name _____

Directions:

Name _____   **Sing-Along School Bus Finger Play Poem**

Read the finger play poem. Perform the finger movements as you read the poem again. You may wish to repeat the poem several times.
Color the picture.

SCHOOL BUS FINGER PLAY POEM

Bus driver, bus driver, sing us a song!	(All fingers up)
"I will," said the driver,	
"If you'll sing along."	
The bus driver sang,	(Hold up thumb)
"I love to go running."	(Fingers run)
The first child sang,	(Hold up 1 finger)
"I like beaches and sunning."	(Turn face up to sun)
The second child crowed,	(Hold up 2 fingers)
"I love to climb trees."	(Hands climb tree)
The third child chanted,	(Hold up three fingers)
"I love a good breeze."	(Puff cheeks and blow)
The fourth child warbled,	(Hold up four fingers)
"I love rowing boats."	(Hands pull oars)
The fifth child sang,	(Hold up five fingers)
"I love ice cream floats."	(Sip a straw)
The sixth child chirped,	(Hold up six fingers)
"I love to feed the birds."	(Flap arms like wings)
The seventh child whistled;	(Hold up seven fingers)
He could think of no words.	(Whistle)
Said the driver,	
"We each like a different thing.	(Hold up 7 fingers and a thumb)
But one thing's for sure -	
We all like to sing!"	(Open mouth, open arms wide)

© Carson-Dellosa Publ. CD-0946

Name _____   **School Bus Art Project**

1. Color and cut out all of the pieces.
2. Glue each wheel to a half circle on the bottom of the bus. (See example.)
3. Glue the girl's head to the body on the left. (See example.)
4. Glue the boy's head to the body on the right. (See example.)

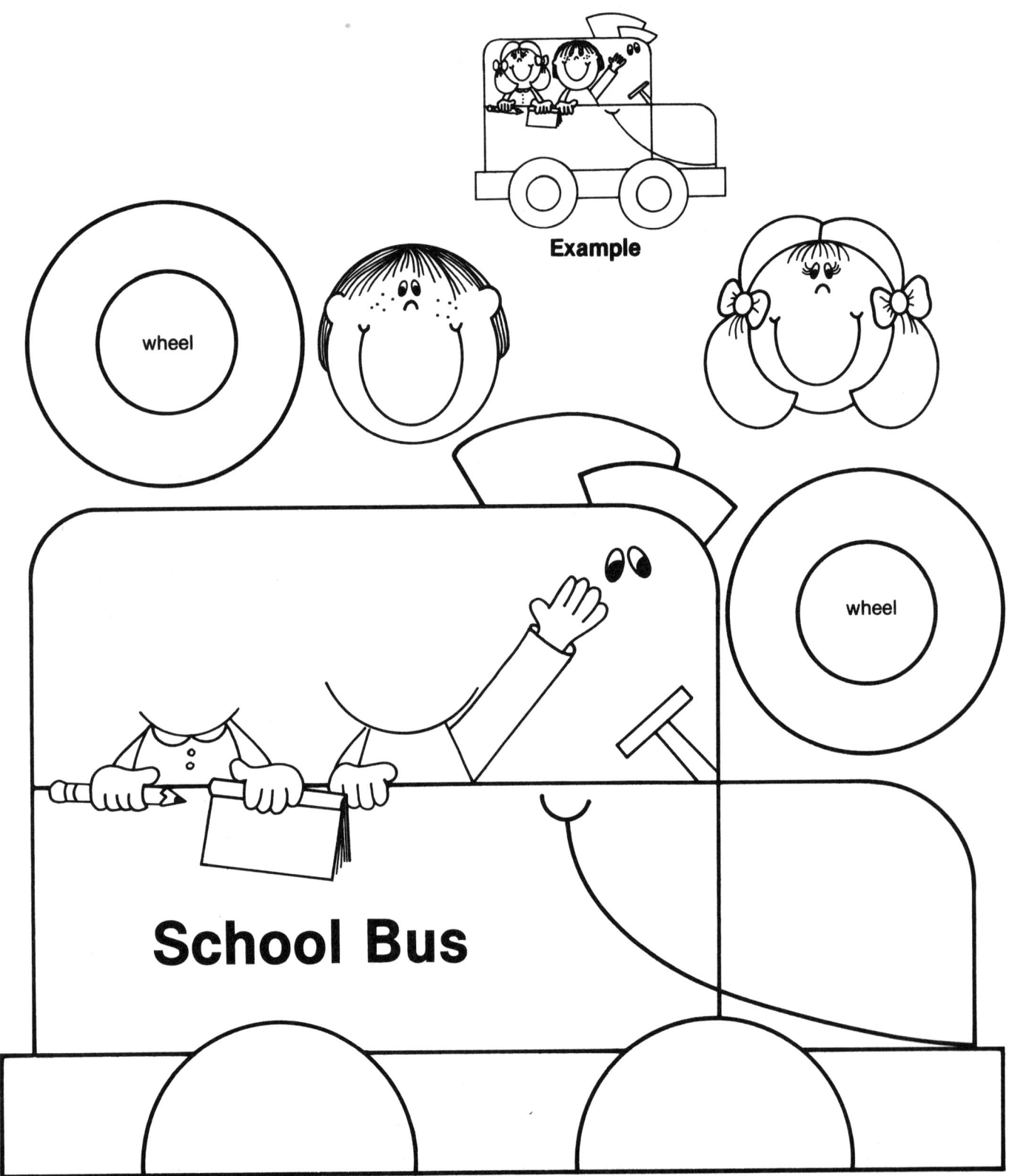

Example

wheel

wheel

School Bus

Name _____

```
a o e r o t
c u r i u g
o t s v n a
r i m o e s
n u t s o n
m a f a r e
l e a v e s
    l i t o
    l a e f
```

Circle the hidden words:
acorn, nuts, leaves, fall

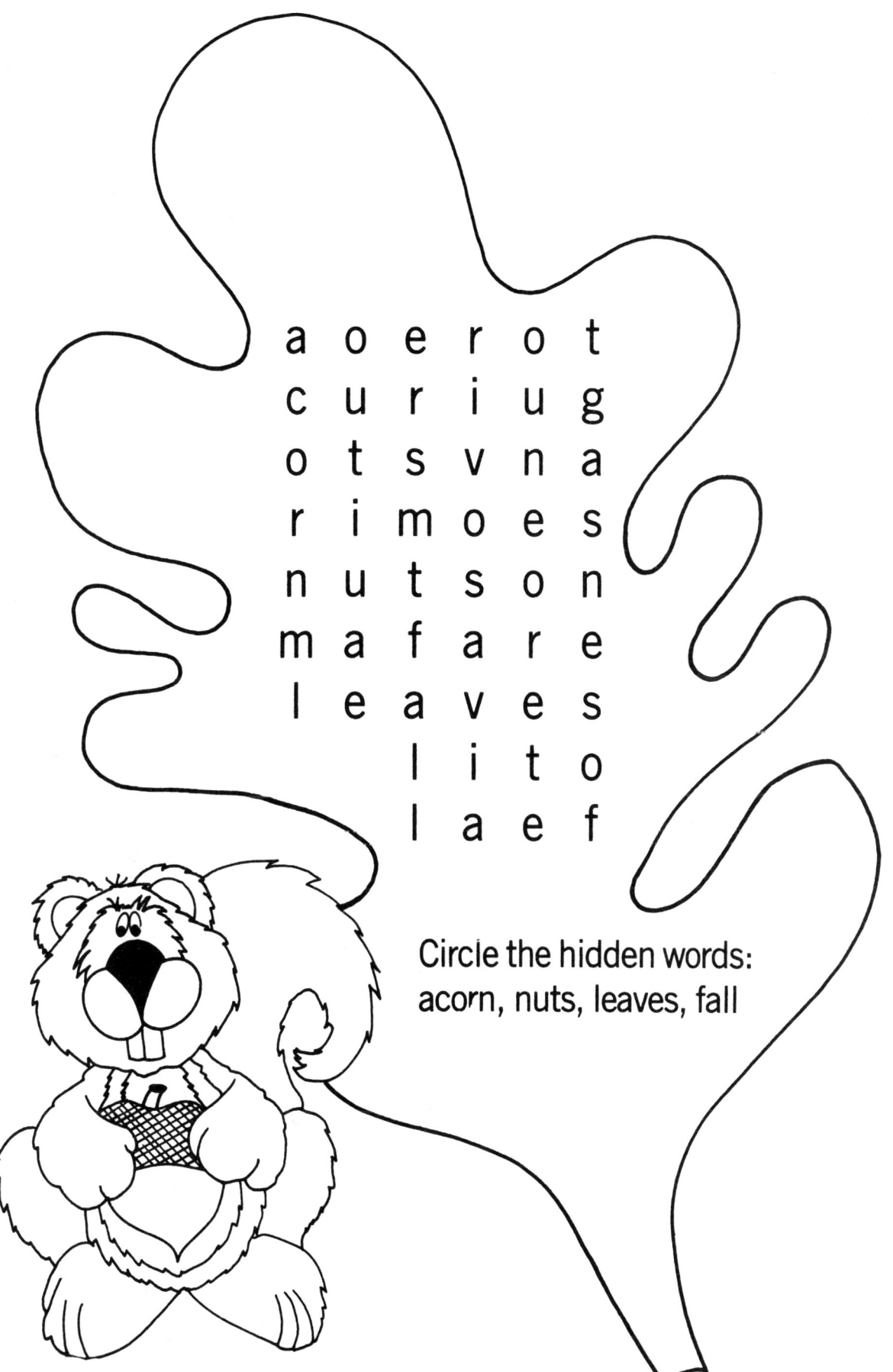

Name _____

Count the crows.
There are _____ crows.

64

© Carson-Dellosa Publ. CD-0946

Name _____

Directions:

65

Name _____   **Scarecrow Lady Art Project**

1. Color and cut out all of the pieces on pp. 66-67.
2. Glue the head to the collar of the dress. (See example.)
3. Glue the arms to the body by placing an arm behind each side of the body. (See example.)
4. Glue a hand to the bottom of each arm by placing the hand behind the arm. (See example.)
5. Glue the body to the pole. (See example.)

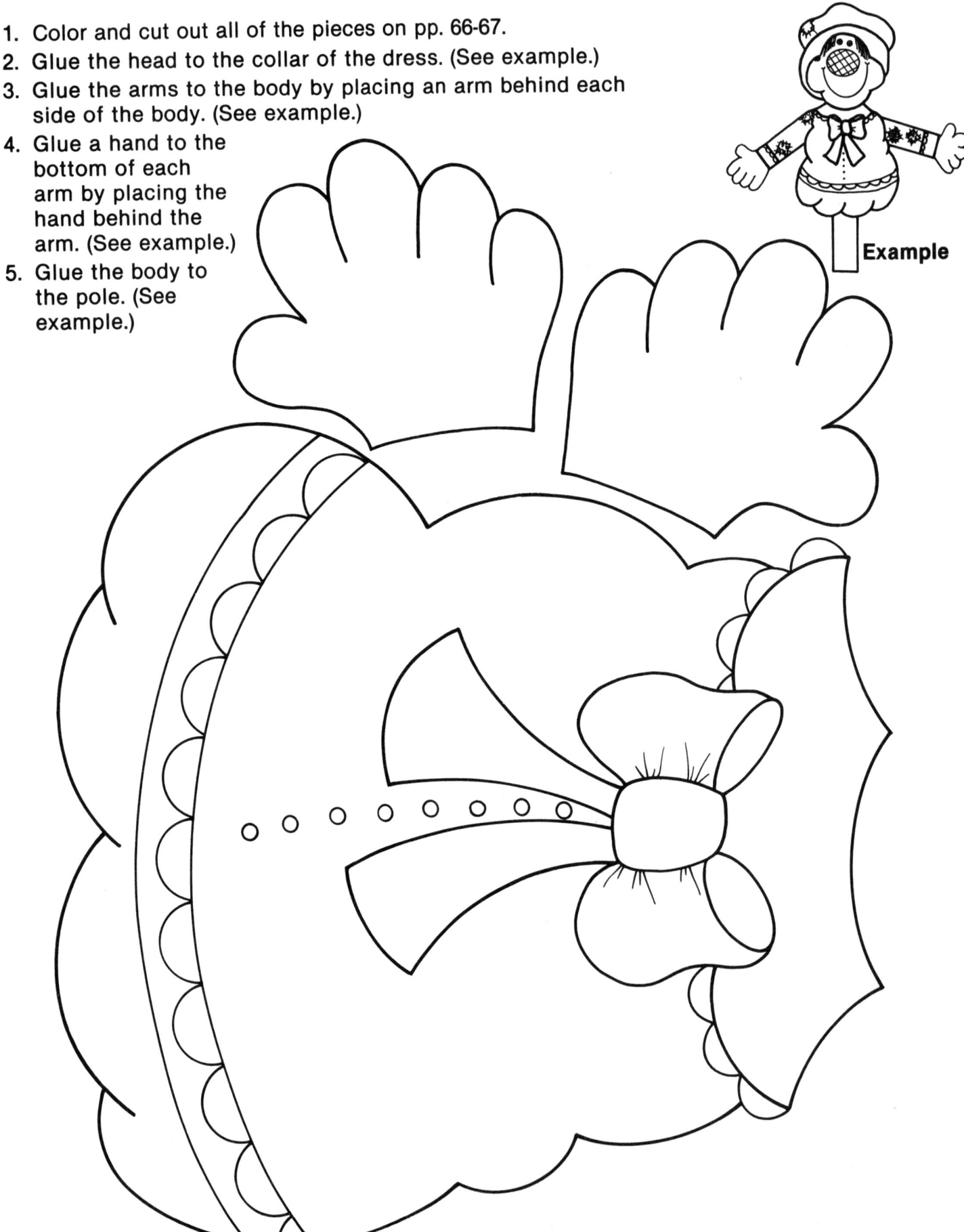

Example

© Carson-Dellosa Publ. CD-0946

66

Name _____ **Scarecrow Lady Art Project**

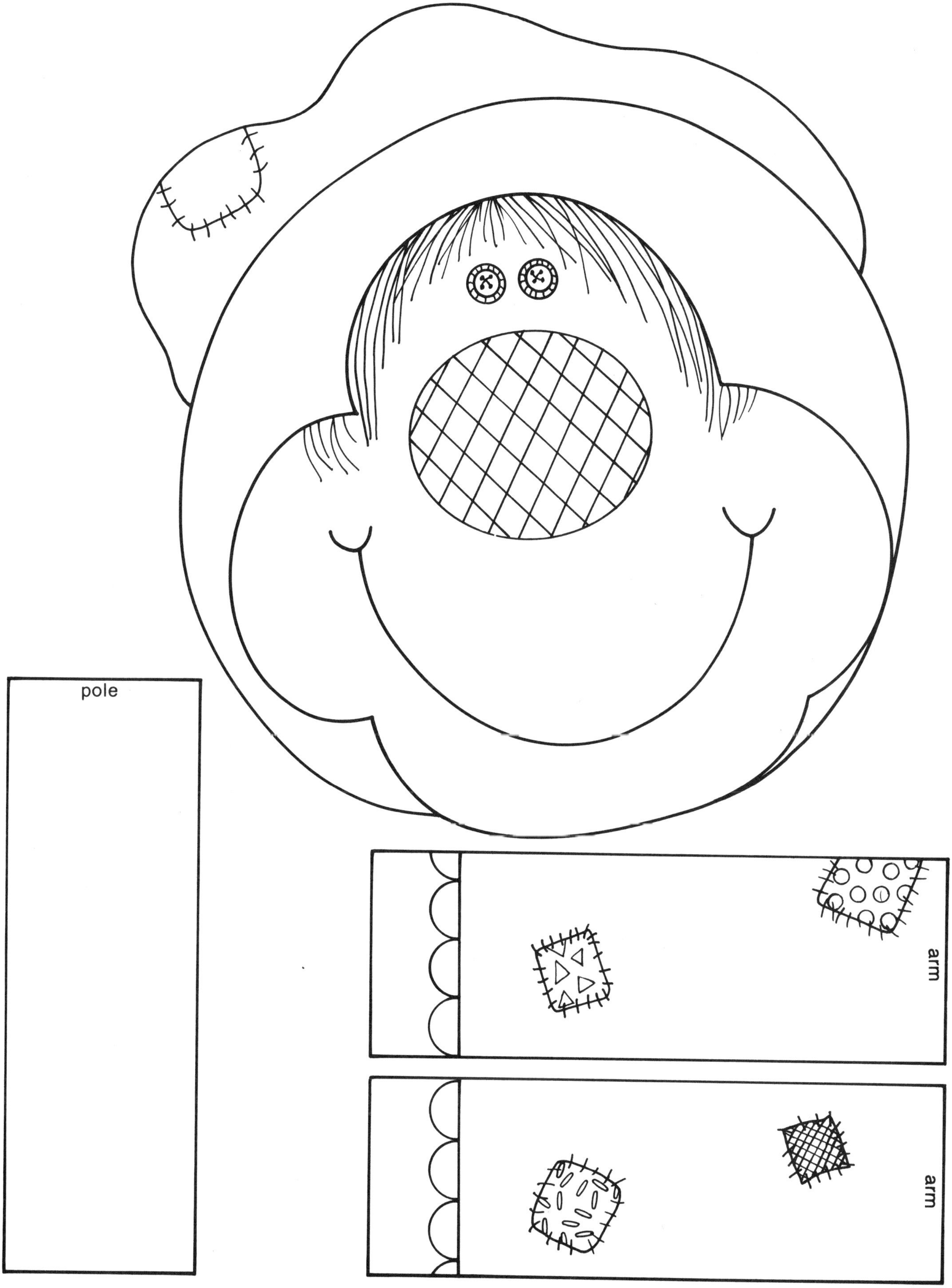

pole

arm

arm

© Carson-Dellosa Publ. CD-0946

67

Name _____ **Scarecrow Man Art Project**

1. Color and cut out all of the pieces on pp. 68-69.
2. Glue the head to the scarf. (See example.)
3. Glue the hat to the top of the head. (See example.)
4. Glue the arms to the body by placing an arm behind each side of the body. (See example.)
5. Glue a hand to the bottom of each arm by placing the hand behind the arm. (See example.)
6. Glue the body to the pole.

Example

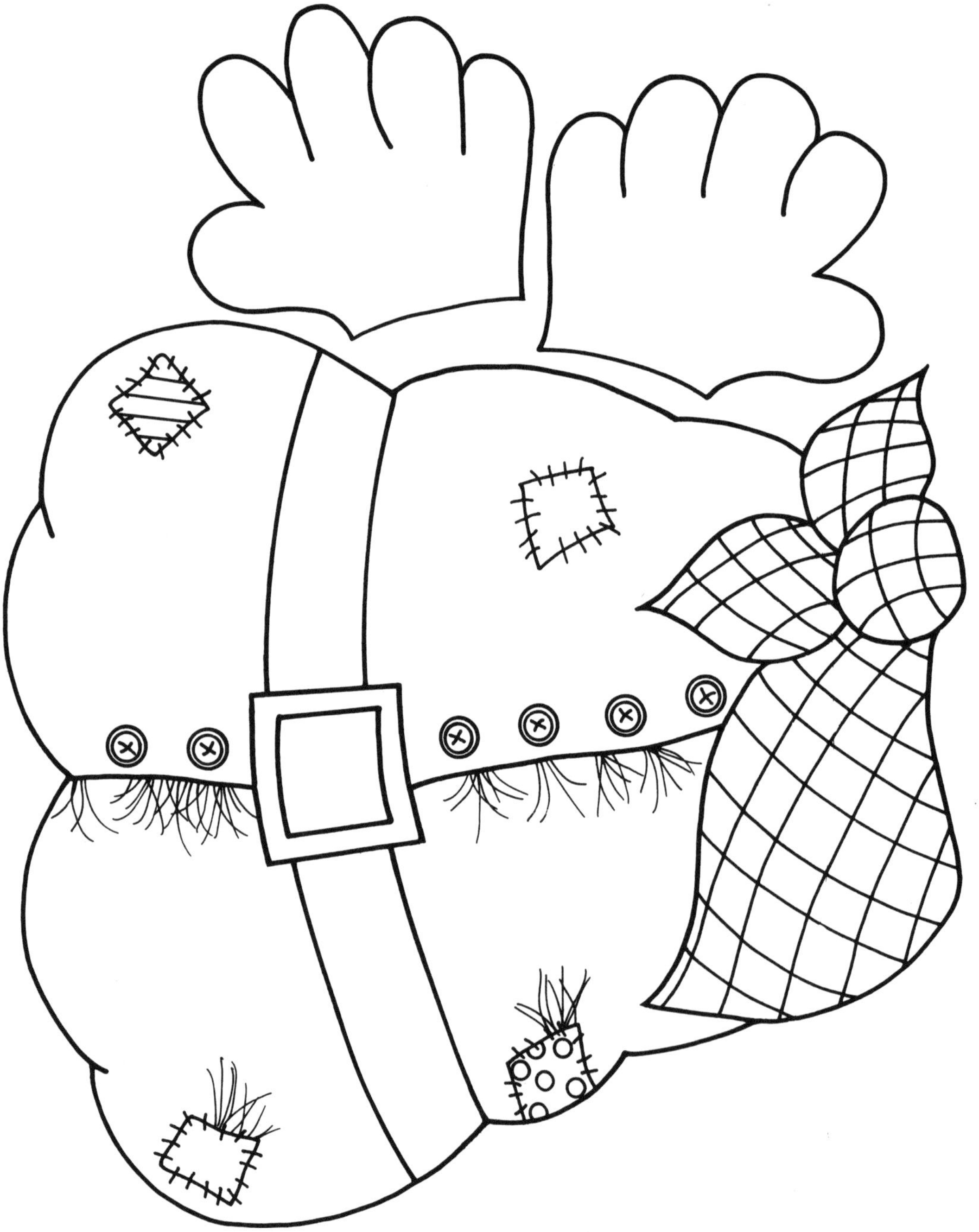

Name _____   **Scarecrow Man Art Project**

69

Name _____

```
a m c e a d
f a r m e r
i t o e t s
e u w e h i
l a n f a n
d t o a y e
```

Circle the hidden words:
field, farmer, crow, hay

Name _____
Directions:

Name _____

1. rcon _____
2. wcor _____
3. tsawr _____
4. lafl _____

Can you unscramble the words on the scarecrow?

Answers: 1. corn, 2. crow, 3. straw, 4. fall

Name_____
Directions:

Name _____

Halloween Bat Story Starter

Write a "bat-tale" on the lines below. The words on the bat will help you get started!

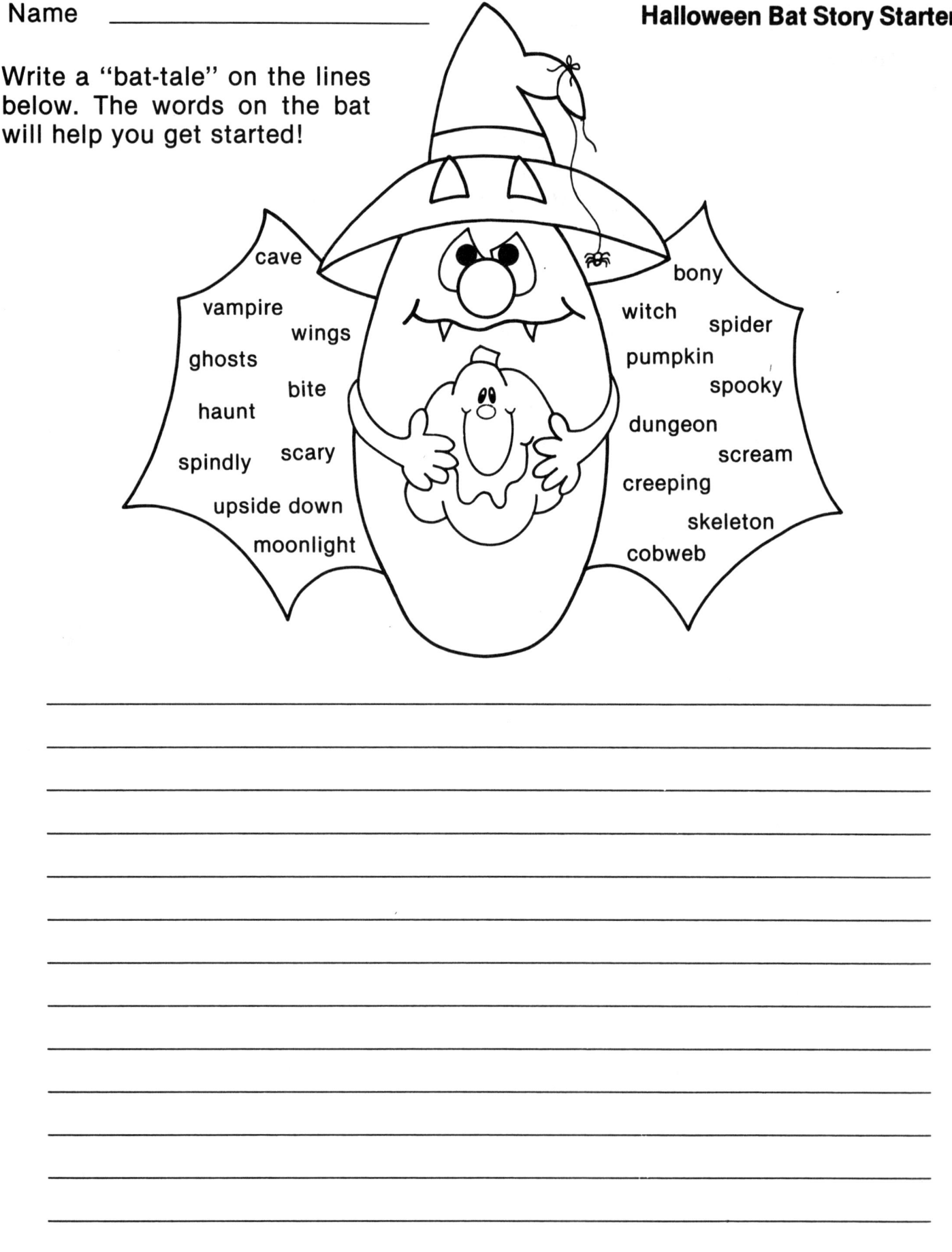

74

© Carson-Dellosa Publ. CD-0946

Name _____
Directions:

Name _____ **WONDERFUL WINDOW WEB**

Directions:

1. Cut out the square on the solid lines.
2. Fold the square in half diagonally on the dotted line.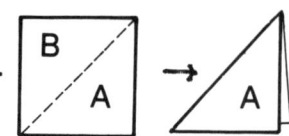
3. Unfold the square.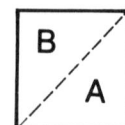
4. Fold A towards the center dotted line until A (the bottom edge of the square) is lined up on the dotted line.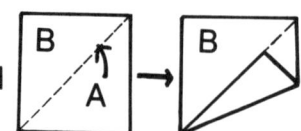
5. Fold B towards the center dotted line until B (the left edge of the square) is lined up on the dotted line.
6. Cut off the top, unfolded section.

   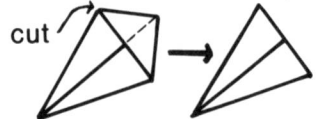

7. Fold the paper in half again.

8. Draw this pattern on the folded section. **Make sure the open end is facing down.** Notice that the shaded parts do not extend to the top fold.

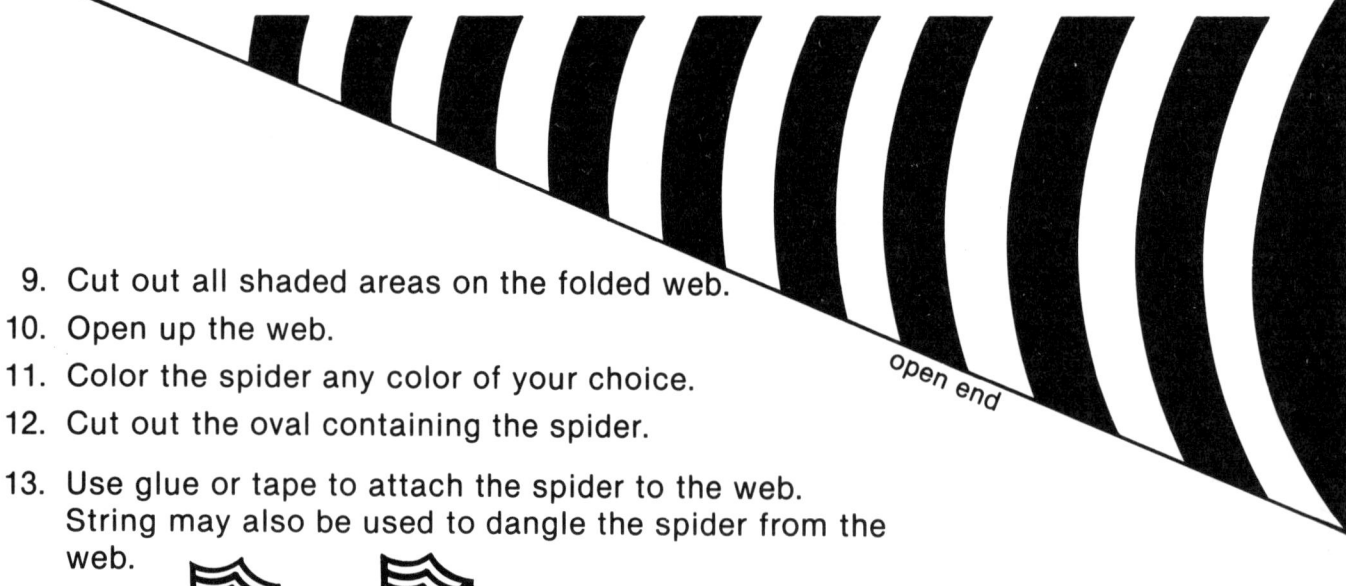

9. Cut out all shaded areas on the folded web.
10. Open up the web.
11. Color the spider any color of your choice.
12. Cut out the oval containing the spider.
13. Use glue or tape to attach the spider to the web. String may also be used to dangle the spider from the web.
14. Tape the web and the spider to the corner of a window.

Name _____

WONDERFUL WINDOW WEB
Create a spider and web to decorate any corner of a window!

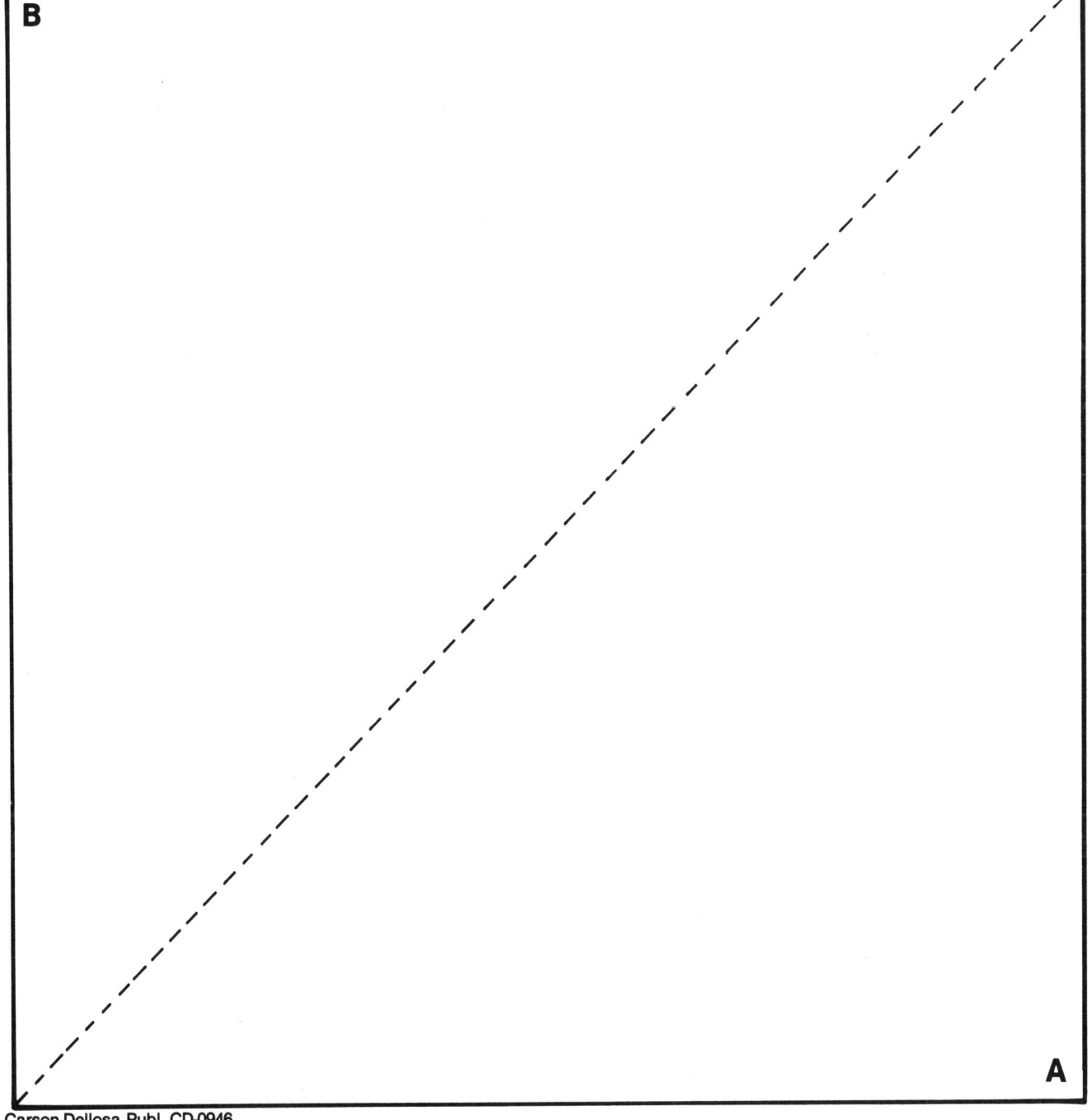

Name _____
Directions:

78 © Carson-Dellosa Publ. CD-0946

Name _____

Match the letters to the numbers on the vampire's cape. Find the message in the secret code.

1. B   2. O   3. A   4. G   5. U

Match the letters to the numbers on the vampire's cape. Find the message in the secret code.

1. T 2. A 3. M
4. B 5. Y 6. D
7. E 8. I 9. O
10. V 11. U 12. R

__ __ __ __ __ __ __ __ __ __ __ __
5 9 11 6 12 8 10 7 3 7 4 2 1 1 5

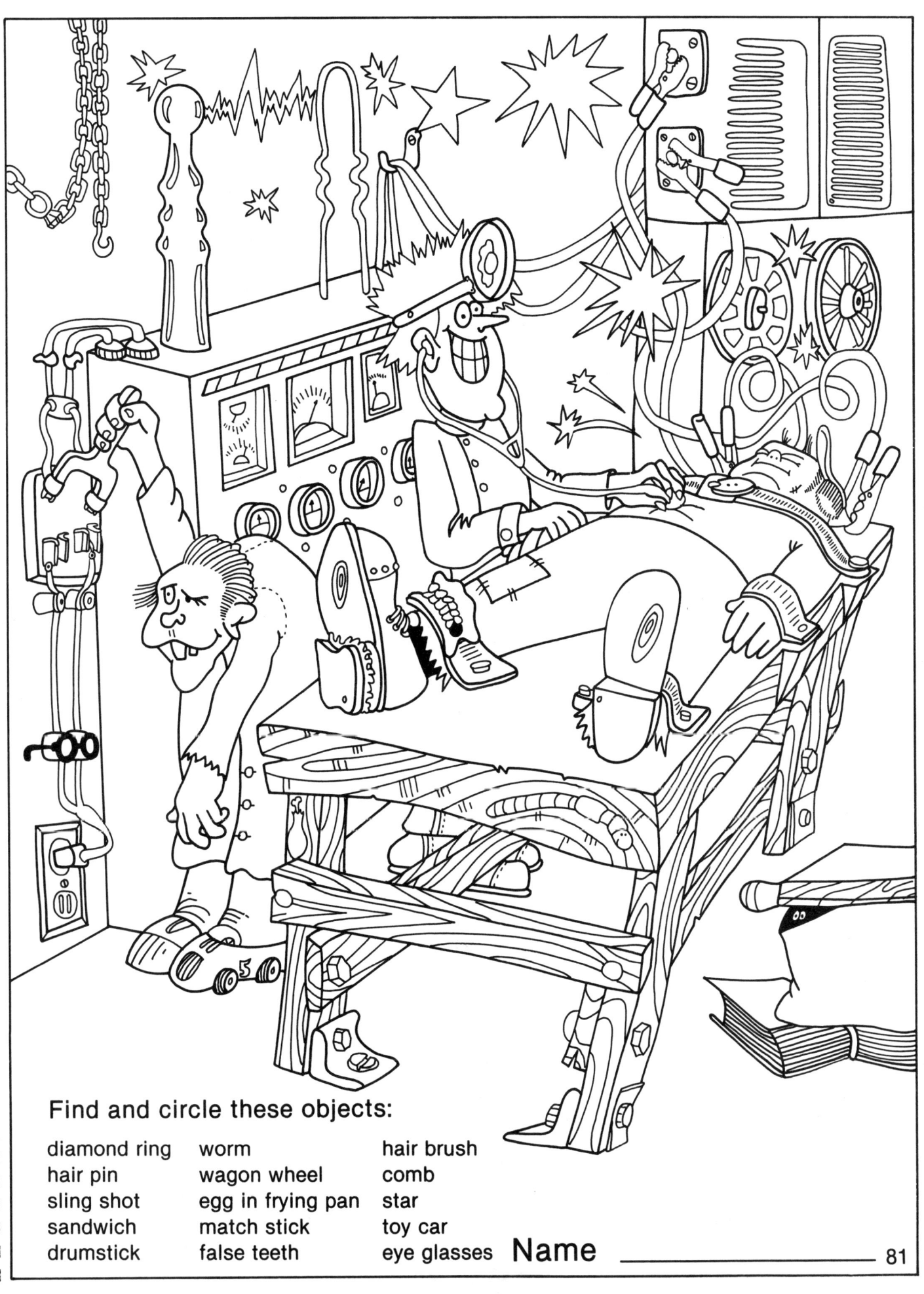

Find and circle these objects:

diamond ring, worm, hair brush
hair pin, wagon wheel, comb
sling shot, egg in frying pan, star
sandwich, match stick, toy car
drumstick, false teeth, eye glasses

Name _____

Monster Paper Bag Puppet

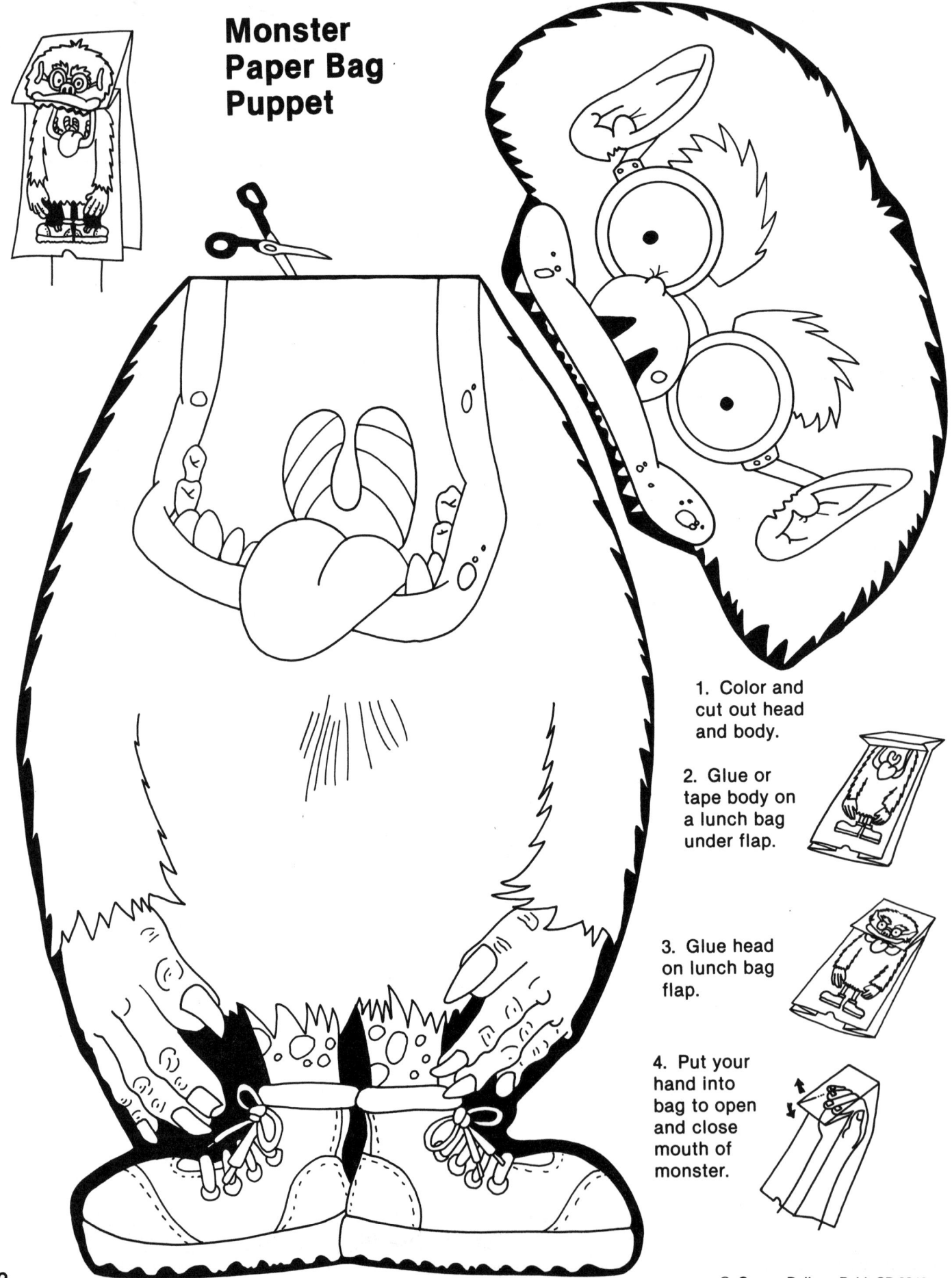

1. Color and cut out head and body.

2. Glue or tape body on a lunch bag under flap.

3. Glue head on lunch bag flap.

4. Put your hand into bag to open and close mouth of monster.

Name _____

1. ysrca _____
2. nrfhgiet _____
3. untah _____
4. nkppmui _____
5. aenlHlowe _____
6. onntrelaajkc _____
7. neacld _____
8. eacsr _____
9. vcrea _____
10. thgso _____

Unscramble the words:

ghost	frighten
scare	carve
Halloween	candle
pumpkin	haunt
jack-o'-lantern	scary

Name _____   **Halloween Story Starter**

Use some of the words below to write a Halloween story.

ghost   dunk   carve   costume   knock
bushes   games   hobos   creaking   demon
party   witch   neighborhood   grab
sack   candy   shriek   variety
scary   mask   monsters   dark
trick   treat   glowing
seeds   pumpkins   candles   faces
cider   giggle   jack-o'-lantern
doorbell   cobwebs
mischief   groups

Name _____

Name _____

```
r  b  t  m  n  f  r  f
s  g  f  s  z  r  y  i
p  u  m  p  k  i  n  a
r  s  o  o  x  g  r  c
b  o  o  h  j  b
r  k  w  t  k  a
r  g  t  r  e  a  t
```

Circle the hidden words:
pumpkin, boo, treat, spook, fright, bat

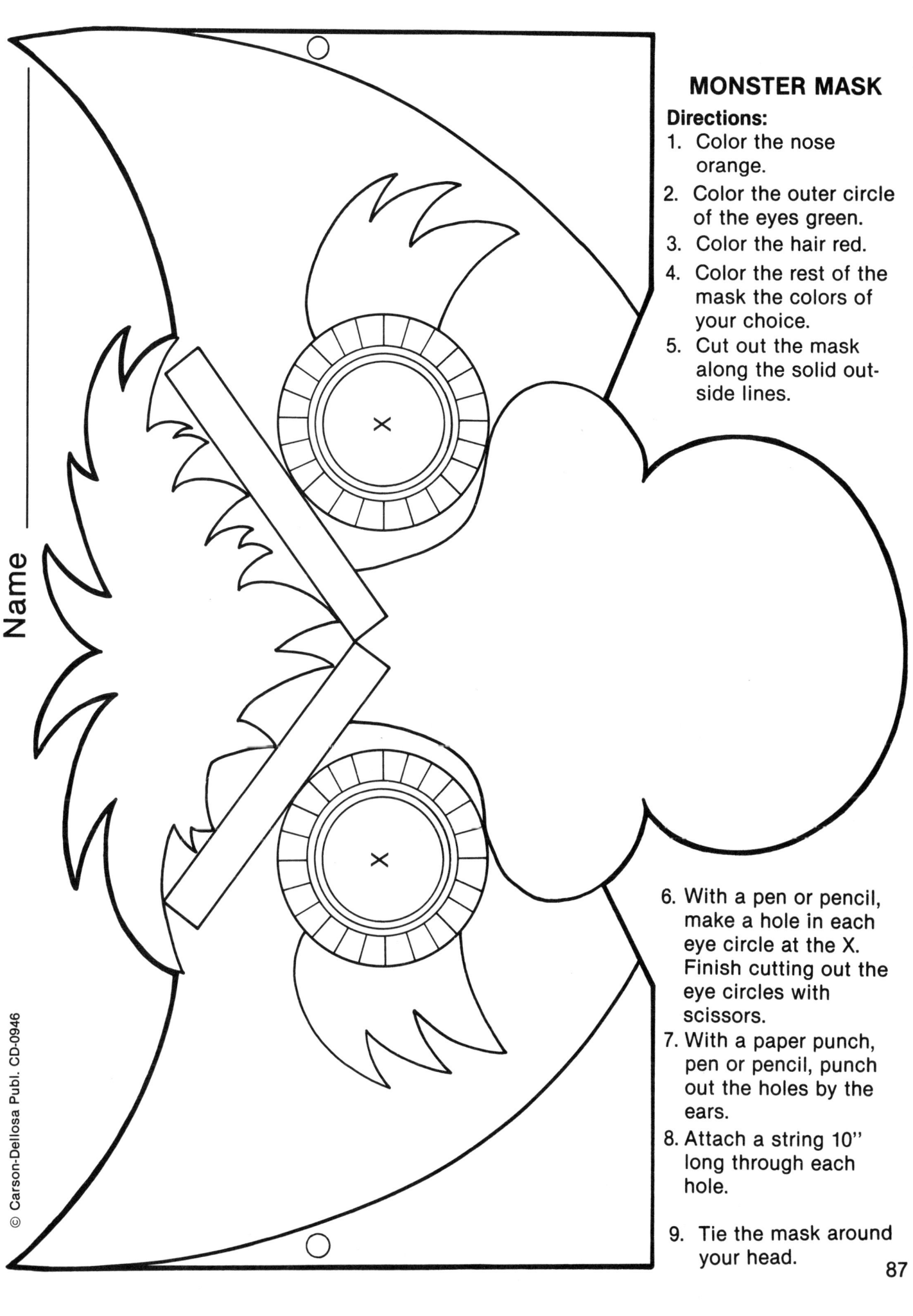

MONSTER MASK

Directions:
1. Color the nose orange.
2. Color the outer circle of the eyes green.
3. Color the hair red.
4. Color the rest of the mask the colors of your choice.
5. Cut out the mask along the solid outside lines.
6. With a pen or pencil, make a hole in each eye circle at the X. Finish cutting out the eye circles with scissors.
7. With a paper punch, pen or pencil, punch out the holes by the ears.
8. Attach a string 10" long through each hole.
9. Tie the mask around your head.

Name _____

Use your pencil to follow the dots to see who or what is watching Fido's dish.

88
Carson-Dellosa Publ. CD-0946

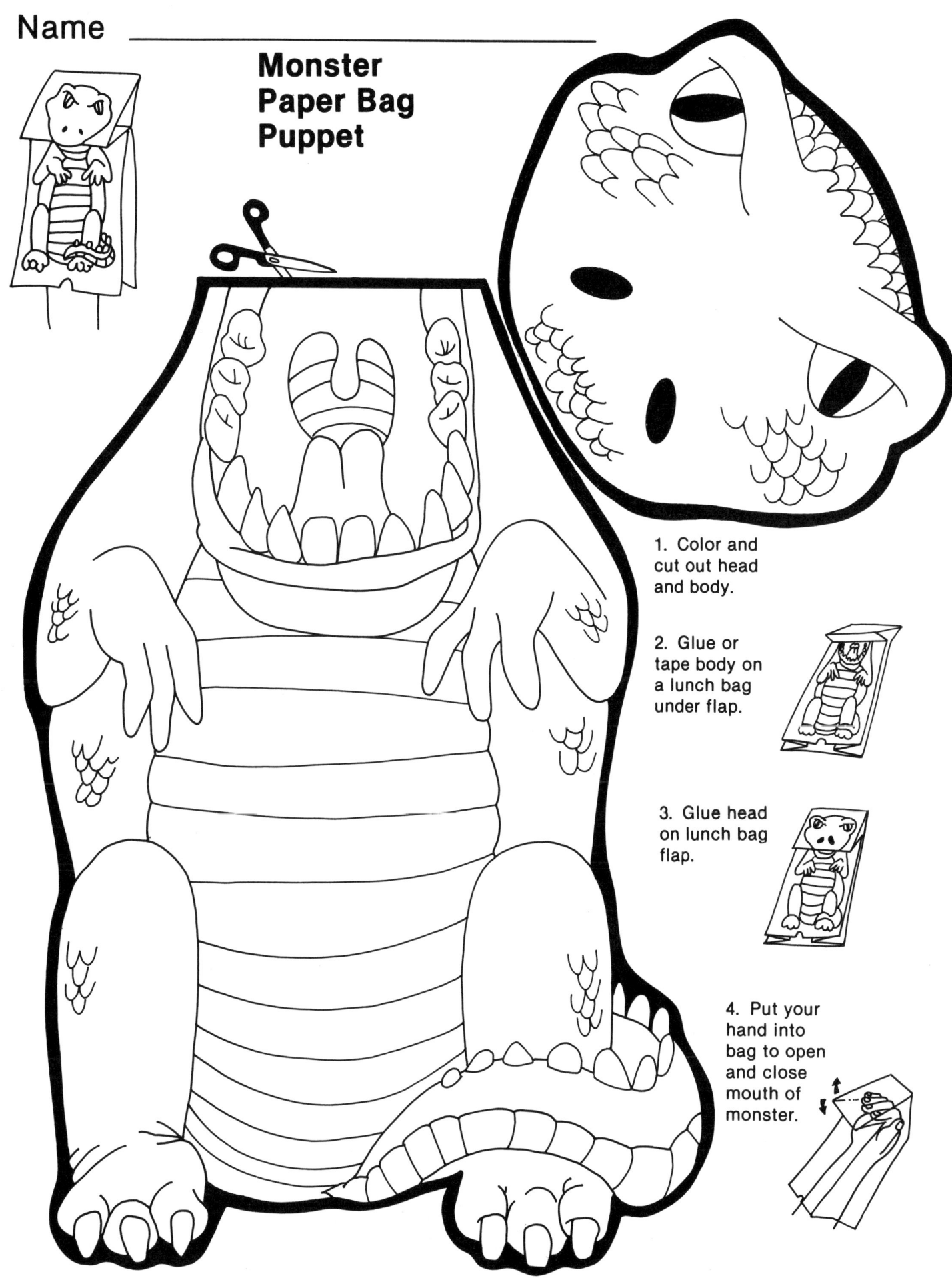

Name _____

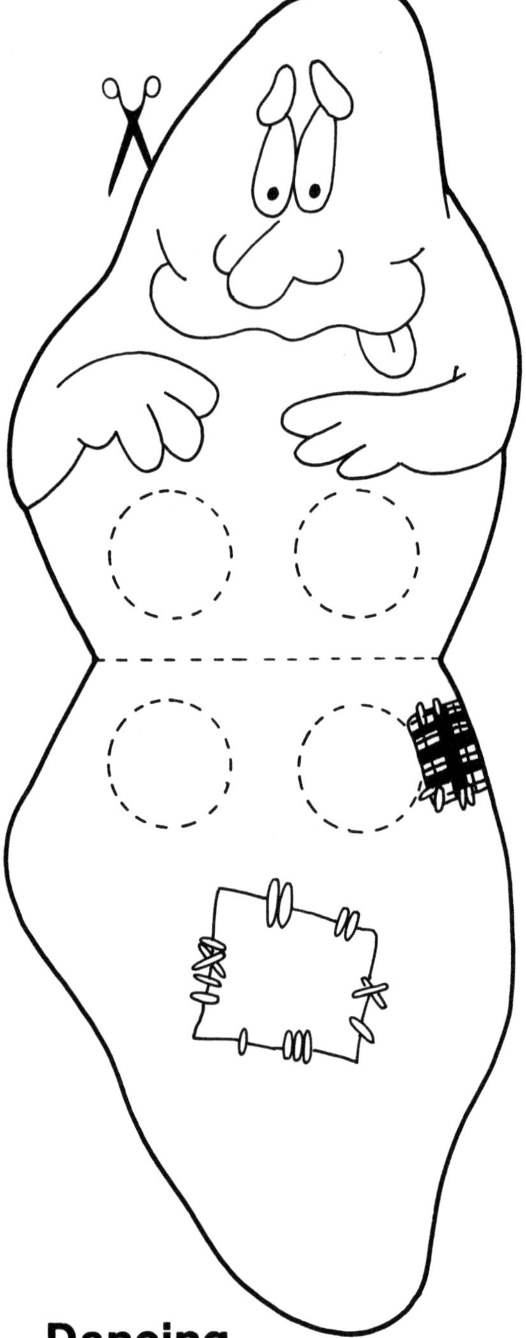

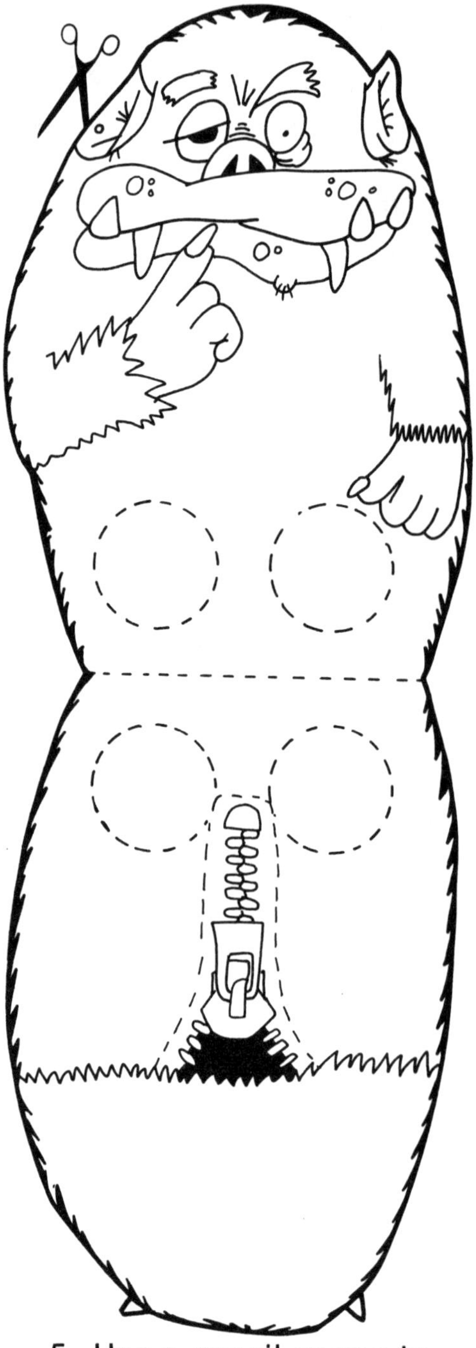

Dancing Monster Finger Puppets

Follow these easy directions to make each puppet:
1. Color puppet.
2. Cut puppet on heavy black line.
3. Fold puppet in half on dotted centerfold line.
4. Connect front and back sections of puppet by gluing or taping at top of head.  
5. Use a pencil or pen to punch holes in finger openings which are indicated by dotted circles. 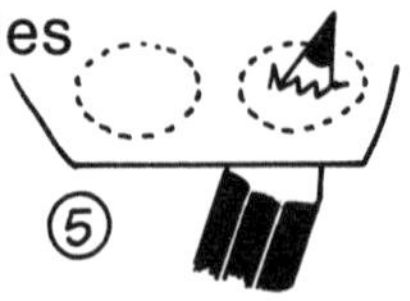
6. Use scissors to finish cutting out finger openings.
7. Put your fingers through the finger holes and make puppet dance by moving your fingers.

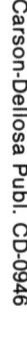

Name_____

Directions:

Name _____

My "mummy's" cookies

Use the recipe below to make a batch of Halloween cookie treats. Color the picture while your cookies are baking.

Halloween Cookie Treats

Batter Recipe
- 1 cup soft shortening (butter or margarine)
- 1½ cups sugar
- 2 eggs
- 2¾ cups flour
- 2 teaspoons cream of tartar
- 1 teaspoon baking soda
- ¼ teaspoon salt

Topping Recipe
- 2 tablespoons sugar
- 2 teaspoons cinnamon

1. Heat oven to 375°.
2. Mix the shortening, sugar and eggs listed in the batter recipe.
3. Blend in remaining dry ingredients listed in the batter recipe.
4. Place walnut-sized balls of dough 2 inches apart on an ungreased baking sheet.
5. Combine topping ingredients in a small bowl.
6. Sprinkle topping mixture on each cookie.
7. Bake 8 to 10 minutes.

© Carson-Dellosa Publ. CD-0946

Name _____

Find and circle the hidden words from the word list. The words are printed up, down, across or diagonally. Some words share a letter.

WORD LIST

GHOST
SKELETON
BAT
WITCH
MUMMY
GHOUL
SCREAM
BOO
HAUNTED
TRICK-OR-TREAT
GOBLIN
PUMPKIN
SCARE
SPOOKY
MONSTER
HALLOWEEN

```
B J C V G Y U I M G R T F V H S
B G H O S T M G R D A K N F A K
V D E R F G Y H B E K M M X L Z
P U M P K I N A R D G U O V L P
C D E R G H I T C R T G N W O C
E B C E A T R U B I C I S B W M
N E X U K O N W A B E K T C E S
X G Y C K X W I T C H N E J E C
N W I C S B U R M S R Y R C N A
V U I M S K E L E T O N Z P Q R
C R W B U P N E X Y B J O P A E
T X I G B K Y H A U N T E D N Q
V I S O G U I P M S W Z C R N H
C E Y B Z S J P L S R V T Y I H
X T O L B D C H P Q P D E V G T
E Y N I X W U R B W U O M X T K
C Y B N M F G K E X U V O E B I
X N O S L O W M A V S J K W B
G H O U L W V Y B O M U M M Y C
```

93

Name _____

**Halloween
Finger Play Poem**

Read the finger play poem. Perform the finger movements as you read the poem again. You may wish to complete the finger puppets on p.95 to use with the poem.

Color the picture.

FIVE LITTLE WITCHES
by Katherine Oana

One little witch was fixing her black shoe.
    (Fix shoe)

Another came to help, and then there were two.
    (Hold up 2 fingers)

Two little witches climbed high in the tree.
    (Fingers climb up)

Another started climbing, and then there were three.
    (Hold up 3 fingers)

Three little witches said,
"More brooms. We need more."
    (Fingers sweep)

Another brought her broom,
And then there were four.
    (Hold up 4 fingers)

Four little witches said,
"Through the sky let's dive."
    (Fingers dive)

Another came along, and then there were five.
    (Hold up 5 fingers)

Five little witches flying high in the sky.
"To the moon!" they said.
"To the moon let's fly!"
    (Five fingers fly
    in the air)

© Carson-Dellosa Publ. CD-0946

Name _____ **Witch Finger Puppets**

Complete these finger puppets to use with the finger play poem on p. 94.
1. Color and cut out the finger puppets.
2. Glue or tape the tabs together so that the puppet fits around your finger.

© Carson-Dellosa Publ. CD-0946

Name _____

Halloween Witch Art Project

1. Color and cut out all of the pieces.
2. Glue the hair to both sides of the head. (See example.)
3. Glue the hat brim to the hat. (See example.)
4. Glue the hat to the top of the head. (See example.)

Example

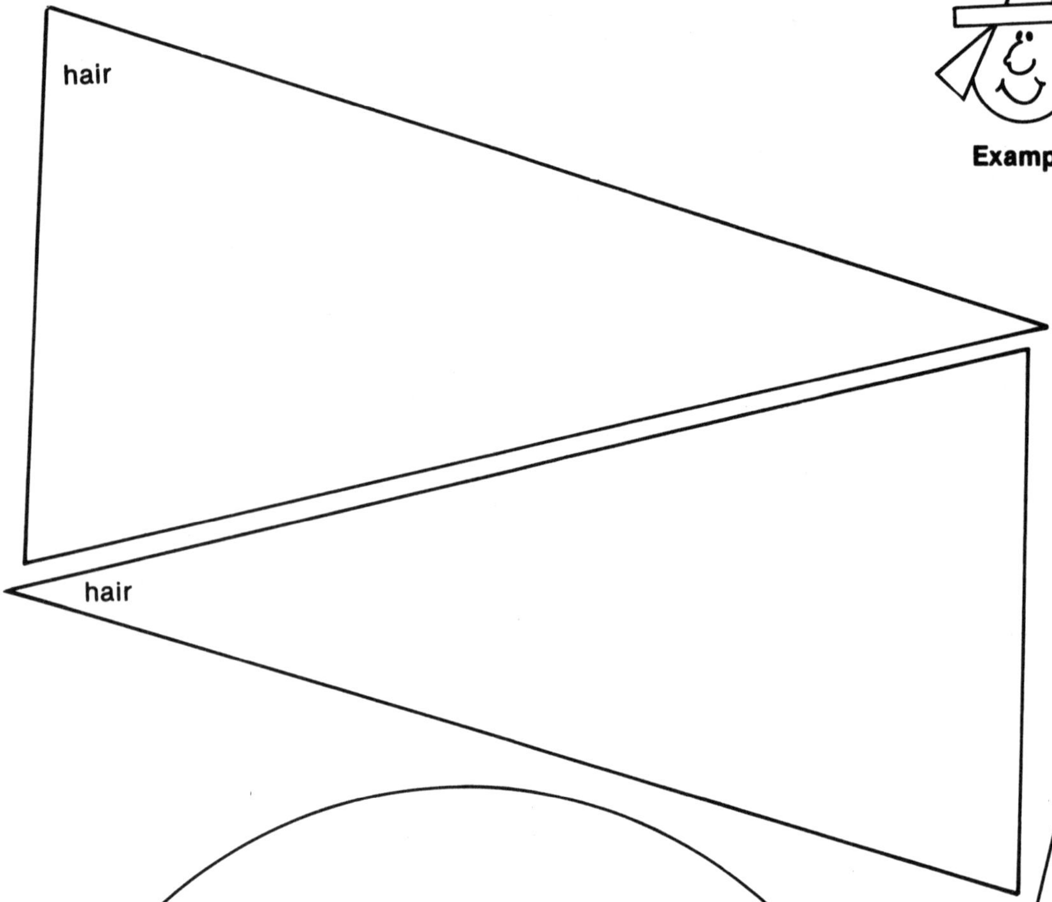

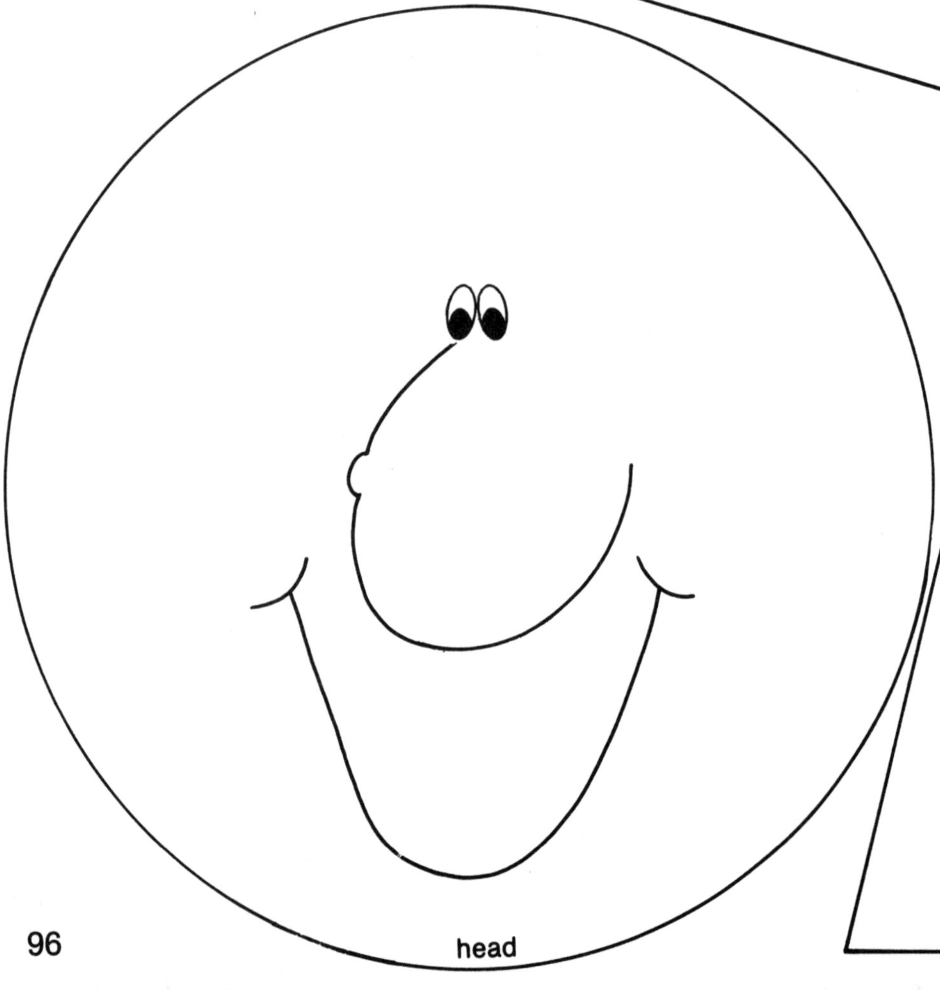

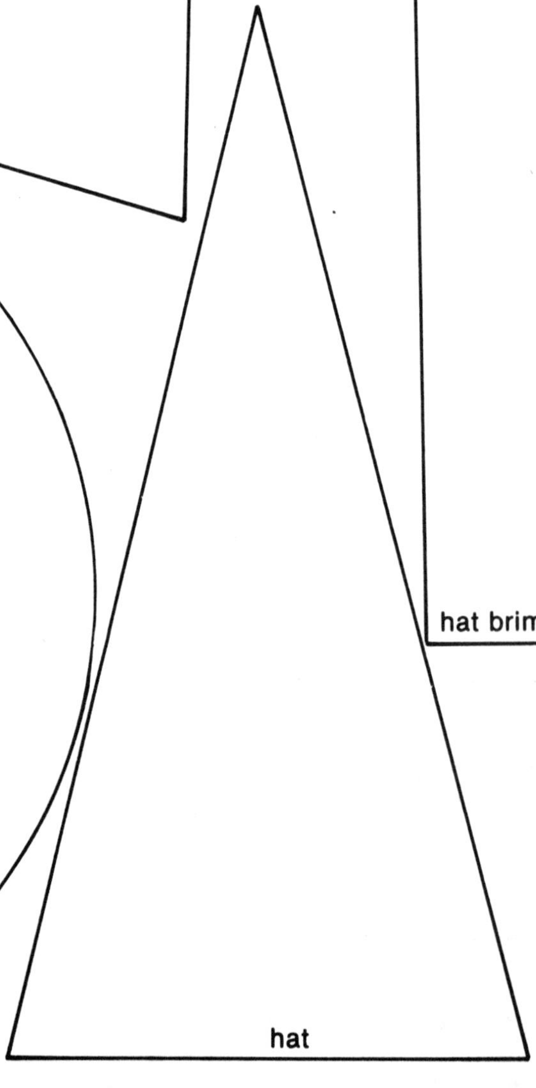

hair

hair

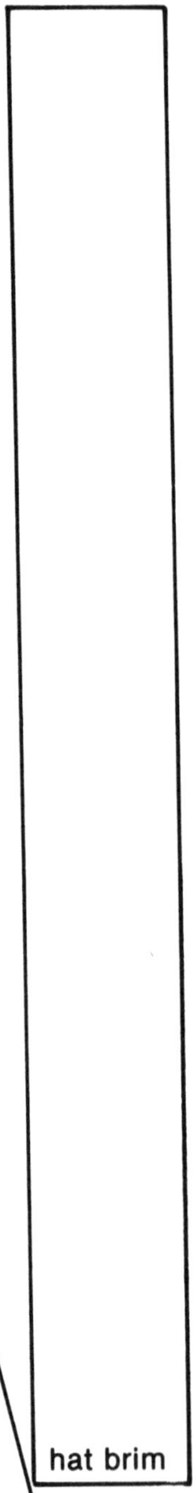

head

hat

hat brim

96

© Carson-Dellosa Publ. CD-0946

Name _____

Boning Up for Fun

Use these directions to construct the skeleton pictured on the following pages. Use the diagram at the left to help you.

1. Cut out all skeleton parts on pages 97-99 except for the complete skeleton at the left.
2. Use tape, glue or metal fasteners to connect matching numbers at dotted line circles. (Use pen or pencil to punch holes in the dotted circles before inserting fasteners.)

Suggestions for Use:

1. Hang your skeleton on the front door or your bedroom door.
2. Attach a string to the head and hang your skeleton from the ceiling.

Do not cut out this skeleton.

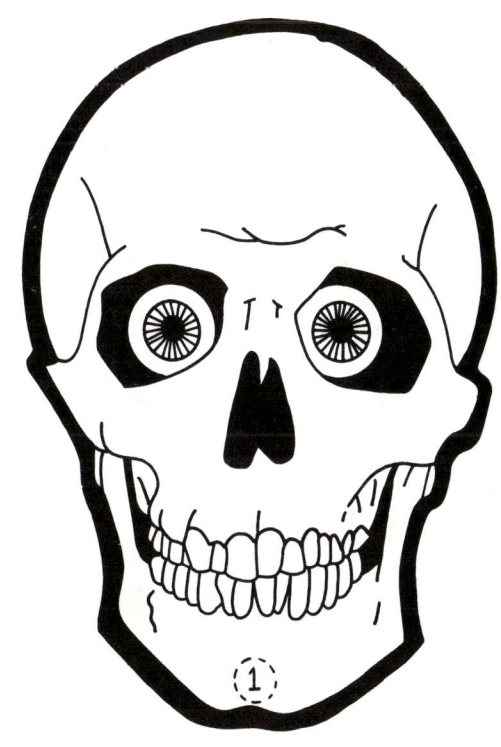

© Carson-Dellosa Publ. CD-0946

97

Name _____

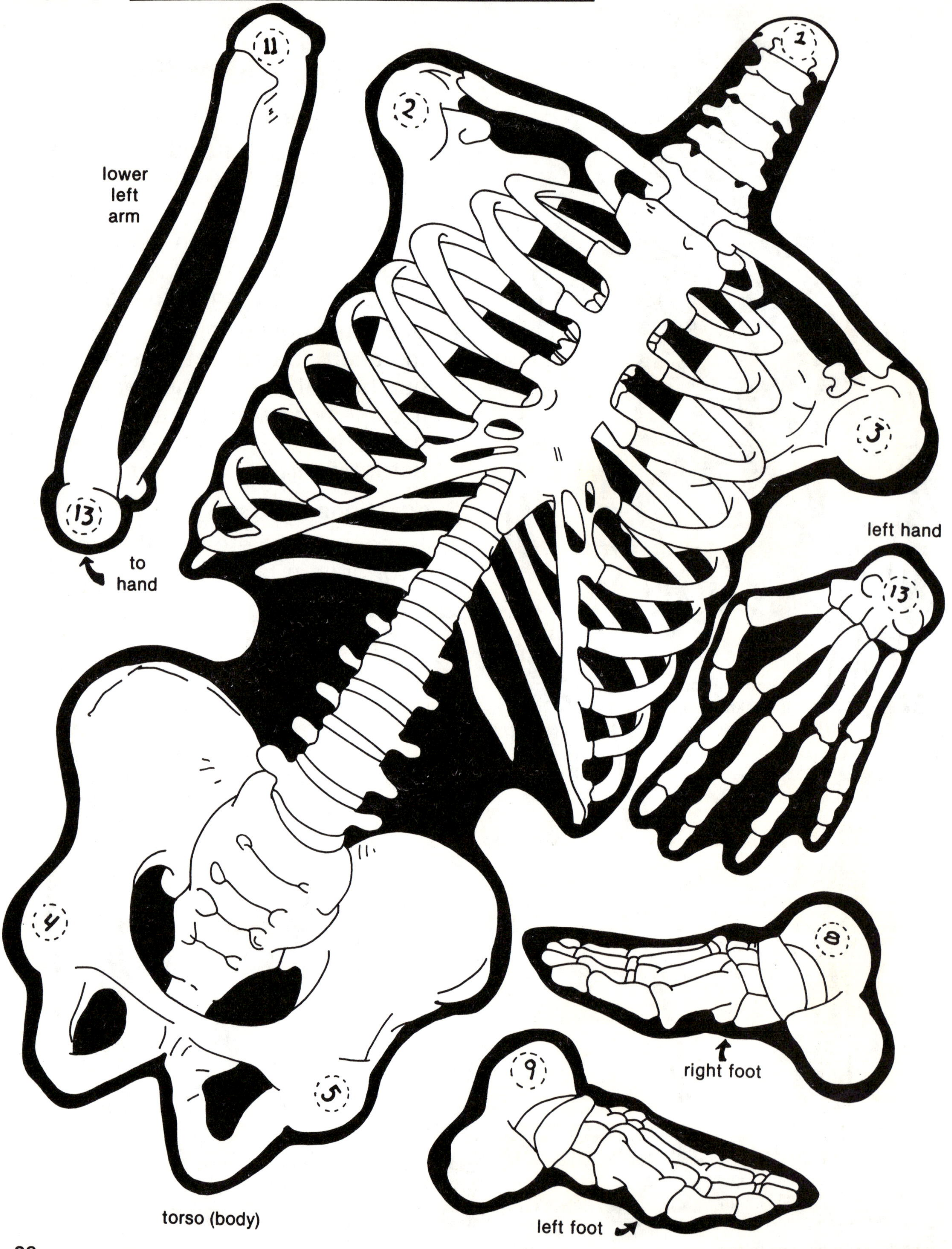

lower left arm

to hand

left hand

torso (body)

right foot

left foot

98

© Carson-Dellosa Publ. CD-0946

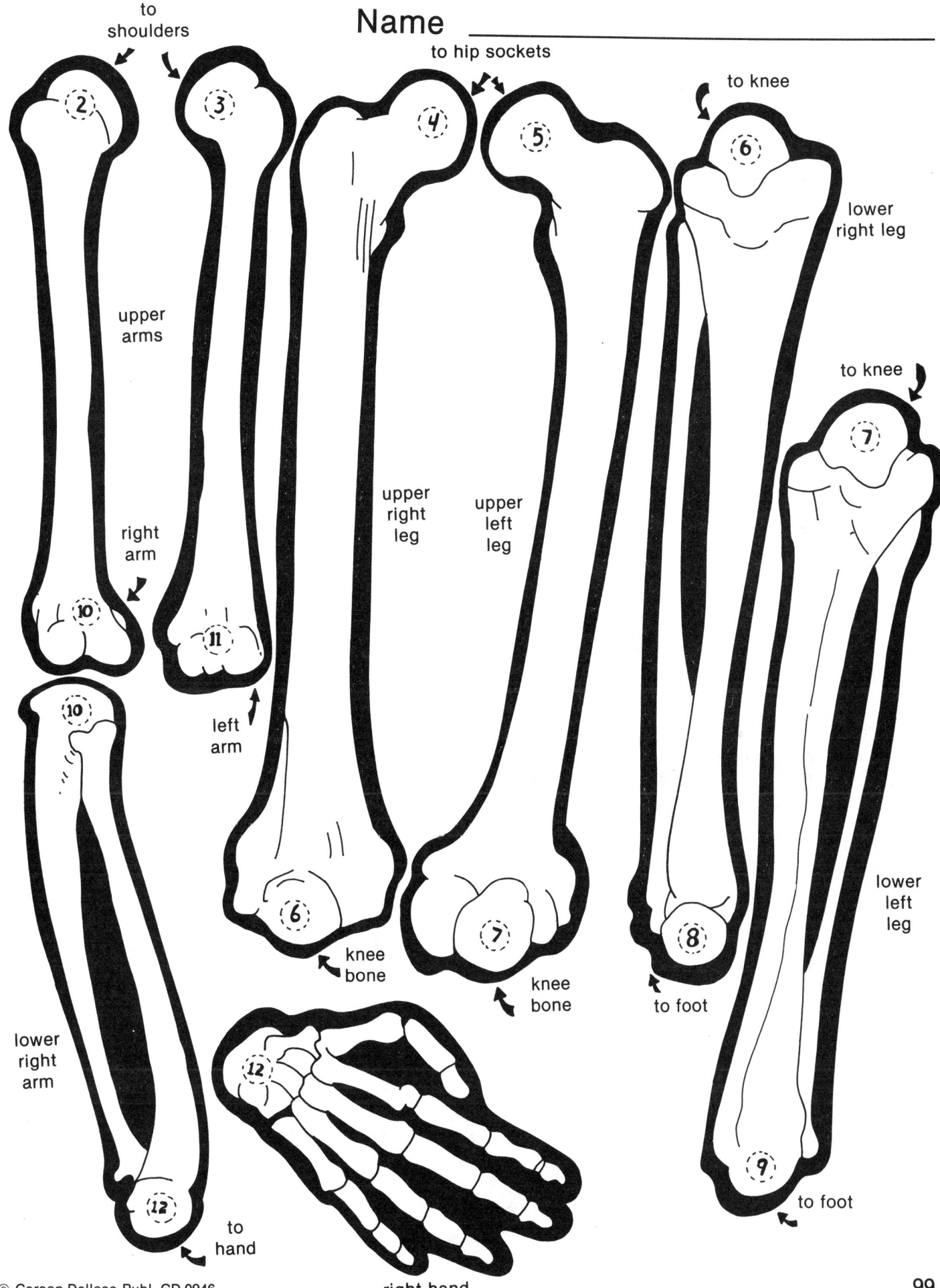

Name _____

Skeleton Story Starter

Use some of the words on the skeleton to write a story about Halloween.

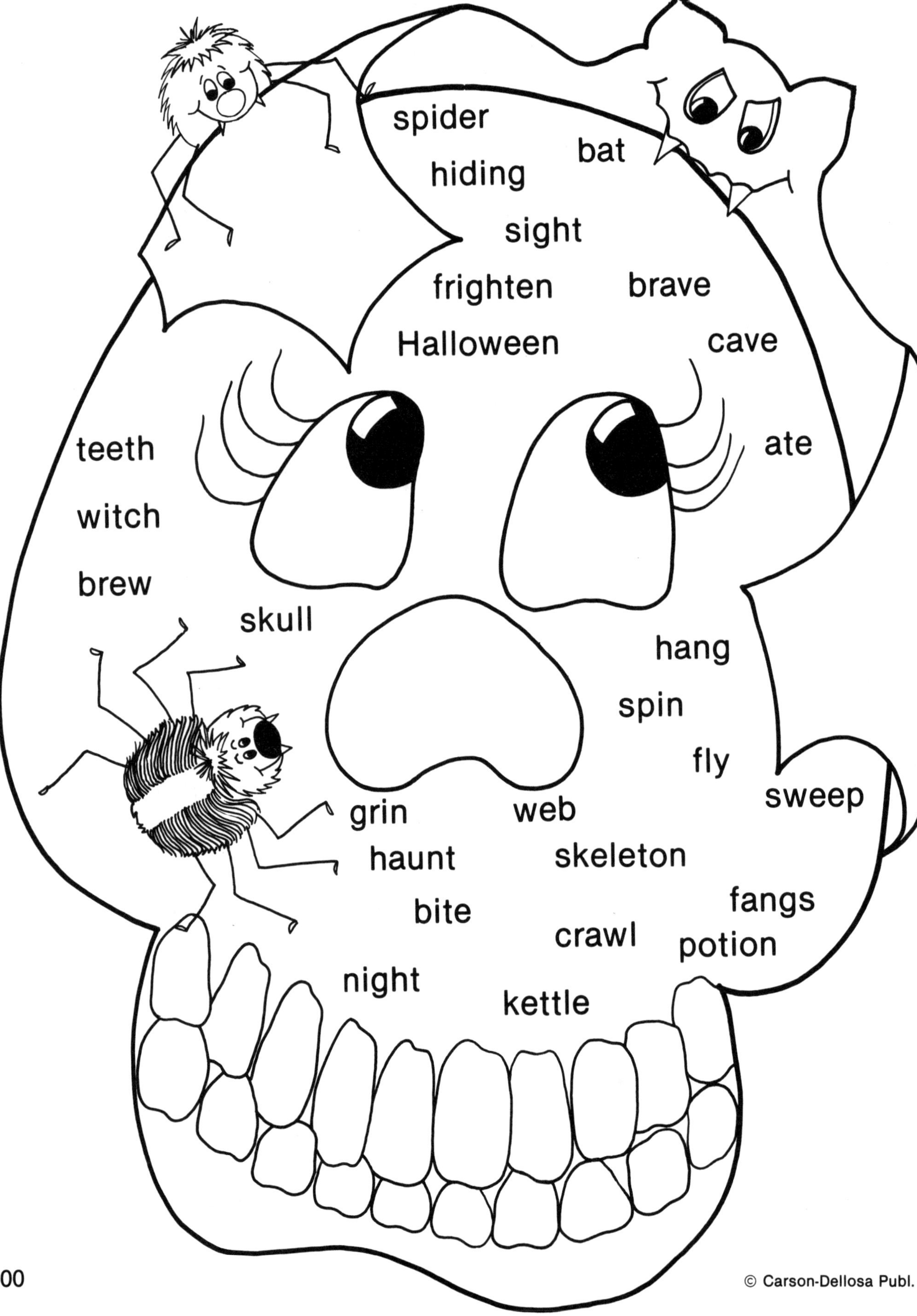

spider
bat
hiding
sight
frighten   brave
Halloween   cave
teeth
ate
witch
brew
skull
hang
spin
fly
sweep
grin   web
haunt   skeleton
bite   fangs
crawl   potion
night   kettle

Name _____

Monsters

How to Use

Related Poems
Enlarge any of the patterns to use as the center of a bulletin board. Direct students to copy a related poem. Display the papers on the bulletin board.

Award Sayings
Use an award saying with its related pattern to create student awards.

Related Poems

Imagine how men from space
    might look.
I'm sure you've seen one in a book.
My dad sells shoes and he'd like
    to meet
A monster who has at least
    eight feet.

We think of monsters as something
    quite shocking.
Well, I found one down in my
    Christmas stocking
Now you can be sure, it was quite
    a surprise
To see that big tooth and those
    purple eyes!

Monsters can have horns or wild
    stringy hair.
They can have scales or
    warts everywhere.
Fortunately, things are not as
    they seem.
'Cause we only see monsters if
    we dream.

Award Sayings

Monstrously Good Work!

_____ is a
Monstrous Success

Hauntingly Helpful

I'm a Monstrously Good Student!

Name _____   **Monsters**

Halloween

How to Use

Related Poems
 Enlarge any of the patterns to use as the center of a bulletin board. Direct students to copy a related poem. Display the papers on the bulletin board.

Award Sayings
 Use an award saying with its related pattern to create student awards.

Related Poems

Sitting high up in a large oak tree,
His big round eyes surely frighten me.
But it's when he lets out his owly hoot,
That I get going and really scoot!

Did you see that strange-looking cat
Walking around in a witch's hat?
If he came with us Halloween night
Would he come on a broom?
I think he just might.

He's not well-liked, this poor little guy,
And so often I have wondered why.
He asks so little - a fly or two!
He's no bother to me -
Does he bother you?

Tall hats
Stringy hair
Stirring brew
Scaring you,
 - Witches!

Award Sayings

I give a "hoot" about my grades.
Whoo-ray for a job well done!
I'm worth "hooting" about.

Clever kitty
I'm the cat's meow!

I'm spinning a web of good work!
My web is filled with good grades.

Bewitching Good Worker!
I've cast a spell on you.

Name _____   **Halloween**

105

The BAT AWARD goes to

_____

for great work!

Signed _____

© Carson-Dellosa Publ. CD-0946

_____ is the CAT'S MEOW for "Purrfect" Work!

© Carson-Dellosa Publ. CD-0946

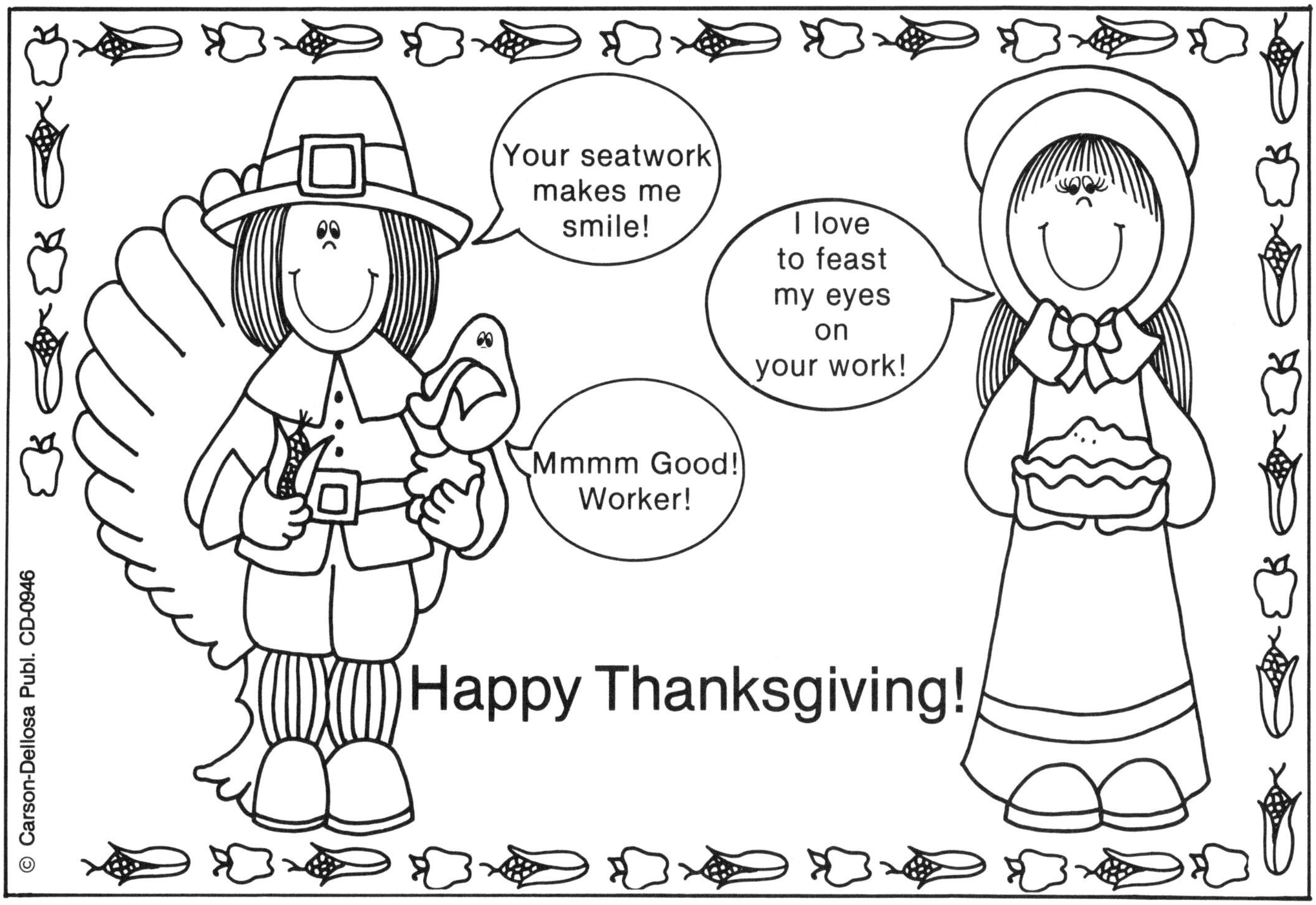
Your seatwork makes me smile!
I love to feast my eyes on your work!
Mmmm Good! Worker!
Happy Thanksgiving!
© Carson-Dellosa Publ. CD-0946

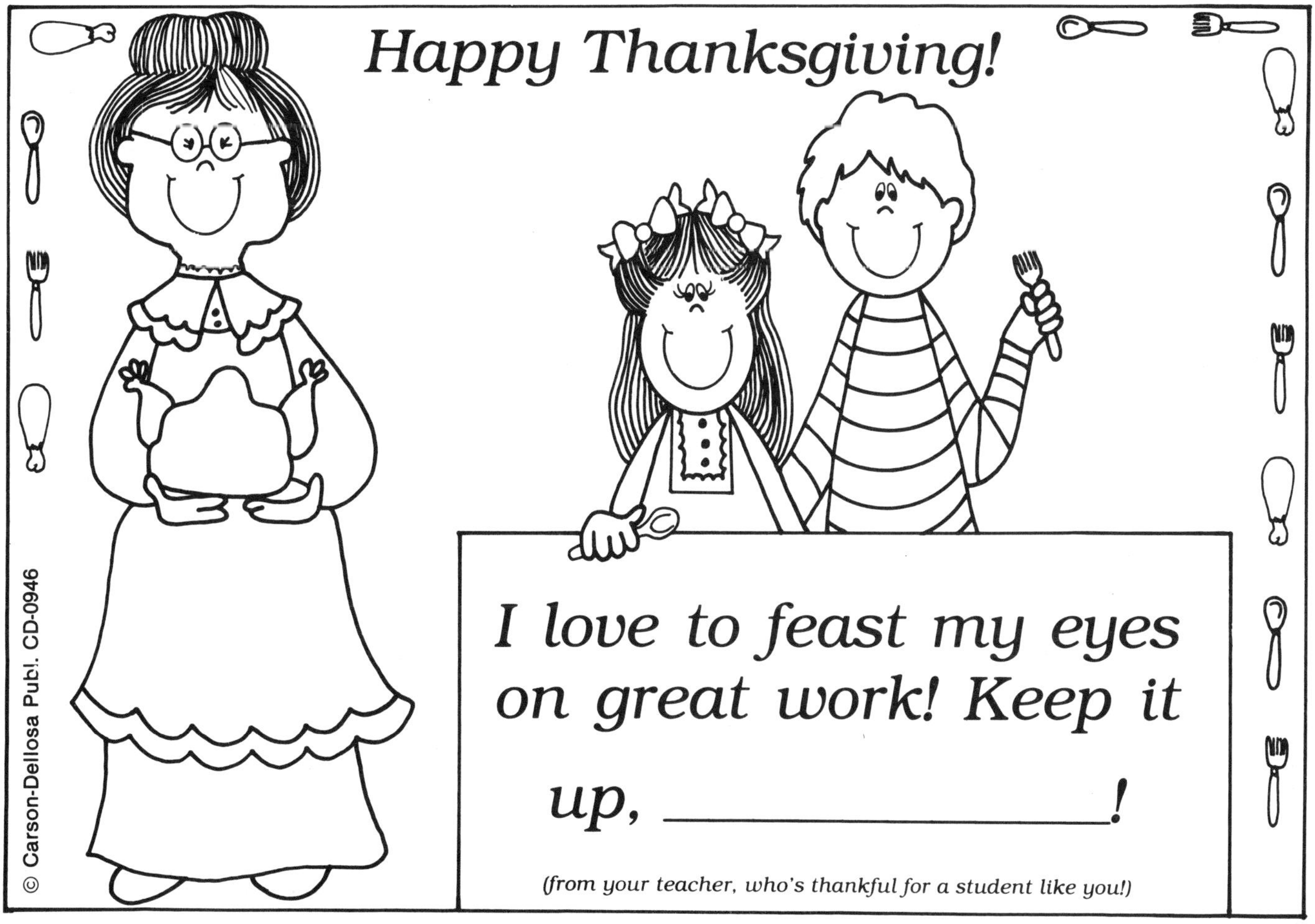
Happy Thanksgiving!
I love to feast my eyes on great work! Keep it up, ____________!
(from your teacher, who's thankful for a student like you!)
© Carson-Dellosa Publ. CD-0946

Name _____   **Thanksgiving Story Starter**

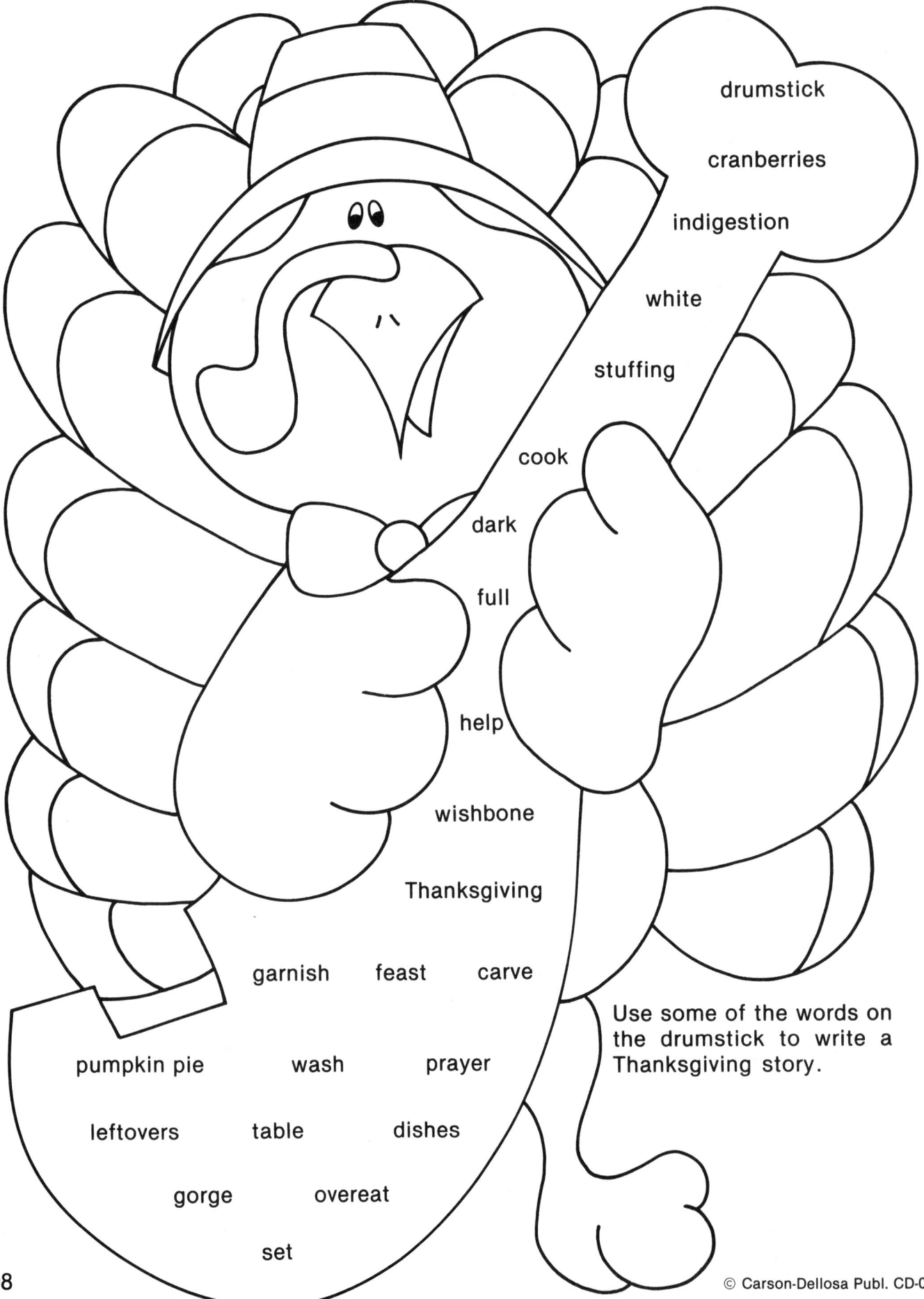

drumstick
cranberries
indigestion
white
stuffing
cook
dark
full
help
wishbone
Thanksgiving
garnish feast carve
pumpkin pie wash prayer
leftovers table dishes
gorge overeat
set

Use some of the words on the drumstick to write a Thanksgiving story.

Name _____

Name _____

Thanksgiving Story Starter

Use some of the words on the pumpkin pie to write a Thanksgiving story. Color the picture.

fork, bib, turkey, feast, chick, fat, smell, pie, flavor, tasty, oats, hat, tough, knife, hide, corn, napkin, Thanksgiving, food, pilgrim, stuffing, feathers, dripping, colorful

Name _____

Name_____

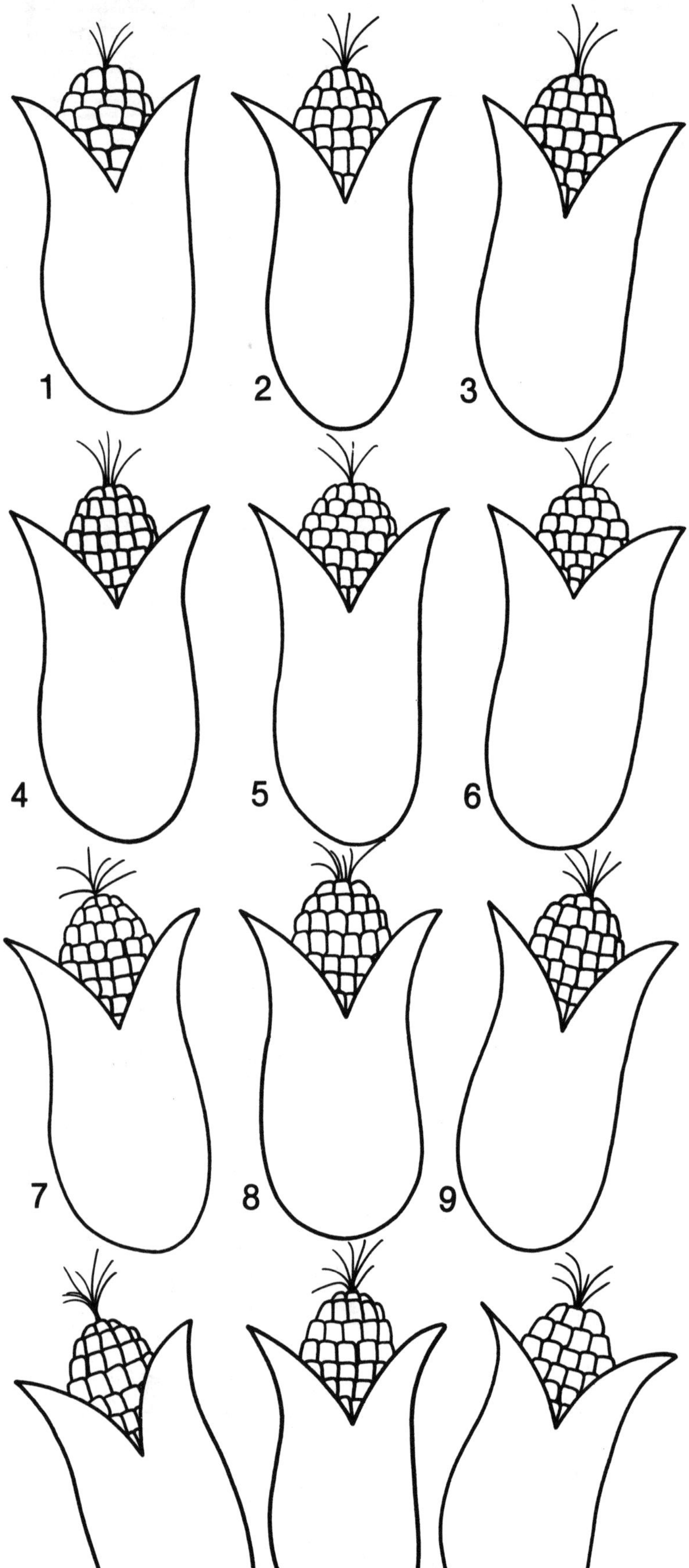

Directions:

1 2 3
4 5 6
7 8 9
10 11 12

112

© Carson-Dellosa Publ. CD-0946

Name_____

1. rcon _____
2. kutrye _____
3. eder _____
4. kpnimpu _____
5. refteahs _____
6. giwawm _____
7. inIdan _____
8. gmilriP _____
9. sefat _____

Unscramble the words:
deer
feathers
Indian
feast
corn
pumpkin
wigwam
turkey
Pilgrim

Name _____

Word Wizardry

How many three and four-letter words can you make by using the letters from the phrase below? You may use any letter combination.

Thanksgiving Dinner

Name _____

Directions:

Name_____

Directions:

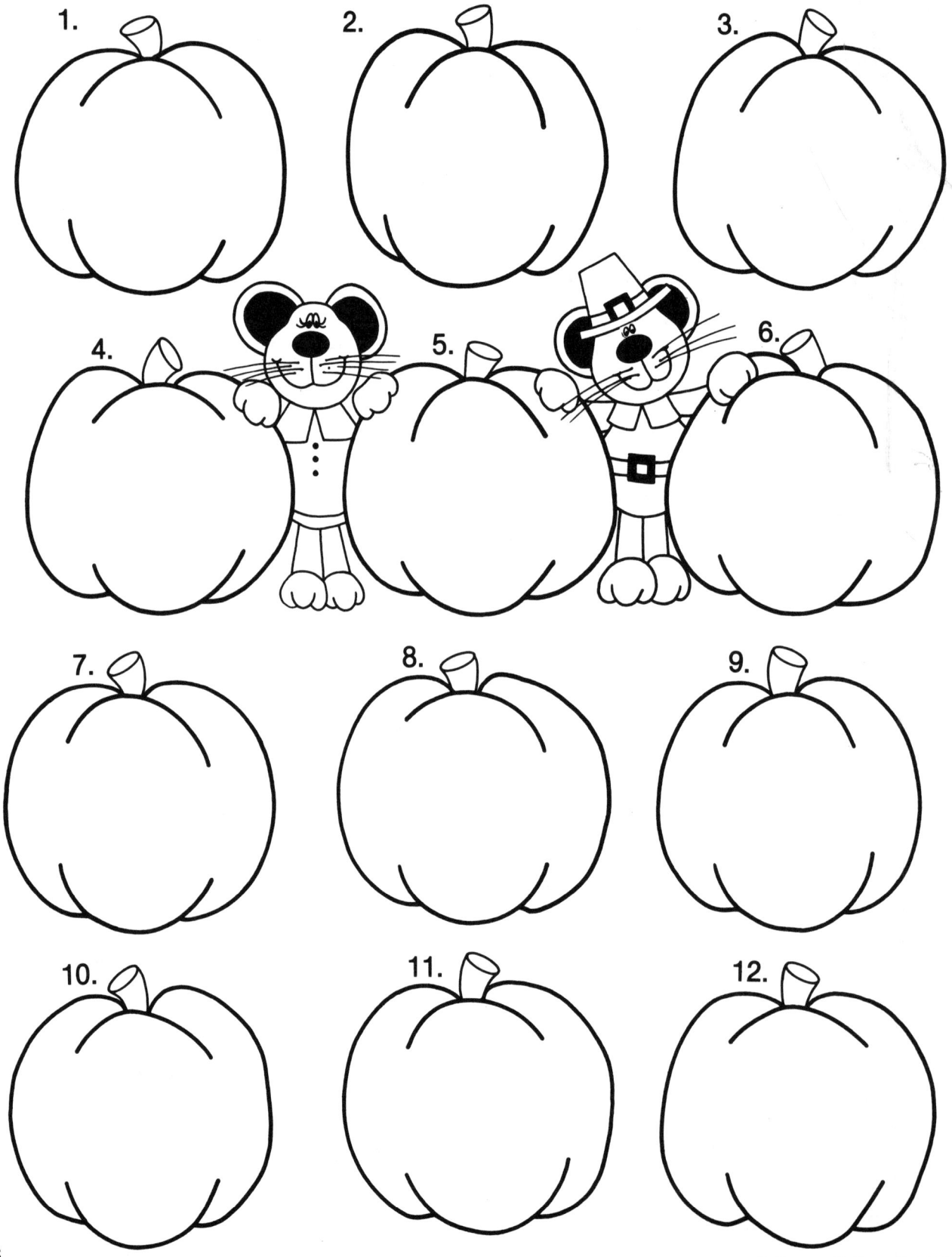

Name_____

Put a circle around:
Pilgrim corn
drumstick turkey
feather pumpkin
feast

```
   t b c o l m n
p  u m p k i n o d a
f  r s s w t y a c u
c  k e x d f p d o r
f  e a t h e r o r s
o  y n g u a u b n d
   d r u m s t i c k
   a o s d t c r i j
   P i l g r i m p
```

Thanksgiving

How to Use

Related Poems
 Enlarge any of the patterns to use as the center of a bulletin board. Direct students to copy a related poem. Display the papers on the bulletin board.

Award Sayings
 Use an award saying with its related pattern to create student awards.

Related Poems

Come with me for a little walk.
You should see this huge cornstalk!
Sh! I think it can really hear,
'Cause I see it has a great big ear.

Award Sayings

A"maize"ing Student
Shucks, I'm Smart!

I'm an Indian maiden with jet black hair.
Tending my teepee with loving care.
The moccasins that I proudly wear
I make with leather, beads and care.

Proud Princess!
Mighty Maiden

I'm an Indian warrior bold.
About me many things are told.
I helped the white man with his living;
This is why we have Thanksgiving.

Bravo Brave
Super Chief
High Marks Chief

Name _____ **Thanksgiving**

(Instructions on previous page)

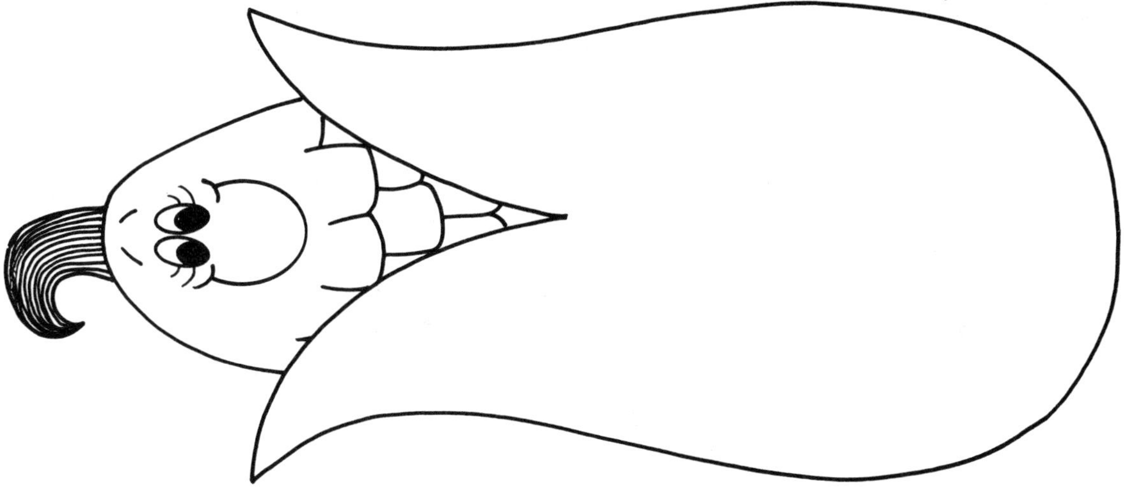

© Carson-Dellosa Publ. CD-0946

119

Thanksgiving

How to Use

Related Poems
 Enlarge any of the patterns to use as the center of a bulletin board. Direct students to copy a related poem. Display the papers on the bulletin board.

Award Sayings
 Use an award saying with its related pattern to create student awards.

Related Poems

Award Sayings

When you see me in the fields,
My orange glowing in the sun,
It's time to say goodbye to summer
And hello to autumn fun!

Pumpkin Pickin' Worker!
I'm pleased as a pumpkin about my work.

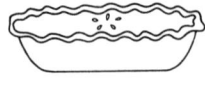

There isn't a smell anywhere -
Nowhere an aroma so fair.
Such lusciousness - oh me, oh my!
The temptation of a freshly-baked pie.

My work is quite a treat!
I'm a sweetie-pie!

A pilgrim boy of long ago
Helped his dad the corn to grow.
The pilgrim girl, with much care taking,
Helped her mom with candlemaking.

Purely Perfect
Proud Pilgrim

Name _____

Thanksgiving

(Instructions on previous page)

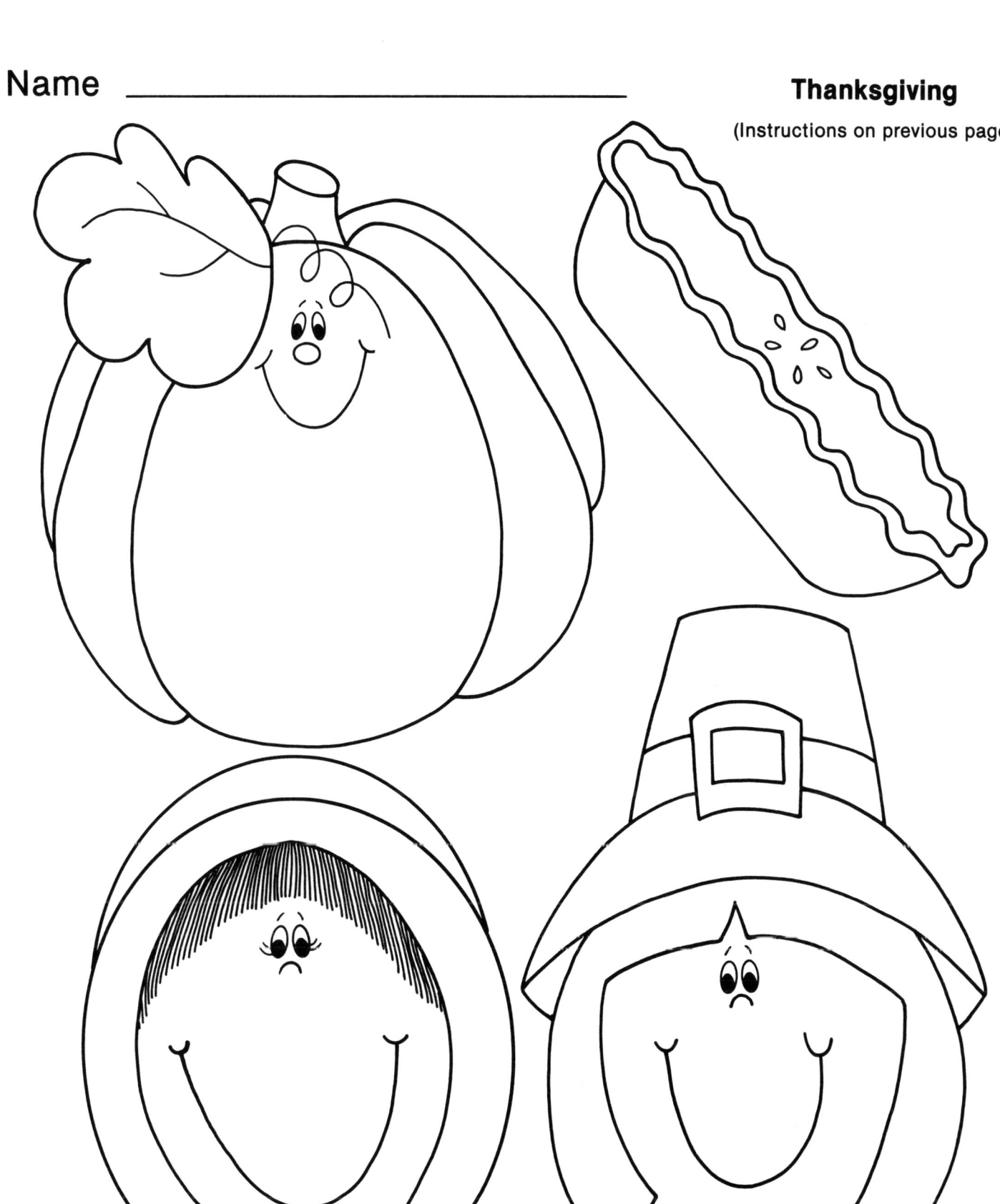

© Carson-Dellosa Publ. CD-0946

121

Name _____

Thanksgiving Story Starter

Use some of the words on the pilgrim to write a Thanksgiving story.

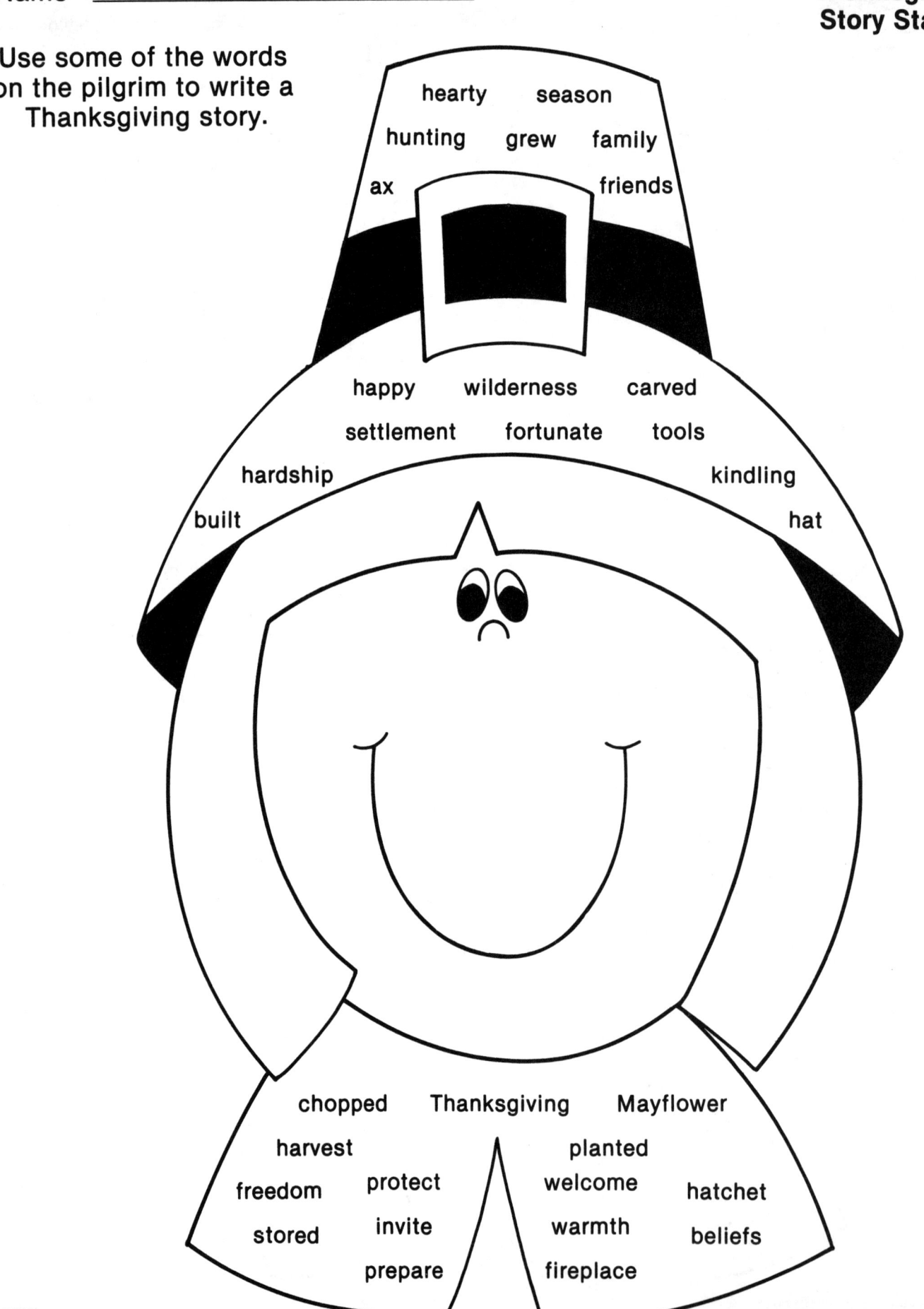

122
© Carson-Dellosa Publ. CD-0946

Name_____

Name _____

Thanksgiving Story Starter

Use some of the words on the pilgrim to write a Thanksgiving story.

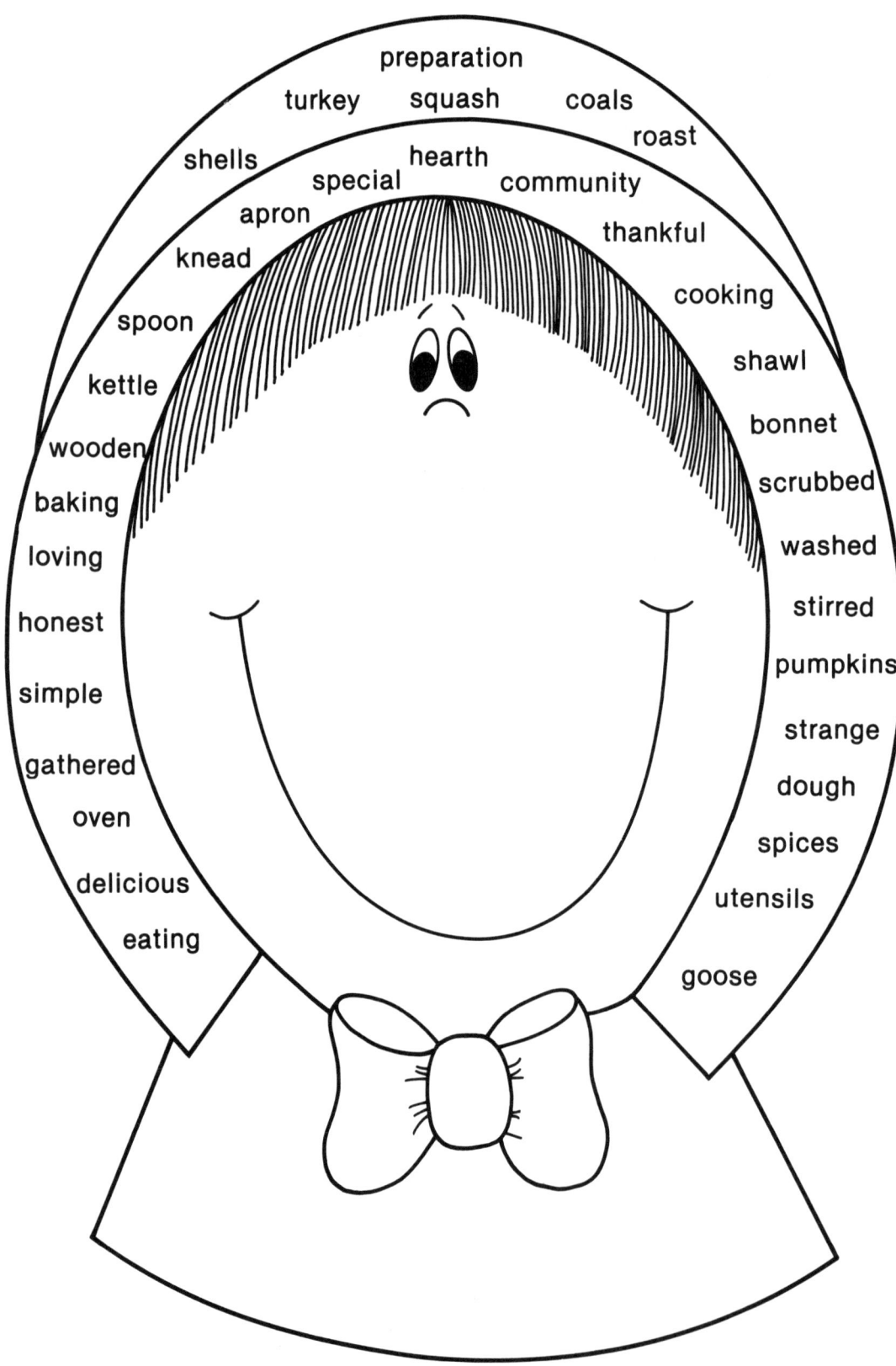

124
© Carson-Dellosa Publ. CD-0946

Name _____

Name _____

Did you ever wish you could make something really special to add to your family's Thanksgiving dinner? Now you can, and it's simple. You're lucky today. Unlike the Pilgrims, you don't have to start with a real pumpkin. You also probably won't need to bake your dessert in a fireplace. Follow the recipe below to make delicious pumpkin bars. Color the picture while the bars are baking.

Pilgrim Pumpkin Bars

2 eggs
½ cup sugar
½ cup brown sugar
½ cup vegetable oil
1 cup canned pumpkin
1 cup all-purpose flour
1 teaspoon baking powder
1 teaspoon cinnamon
½ teaspoon baking soda
¼ teaspoon salt

½ teaspoon ground nutmeg
¼ cup raisins
¼ cup chopped nuts

Frosting Ingredients
⅓ cup margarine
1¾ cup powdered sugar
1 teaspoon vanilla
1 to 1½ tablespoons hot water

Heat oven to 350°. Lightly grease and flour a 9" square pan. Beat together eggs, sugars, oil and pumpkin. In a separate bowl, mix together flour, baking powder, cinnamon, baking soda, salt and nutmeg. Add to egg mixture. Stir well. Mix in raisins and nuts. Pour into pan. Bake 35 minutes or until lightly browned. Cool. Spread with frosting. Cut into 1" x 3" bars. Refrigerate. Makes 27 bars.

Browned Butter Frosting: Melt margarine over low heat until light brown. In large bowl, beat together powdered sugar and vanilla. Gradually add hot water, beating until frosting is smooth enough to spread.

Name _____

Crack the Code

Using the key at the bottom, unlock the secret code to learn some real secrets about the first Thanksgiving! Write the words on another sheet of paper.

$\overline{26}\ \overline{19}\ \overline{1}$ $\overline{17}\ \overline{16}\ \overline{6}\ \overline{7}\ \overline{25}\ \overline{13}\ \overline{5}\ \overline{11}\ \overline{24}\ \overline{11}\ \overline{7}\ \overline{5}$ $\overline{8}\ \overline{11}\ \overline{7}\ \overline{7}\ \overline{20}\ \overline{1}$' $\overline{13}\ \overline{19}$ $\overline{6}\ \overline{13}\ \overline{17}\ \overline{19}\ \overline{7}\ \overline{11}\ \overline{13}\ \overline{16}\ \overline{20}\ \overline{8}$ $\overline{6}\ \overline{15}$ $\overline{11}$'

$\overline{17}\ \overline{16}\ \overline{20}\ \overline{22}\ \overline{16}\ \overline{6}\ \overline{8}$ $\overline{7}\ \overline{19}$ $\overline{2}\ \overline{16}\ \overline{7}\ \overline{18}\ \overline{20}\ \overline{1}\ \overline{1}\ \overline{22}$ $\overline{13}\ \overline{6}\ \overline{12}\ \overline{2}\ \overline{20}$ $\overline{6}\ \overline{7}\ \overline{8}$ $\overline{7}\ \overline{19}$ $\overline{9}\ \overline{12}\ \overline{15}\ \overline{9}\ \overline{25}\ \overline{11}\ \overline{7}$ $\overline{9}\ \overline{11}\ \overline{20}$!

$\overline{17}\ \overline{16}\ \overline{19}\ \overline{13}\ \overline{20}$ $\overline{9}\ \overline{11}\ \overline{10}\ \overline{5}\ \overline{1}\ \overline{11}\ \overline{15}\ \overline{13}$ $\overline{6}\ \overline{17}\ \overline{20}$ $\overline{10}\ \overline{19}\ \overline{18}\ \overline{13}\ \overline{17}\ \overline{20}\ \overline{1}$' $\overline{8}\ \overline{1}\ \overline{11}\ \overline{20}\ \overline{8}$ $\overline{26}\ \overline{1}\ \overline{12}\ \overline{11}\ \overline{17}$ $\overline{6}\ \overline{7}\ \overline{8}$

$\overline{2}\ \overline{19}\ \overline{1}\ \overline{7}$.

$\overline{17}\ \overline{16}\ \overline{20}\ \overline{1}\ \overline{20}$ $\overline{3}\ \overline{20}\ \overline{1}\ \overline{20}$ $\overline{19}\ \overline{7}\ \overline{20}$ $\overline{16}\ \overline{12}\ \overline{7}\ \overline{8}\ \overline{1}\ \overline{20}\ \overline{8}$ $\overline{6}\ \overline{7}\ \overline{8}$ $\overline{26}\ \overline{11}\ \overline{26}\ \overline{17}\ \overline{22}$ $\overline{19}\ \overline{7}$ $\overline{17}\ \overline{16}\ \overline{6}\ \overline{17}$

$\overline{17}\ \overline{16}\ \overline{6}\ \overline{7}\ \overline{25}\ \overline{13}\ \overline{5}\ \overline{11}\ \overline{24}\ \overline{11}\ \overline{7}\ \overline{5}$ $\overline{15}\ \overline{19}\ \overline{1}\ \overline{7}$.

$\overline{7}\ \overline{11}\ \overline{7}\ \overline{20}\ \overline{17}\ \overline{22}$ $\overline{3}\ \overline{20}\ \overline{1}\ \overline{20}$ $\overline{11}\ \overline{7}\ \overline{8}\ \overline{11}\ \overline{6}\ \overline{7}\ \overline{13}$ $\overline{3}\ \overline{16}\ \overline{19}$ $\overline{2}\ \overline{6}\ \overline{15}\ \overline{20}$ $\overline{18}\ \overline{22}$ $\overline{13}\ \overline{12}\ \overline{19}\ \overline{1}\ \overline{11}\ \overline{13}\ \overline{20}$.

$\overline{17}\ \overline{16}\ \overline{20}\ \overline{22}$ $\overline{2}\ \overline{6}\ \overline{15}\ \overline{20}$ $\overline{12}\ \overline{7}\ \overline{11}\ \overline{24}\ \overline{11}\ \overline{17}\ \overline{20}\ \overline{8}$' $\overline{16}\ \overline{12}\ \overline{7}\ \overline{5}\ \overline{1}\ \overline{22}$ $\overline{10}\ \overline{19}\ \overline{19}\ \overline{25}\ \overline{13}$ $\overline{11}\ \overline{7}$ $\overline{17}\ \overline{16}\ \overline{20}\ \overline{11}\ \overline{1}$

$\overline{20}\ \overline{22}\ \overline{20}\ \overline{13}$.

,

$\overline{9}\ \overline{10}\ \overline{22}\ \overline{15}\ \overline{19}\ \overline{12}\ \overline{17}\ \overline{16}\ \overline{13}$ $\overline{26}\ \overline{11}\ \overline{24}\ \overline{20}$ $\overline{3}\ \overline{19}\ \overline{15}\ \overline{20}\ \overline{7}$ $\overline{26}\ \overline{20}\ \overline{8}$ $\overline{17}\ \overline{16}\ \overline{20}$ $\overline{3}\ \overline{16}\ \overline{19}\ \overline{10}\ \overline{20}$ $\overline{16}\ \overline{12}\ \overline{7}\ \overline{5}\ \overline{1}\ \overline{22}$

$\overline{18}\ \overline{12}\ \overline{7}\ \overline{2}\ \overline{16}$

"

$\overline{6}\ \overline{13}$ $\overline{17}\ \overline{16}\ \overline{20}\ \overline{22}$ $\overline{13}\ \overline{6}\ \overline{11}\ \overline{8}$ $\overline{17}\ \overline{19}$ $\overline{17}\ \overline{16}\ \overline{20}\ \overline{15}\ \overline{13}\ \overline{20}\ \overline{10}\ \overline{24}\ \overline{20}\ \overline{13}$, "$\overline{6}\ \overline{10}\ \overline{10}$ $\overline{17}\ \overline{16}\ \overline{11}\ \overline{13}$ $\overline{26}\ \overline{19}\ \overline{1}$

$\overline{23}\ \overline{12}\ \overline{13}\ \overline{17}$ $\overline{10}\ \overline{12}\ \overline{7}\ \overline{2}\ \overline{16}$?!"

R	C	W	X	G	A	N	D	P	L	I	U	S
1	2	3	4	5	6	7	8	9	10	11	12	13
Z	M	H	T	B	O	E	Q	Y	J	V	K	F
14	15	16	17	18	19	20	21	22	23	24	25	26

Name _____

Find the two Pilgrim men and the two Pilgrim women that are exactly alike.

Answer: D and H ; E and G

Name _____

Find the two Indians and the two Pilgrim girls that are exactly alike.

Answer: F and J; H and I

129

Name _____ **Instant Pilgrim and Indian Finger Puppets**

These puppets may be used to present the play **"Greedy Henry"** or used in your own Thanksgiving play.

Materials: crayons, pencil and scissors

Directions: Color and cut out each puppet on the dotted lines. Use a pencil to punch a hole through the center of both circles at the bottom of each puppet. Use scissors to cut out the remaining portion of the circles. Place your first two fingers through the holes of a puppet to form the legs. Make the puppet move by moving your fingers.

© Carson-Dellosa Publ. CD-0946

Name _____   **Thanksgiving Play**

Greedy Henry

This play can be performed by as many children as you wish. It requires a minimum of five players, but you may increase the number by casting more children as Indian braves.

Characters: Henry, Pilgrim Boy, Pilgrim Girl, Indian Braves (two or more)

Pilgrim Girl:	I'm so happy we're having this Thanksgiving feast, but I just know Henry is going to embarrass us in front of our Indian friends.
Pilgrim Boy:	He'll eat everything in sight.
Henry:	This is the day I've been waiting for. What's holding up the food?
Pilgrim Girl:	The turkey won't be the only thing that's stuffed! Oh look, here comes the turkey. It's golden brown.
Indian Braves:	We hope you enjoy your first taste of turkey!
Pilgrims:	So this is the glorious bird, Of which we've often heard.
Pilgrim Boy:	Oh no, the Indians are looking at Henry and his tongue hanging out!
Indian Braves:	That boy knows dinnertime is here.
Henry:	It's about time!
Pilgrim Girl:	Let's just hope they keep eating and talking and don't look over at Henry.
Pilgrim Boy:	Would you believe...he just covered his potatoes with gravy and corn and carrots and tomatoes? He said, "Pass me the drumsticks, please, and much more bread and at least fifty peas!"
Pilgrim Girl:	Did you see all that Henry ate? And now he's piling more on his plate. He's crammed with yams, Cranberries and jams. Well, I suppose, if he doesn't hurt, He'll soon be asking for dessert.
Pilgrim Boy:	There's no doubt about that. Henry's a food magician.
Henry:	You bet! Just watch! I can make two pumpkin pies Disappear before your eyes.
Indian Braves:	We see so much food. We've never had so many things to eat. We thank you for inviting us. It really is a treat.
Pilgrim Girl:	You're welcome. (whispering) We're sorry about Henry.
Pilgrim Boy:	There he goes! He's in a hurry. Henry's leaving. He looks sick. We hope he didn't spoil your dinner.
Indian Braves:	We give thanks to Henry, too. He showed what too much food can do. Eating fast and cutting food thickly, Mixing food and getting quite sickly, He has given us a warning - During feasting times and such, Do be thankful for your blessings, But don't eat so very much!

Name _____   **Thanksgiving Word Search**

Find the words in the list by looking down, across or diagonally. Circle each word.

```
F H T N G P E F B T A B L E B F
O O U H P I I E S S N U I A L A
O L R N R E K A S G S T V T E M
D I A K G E N S T I E T A H S T
O D Y S M R E T U R K E Y U S D
N A C N I A Y E F R E R B R I O
R Y F A M I L Y F N G E C S N D
A P L Y D N K R E D L I I D G R
B E A N S E P O D B I M F A L E
Y R G A I H E D I N N E R Y O S
K T P P I M P A F E K P S F A S
I A E K U O P D B L T K A S H I
N B R I N P E N I T N A L B O N
P L I N I C R M L A K L T Y L G
R E E F E U D E H B R E A D D O
K E Y C O R B T M S C O R N N K
T H A N K S G I V I N G O B R E
F O O R M I C E M T U F T F R A
```

WORD LIST

TURKEY	FAMILY
THANKSGIVING	BREAD
MICE	DRESSING
FORK	FEAST
HUNGRY	SALT
TABLE	PEPPER
NAPKIN	BUTTER
CORN	DINNER
BEANS	MILK
PIE	HOLIDAY
FOOD	THURSDAY
BLESSING	STUFFED
THANKS	TABLE

Name _____   **An Indian Word Search**

History tells us that the Indians played a very important part in the first Thanksgiving dinner. Find and circle each of the words in the list by looking down, across or diagonally. Color the picture.

Word List

INDIAN	SQUAW	TEEPEE	CHIEF	BUFFALO	PLAINS
RESERVATION	BRAVE	TREATY	BOW	NATION	DEER
MAIDEN	PAPOOSE	TRIBE	ARROW	BEADS	CUSTOMS
FEATHERS	MOCCASINS	CANOE	DRUMS	POWWOW	TOMAHAWK

Name _____

Use some of the words on the horn of plenty to write a Thanksgiving story.

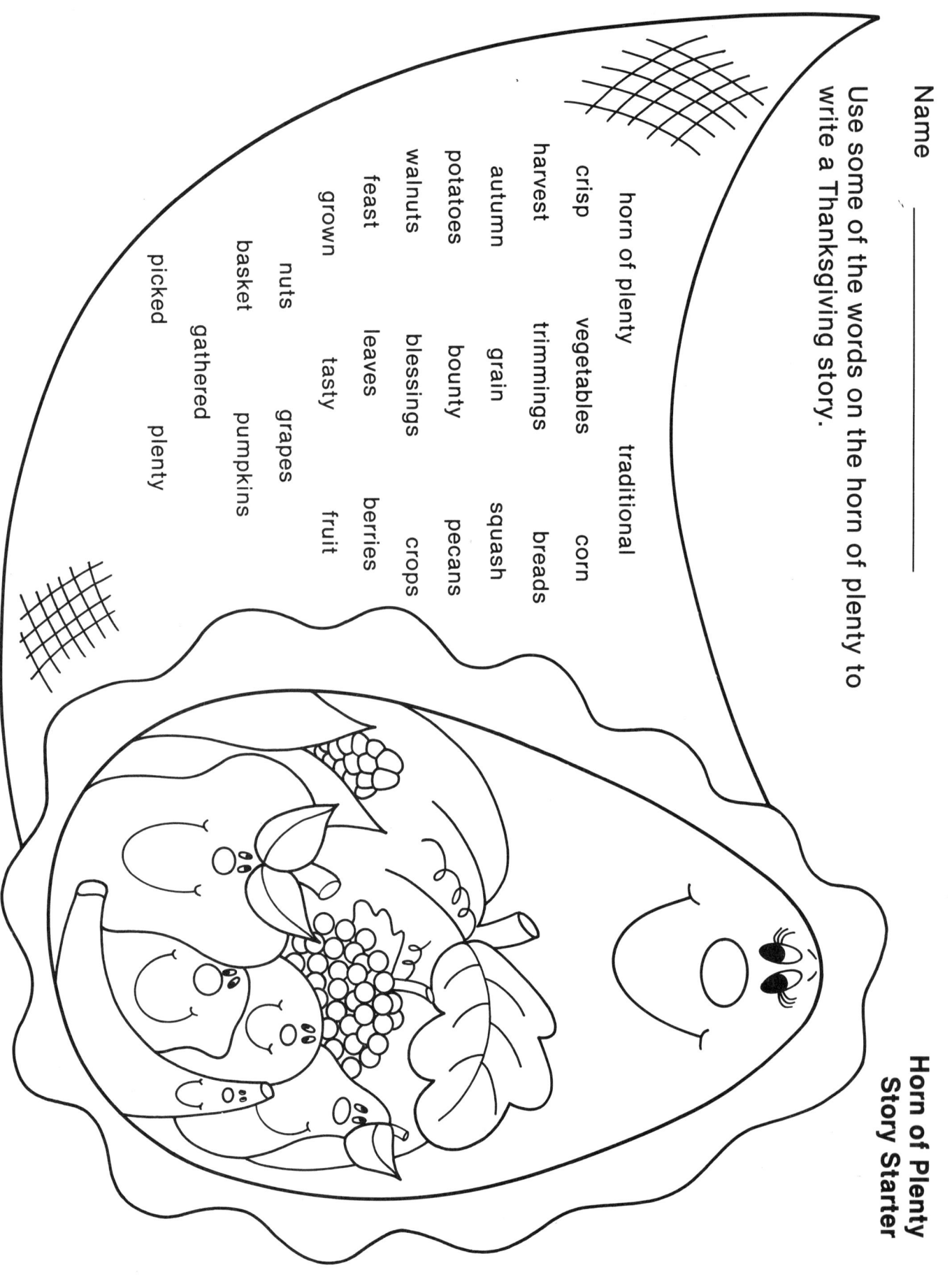

horn of plenty	traditional
crisp	vegetables
harvest	trimmings	corn
autumn	grain	breads
potatoes	bounty	squash
walnuts	blessings	pecans
feast	leaves	crops
grown	tasty	berries	fruit
nuts	grapes
basket	pumpkins
picked	gathered
	plenty

Horn of Plenty Story Starter

Name _____

Find these objects hidden in the picture:

box of matches
feather
chair
Santa
parrot
spiral notepad
baseball bat
wooden spoon
jar of pickles
frying pan
wristwatch
shark
hat
brush
duck

Name _____

Scrambled Food Fun

Directions: Even while the Pilgrims were sailing across the ocean, they might have been thinking about all of the wonderful foods they would have when they reached land. Unscramble each food name below.

1. fistfung _____
2. wallcose _____
3. dramalame _____
4. cribcool _____
5. gnupdid _____
6. rencarsirbe _____
7. yertuk _____
8. samy _____
9. qussah _____
10. drice _____
11. estew astoptoe _____
12. dashem toespota _____
13. kuppnim ipe _____
14. tirfu adals _____
15. leppa trubet _____
16. chotsaucs _____
17. fimfuns _____
18. cranbored _____
19. palepauces _____
20. sneba _____
21. slipcek _____
22. drabe _____
23. dalas _____
24. ryecle _____
25. vargy _____

Word List

beans
yams
cider
bread
squash
salad
gravy
celery
turkey
muffins
pickles
coleslaw
pudding
broccoli
stuffing
succotash
cornbread
applesauce
cranberries
marmalade
apple butter
sweet potatoes
fruit salad
pumpkin pie
mashed potatoes

© Carson-Dellosa Publ. CD-0946

Name _____ "HEAP BIG" FINGER PUPPETS

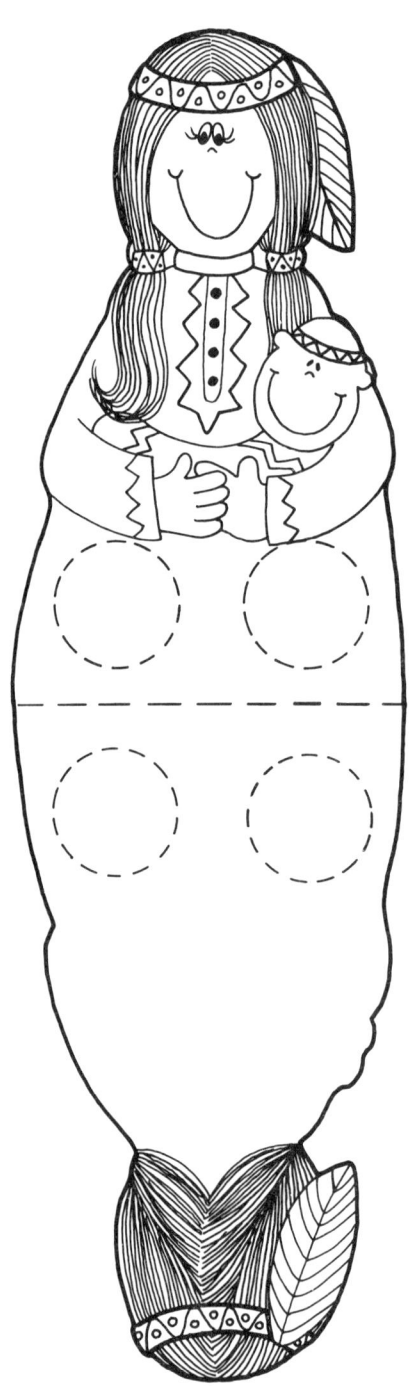
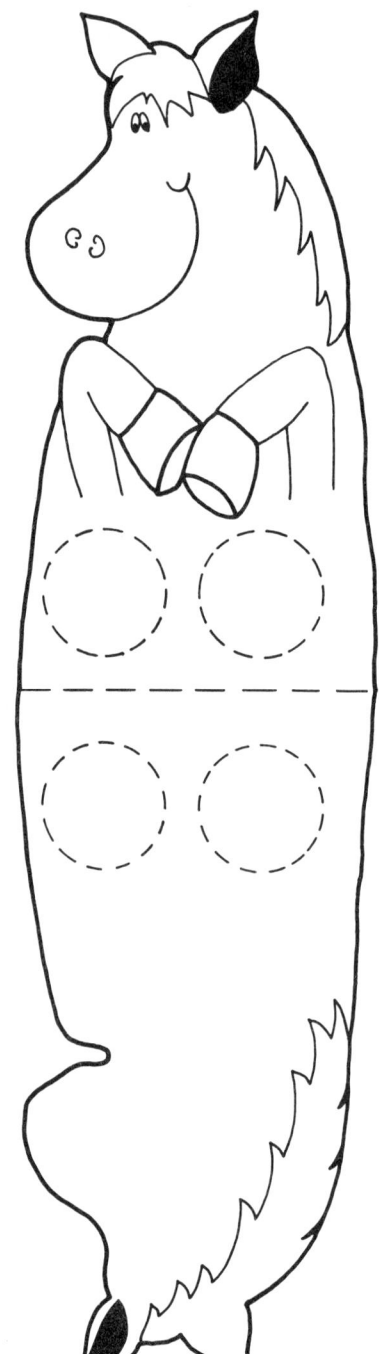
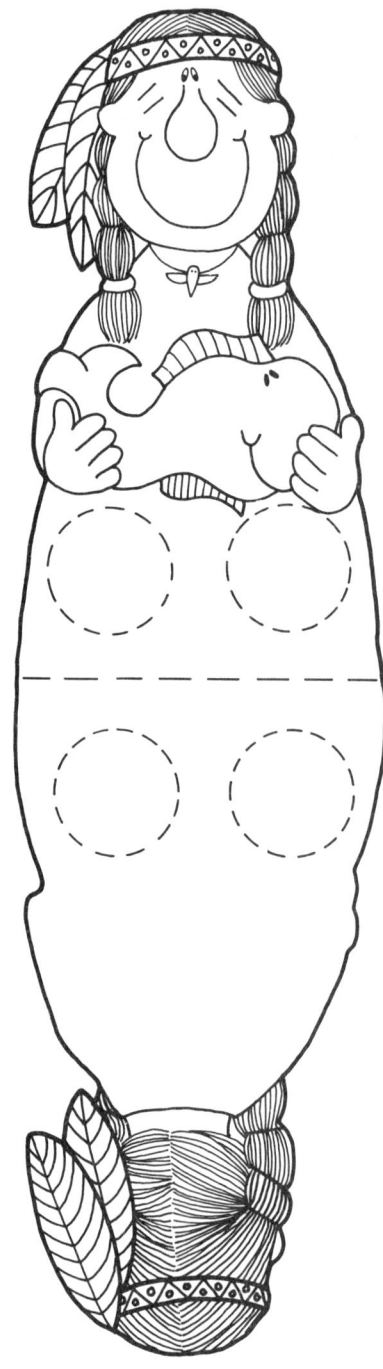

Directions:
1. Color each puppet.
2. Cut out the puppets on the solid outside lines.
3. Fold each puppet in half on the dotted centerfold line.
4. Connect the front and back sections by gluing or taping the tops of the heads together.

5. Use a pencil or pen to punch a hole in each dotted line circle.

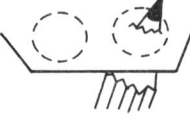

6. Use scissors to finish cutting out these small holes.
7. Put your fingers through these small holes and make your puppet "walk" by moving your fingers.

Thanksgiving Napkin Rings

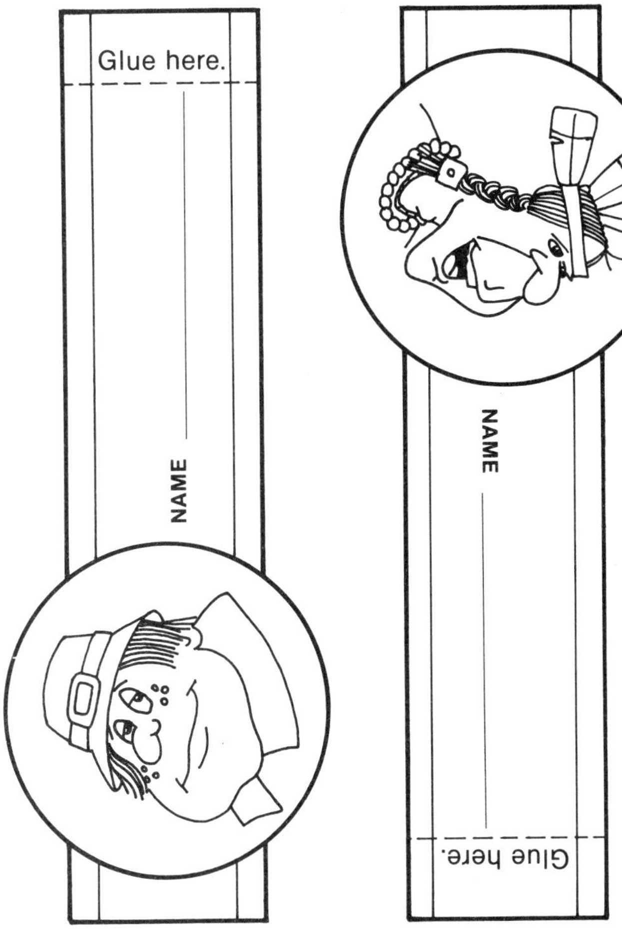

Make festive napkin rings for special guests at your Thanksgiving dinner! First, color each napkin ring and write the name of one of your guests on the line. Cut out each ring along the heavy outside line. Glue the ends together. Slide each napkin ring carefully over a dinner napkin and place them on your table. Now enjoy your dinner and the smiles you'll see.

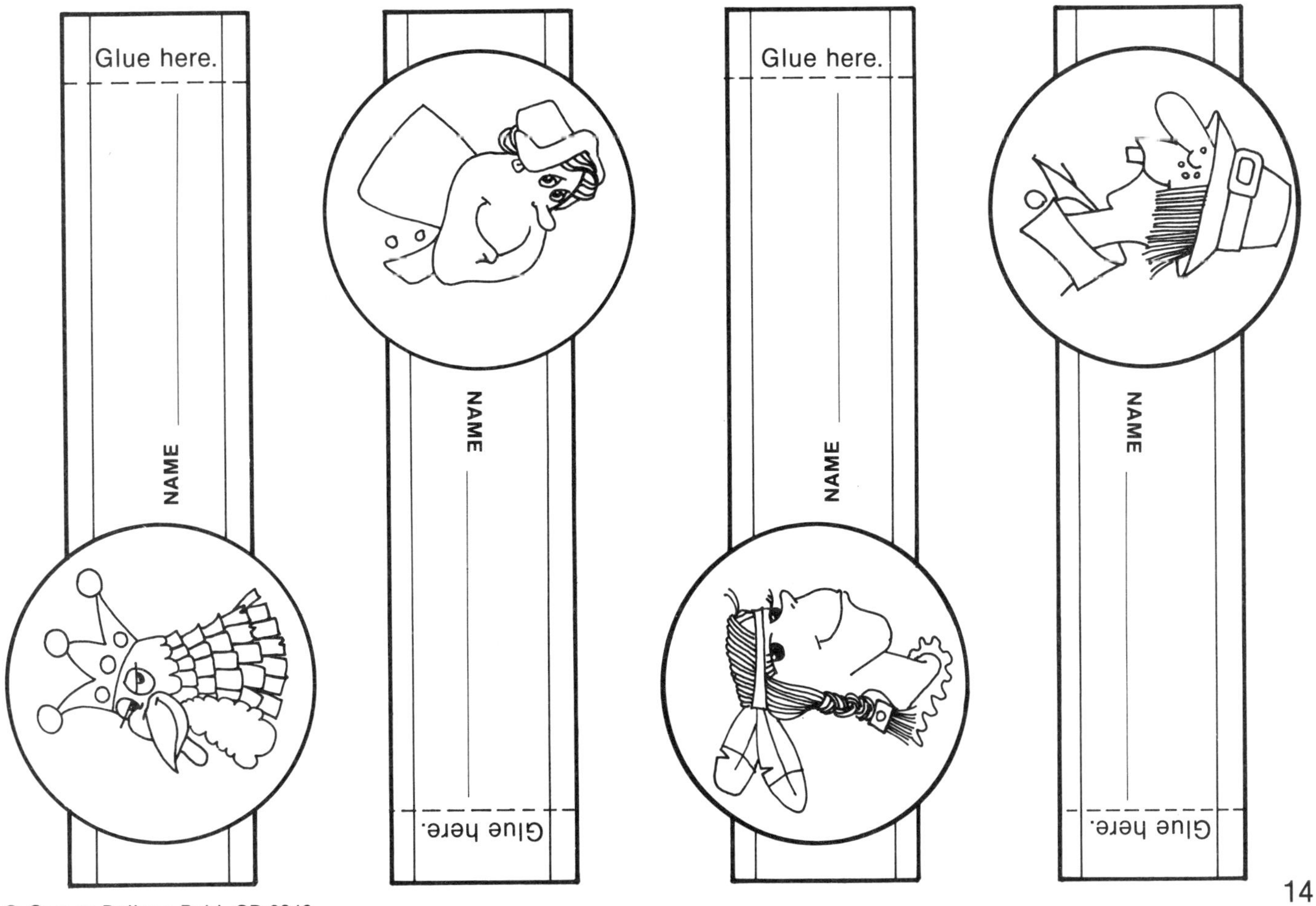

Glue here.

NAME

A THANKSGIVING THANK YOU NOTE TO GRANDMOTHER

Grandma cooked dinner.
    The turkey was fine.
You ate such good food,
    And had a wonderful time!

A Sample Thanksgiving Thank You Note To Grandmother

Dear Grandmother,
    You are the best grandmother anyone can have. The Thanksgiving dinner you cooked was the best ever!
    Thanks for inviting me over for Thanksgiving Day!
    Your grandson,
    Rickie

A THANKSGIVING THANK YOU NOTE

What a Thanksgiving!
You just ate and ate!
It was a fun day -
Thanksgiving was great!

A Sample Thanksgiving Thank You Note

Dear _____,
Thank you for everything. I am glad we could share the holiday.
It was such a wonderful Thanksgiving, thanks to you!
Gratefully,
_____

Directions: Use the stationery provided to copy one of the sample Thanksgiving notes. If you wish, write your own message. Color the picture and send the letter.

Name_____

Use some of the words you find to write a Christmas story. Color the picture.

Put a circle around:
ornaments   bows
bulbs   decorate
star   toy
presents   trim
tree   tinsel
shiny

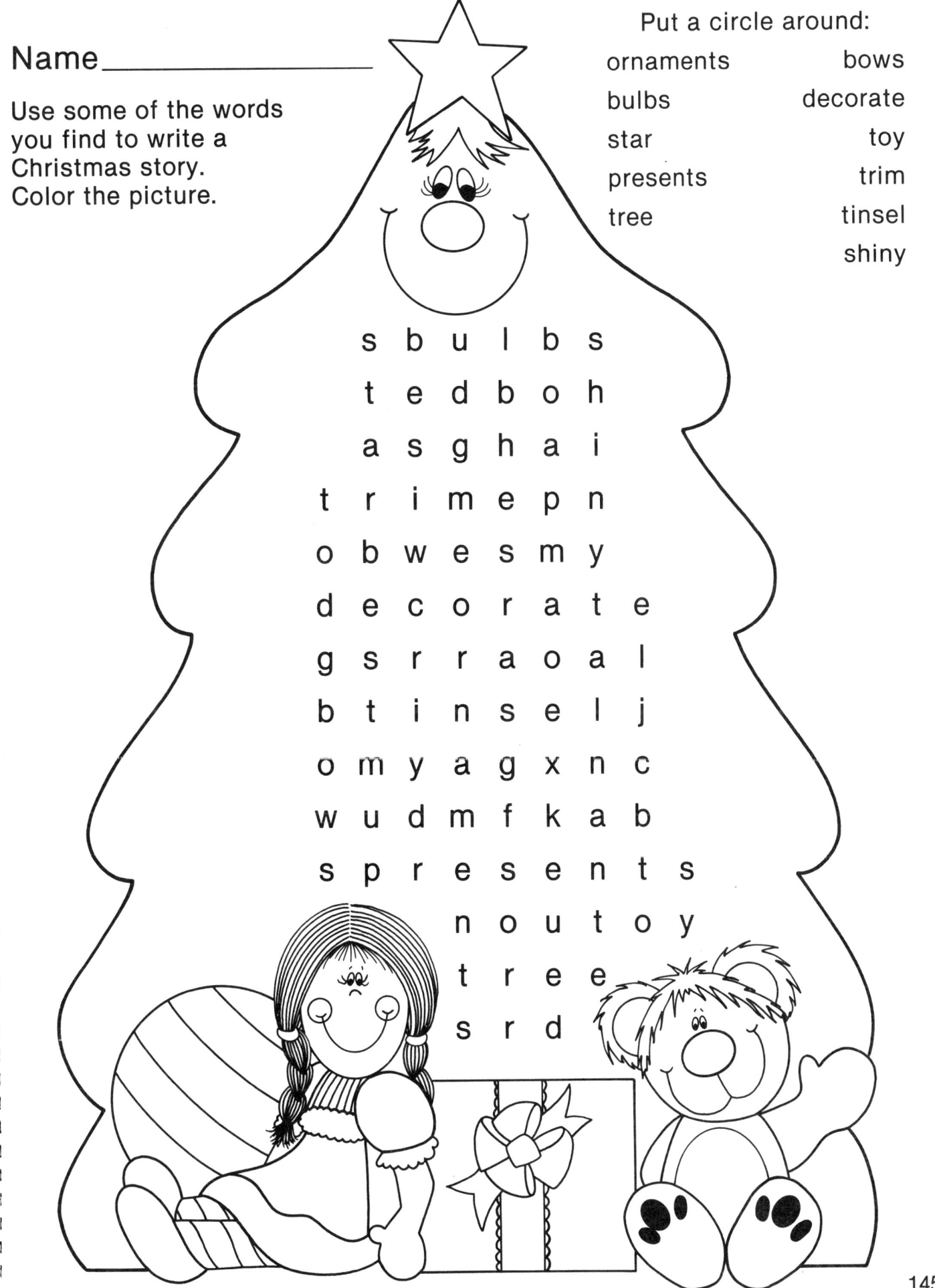

```
s b u l b s
t e d b o h
a s g h a i
t r i m e p n
o b w e s m y
d e c o r a t e
g s r r a o a l
b t i n s e l j
o m y a g x n c
w u d m f k a b
s p r e s e n t s
n o u t o y
t r e e
s r d
```

© Carson-Dellosa Publ. CD-0946

145

Name_____

Name _____

Stick-On Christmas Name Tags and Seals

Materials: crayons or markers, Lepages glue, scissors, water, water container, paintbrush.

1. Color each Christmas seal and name tag.
2. Mix an equal amount of Lepages glue and water together in a small container (paper cup).
3. Use a paintbrush to apply glue mixture to back of this page.
4. Let page dry completely, glue side up.
5. Cut out all name tags and seals.
6. When you are ready to use the seals or name tags, lick the back of each one or use a damp sponge and press to apply.

© Carson-Dellosa Publ. CD-0946

147

Name _____

Directions:

Name_____

Directions:

© Carson-Dellosa Publ. CD-0946

149

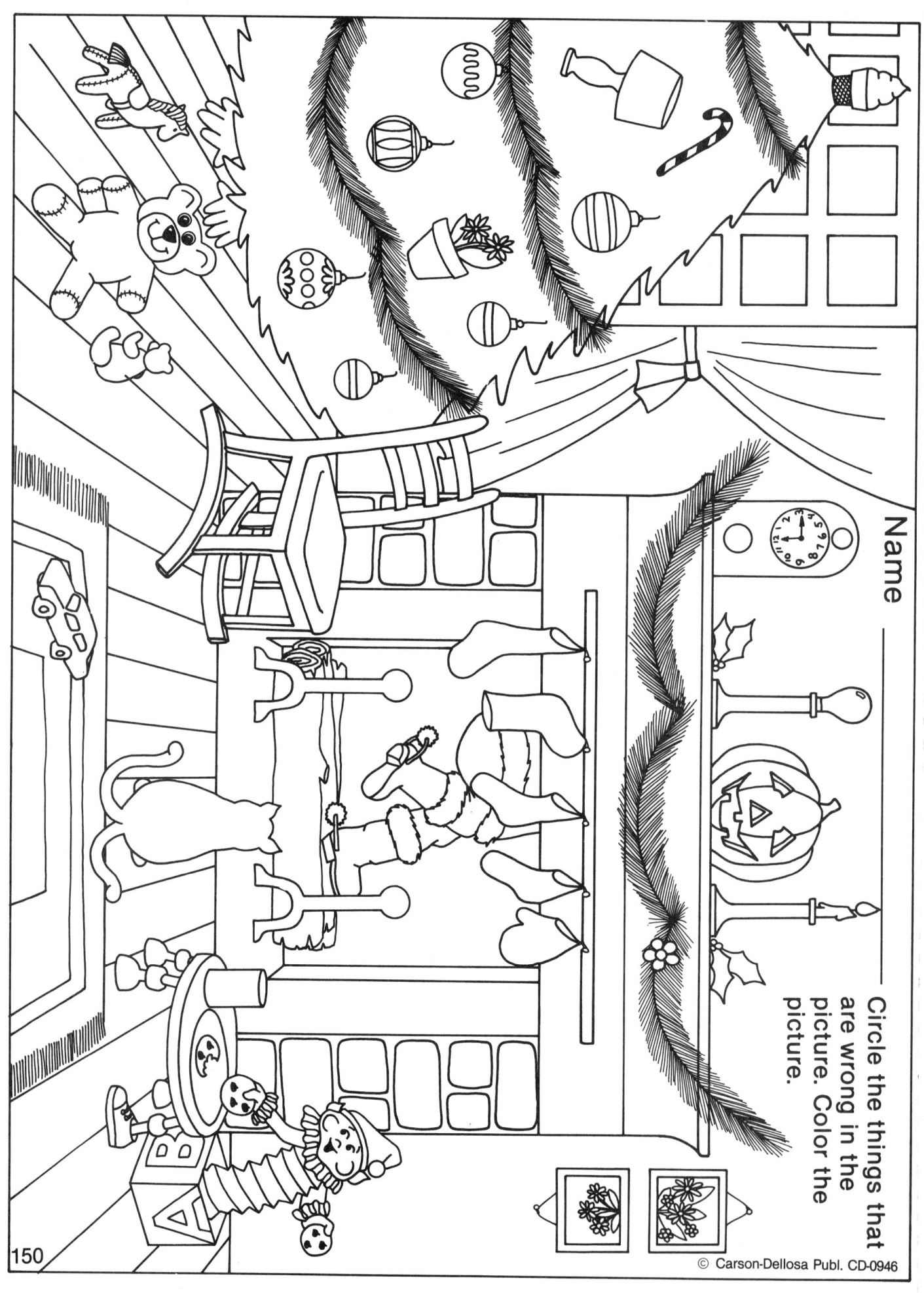

Name _____

Circle the hidden words:

noel   joy   toys
holly   ball   box

```
s j o n e
n o e l t
a y r h a
t u b o x
e b a l l
f e a l s
i t o y s
```

Name _____

Use some of the words below to write a Christmas story.

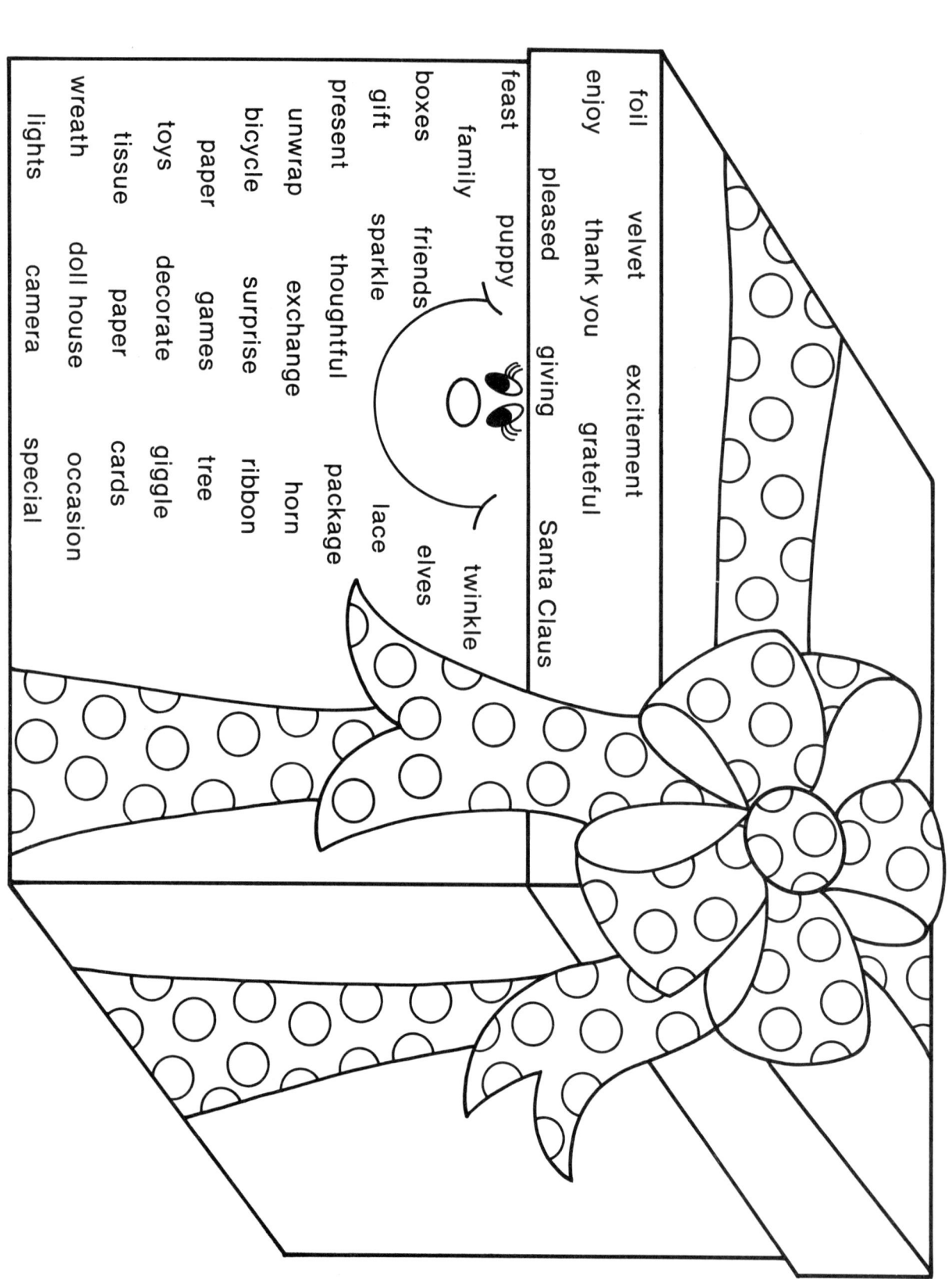

foil	velvet	excitement	
enjoy	thank you	grateful	
pleased	giving		Santa Claus
feast	puppy		twinkle
family	friends		elves
boxes	sparkle	lace	
gift	thoughtful	package	
present	exchange	horn	
unwrap	surprise	ribbon	
bicycle	games	tree	
paper	decorate	giggle	
toys	paper	cards	
tissue	doll house	occasion	
wreath	camera	special	
lights			

Christmas Story Starter

Name_____
Directions:

154
© Carson-Dellosa Publ. CD-0946

Name _____

Christmas Story Starter

Use some of the words below to write a Christmas story.

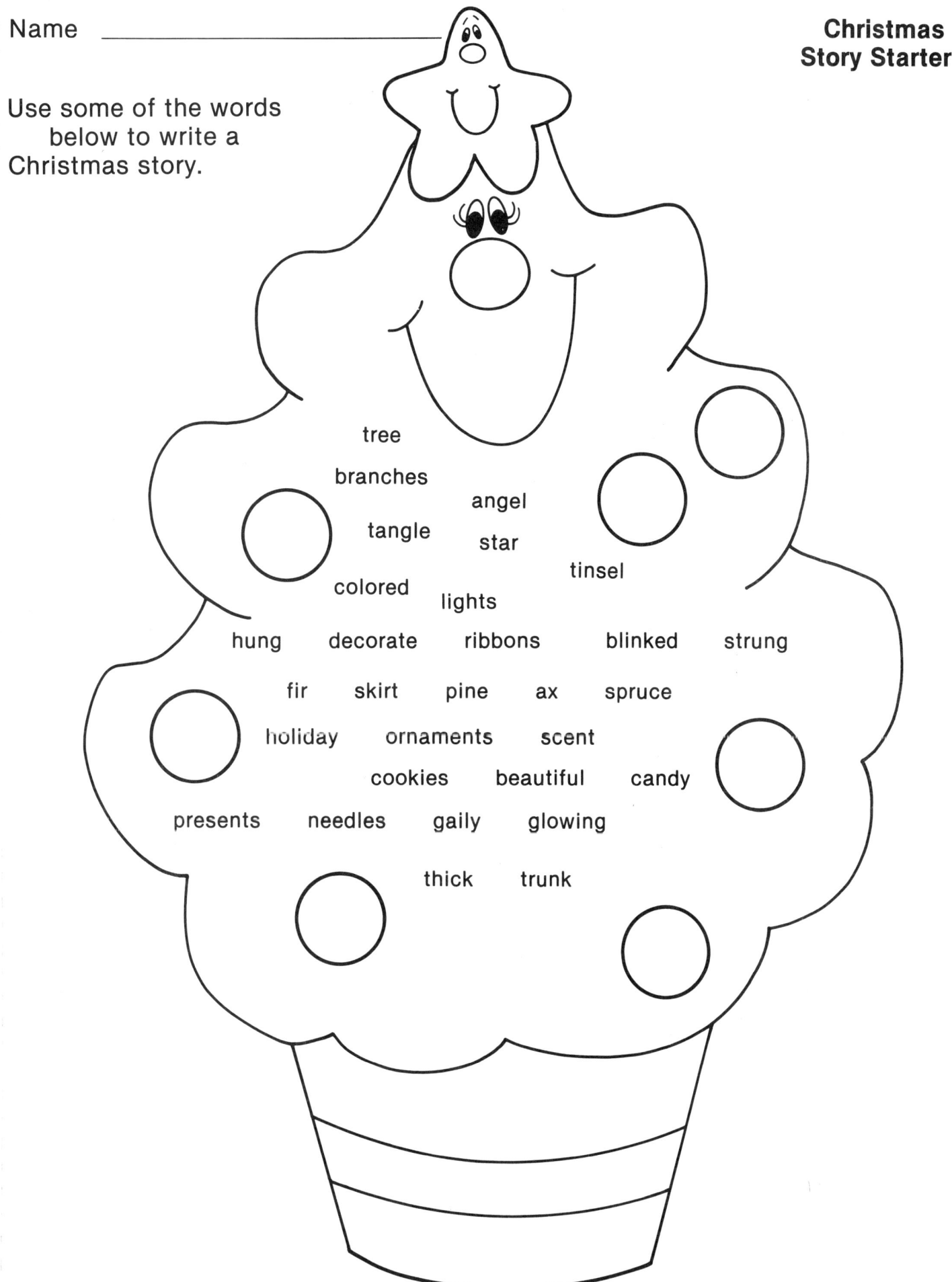

tree
branches
angel
tangle   star
            tinsel
colored
    lights
hung   decorate   ribbons   blinked   strung
fir   skirt   pine   ax   spruce
holiday   ornaments   scent
cookies   beautiful   candy
presents   needles   gaily   glowing
thick   trunk

Name _____

Name _____   Christmas Gift-Token

Give a very meaningful gift for Christmas by making a gift-token stocking. On the back of each of the two candy canes, write a job or favor you'll do for the person to whom you're giving the stocking. Place the candy canes in the stocking and give the gift to a friend. Watch your friend's face beam with delight at your thoughtfulness!

1. Color patterns.
2. Cut out patterns on solid lines.
3. Fold stocking on dotted line.
4. Glue stocking together along edges only.
5. On the back of each candy cane, write a special favor you will do for the person to whom you will give the gift-token stocking.
6. Put candy canes inside stocking.
7. Give stocking as a gift to a friend.

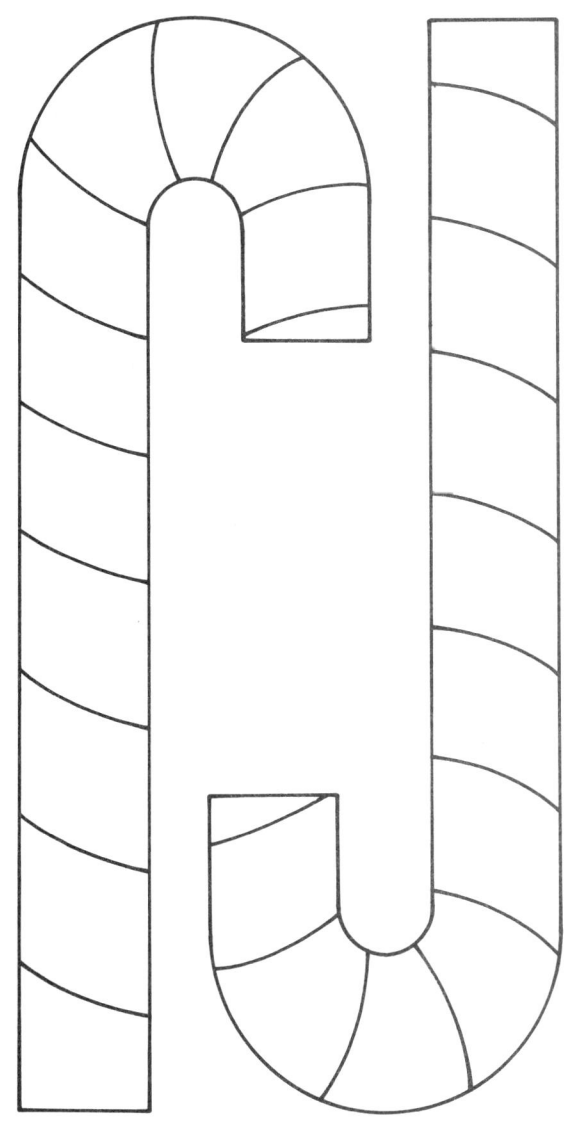

© Carson-Dellosa Publ. CD-0946

157

Name _____

Add to find the hidden combinations. Circle each hidden problem you find.

EXAMPLE:

Name_____
Directions:

Name _____ **Hand-Sewn Tree Ornaments**

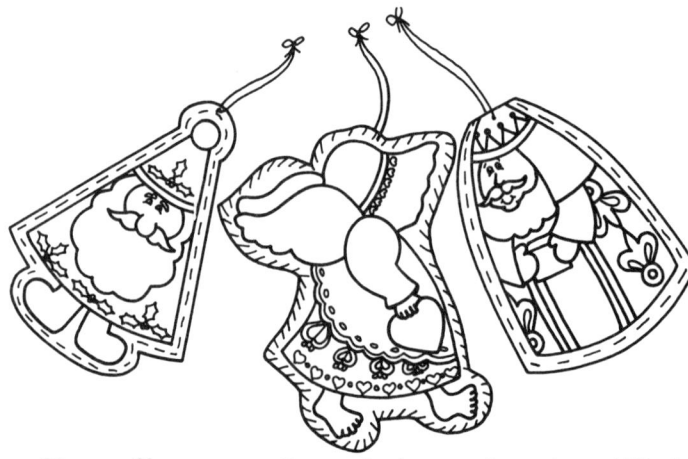

Show off your creative coloring and sewing skills by adding your special touch to these charming tree ornaments. You'll brighten everyone's holiday!

1. Color ornaments brightly. If desired, add your own designs to ornaments.
2. Cut out all ornaments on heavy solid lines.
3. Fold ornament in half on dotted line.
4. Thread needle. Knot thread.
5. Sew together outer edges of ornament, making stitches same size. Leave an inch opening unsewn for stuffing. Do not cut or knot thread.
6. Stuff ornament with small pieces of facial tissue or shredded paper. Use a pencil to aid stuffing. Do not overstuff.
7. Sew opening closed and knot thread.
8. Using threaded needle, attach thread at top of ornament for hanging.
9. Hang ornament on tree or use to decorate house.

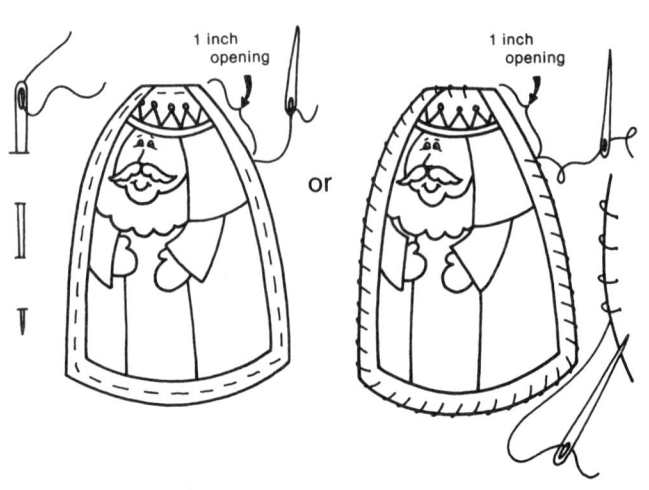

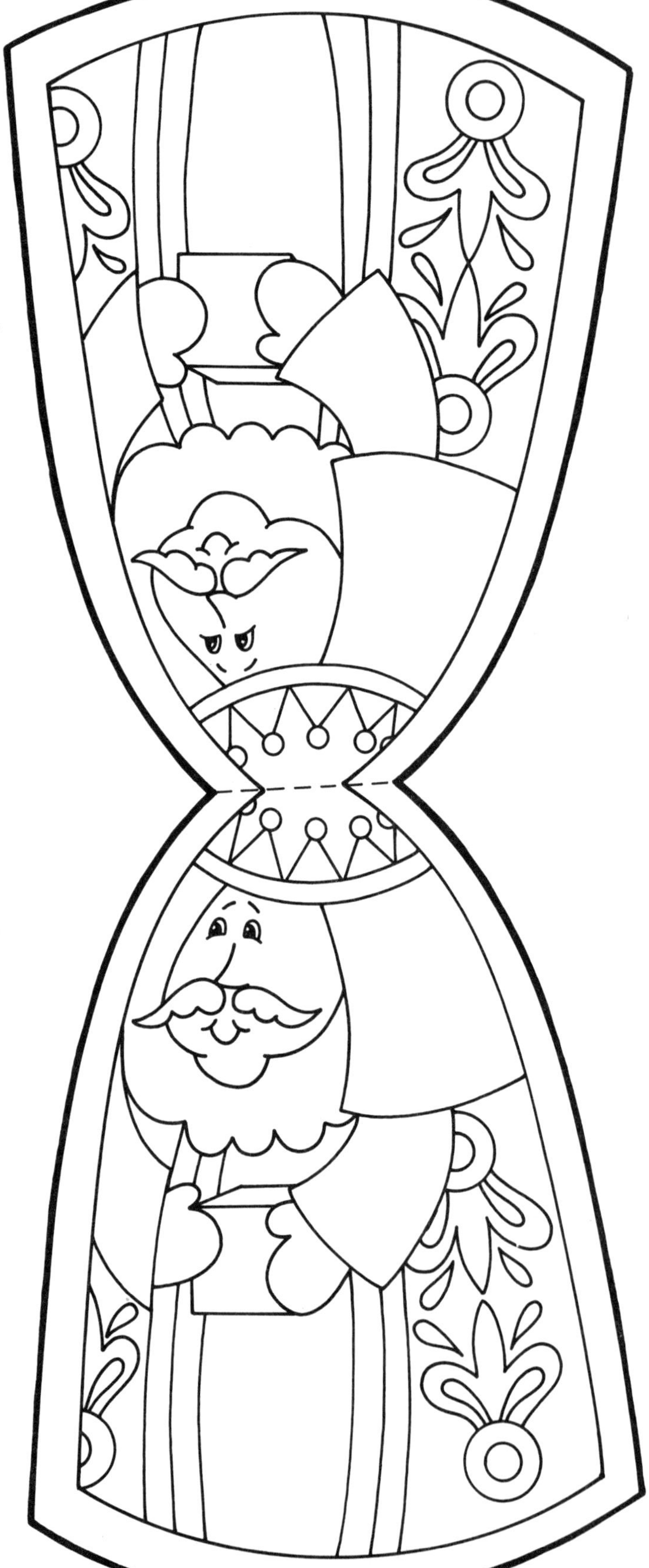

160

© Carson-Dellosa Publ. CD-0946

Name _____

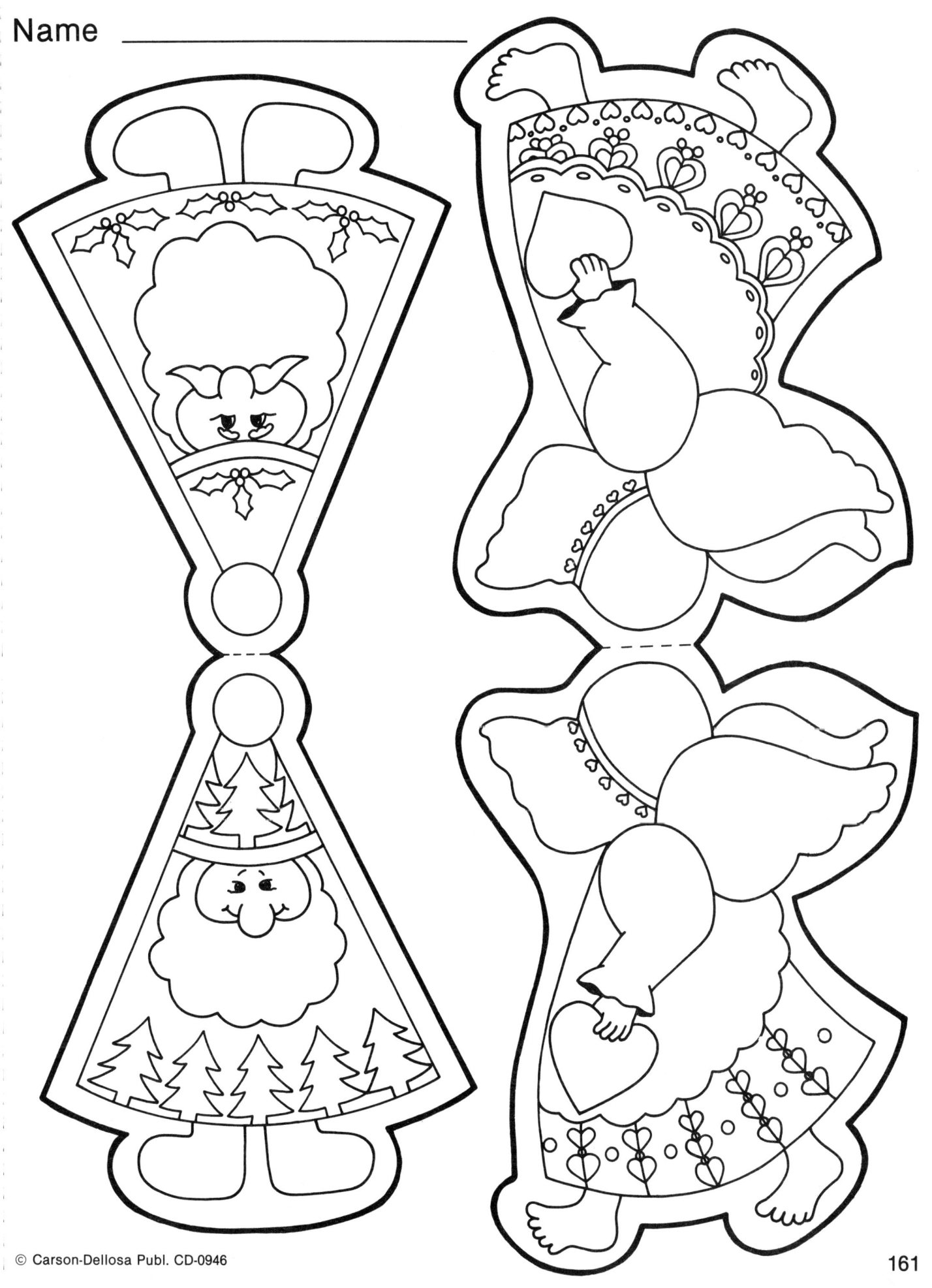

Name _____

Christmas Word Search

Unscramble the words in the scrambled word list. Then locate the answers (unscrambled words) hidden in the puzzle. Circle the hidden words. The words are printed across and down and some words share a letter. An example has been done for you. Use the answer key to check your work. Use some of the words to write a story on the next page.

1. TNSRDCEOIAO DECORATIONS
2. HHMETEBLE _____
3. STILEN _____
4. SSMTARIHC REET _____
5. NTSIA LNHCAOSI _____
6. TLDEEIUY _____
7. LNGEA _____
8. TNNMRAEO _____
9. ESSUJ _____
10. LEON _____
11. REERENDI _____
12. HTWERA _____
13. YLIADHO _____
14. GLNROACI _____
15. AASTN _____
16. TPSEERSN _____
17. HLGSIE _____
18. HPRDLOU _____
19. TRSA _____
20. YTSO _____
21. DLGAANR _____
22. KTSSGNCOI _____
23. YMNCHIE _____
24. EIWS ENM _____
25. TTSLMIOEE _____
26. RMNGAE _____
27. GPPWNIAR _____

```
B E T H L E H E M Y D S R O P L
C H I M N E Y X T I N S E L O G
H I Q A D D U N C V G M O S R B
R T I N O E L Z W R E A T H N V
I J H G M N E S A A L W R T A M
S Y O E L L T R U I P S F K M T
T I L R U O I X N N E D C I E T
M P I F F P D W S A N T A C N J
A R D R G R E I N D E E R X T B
S E A U S T A R D F K I O A K A
T S Y D E O Q J E E K L L D E N
R E C O T Y Z N X M E P I G U G
E N S L I S F G A R L A N D T E
E T P P A S T O C K I N G S B L
C S T H O P S E K J E S U S F R
C S L E I G H Y W R A P P I N G
S A I N T N I C H O L A S D I A
W I S E M E N M I S T L E T O E
H D E C O R A T I O N S W O Q M
```

Answer Key: 1. DECORATIONS 2. BETHLEHEM 3. TINSEL 4. CHRISTMAS TREE 5. SAINT NICHOLAS 6. YULETIDE 7. ANGEL 8. ORNAMENT 9. JESUS 10. NOEL 11. REINDEER 12. WREATH 13. HOLIDAY 14. CAROLING 15. SANTA 16. PRESENTS 17. SLEIGH 18. RUDOLPH 19. STAR 20. TOYS 21. GARLAND 22. STOCKINGS 23. CHIMNEY 24. WISE MEN 25. MISTLETOE 26. MANGER 27. WRAPPING

Name _____ **Christmas Finger Play Poem**

Read the finger play poem. Perform the finger movements as you read the poem again. You may wish to complete the finger puppets on p. 165 to use with the poem. Color the picture.

SANTA'S LITTLE ELVES
by Katherine Oana

One of Santa's little elves trimmed the Christmas tree.
(Hang ornaments on tree)

Two of Santa's little elves baked a cake, you see.
(Put cake in oven)

Three of Santa's little elves stacked blocks on the floor.
(Stack blocks on the floor)

Four of Santa's little elves swept Santa's store.
(Sweep floor)

Five of Santa's little elves hid toys in the nook.
(Hide toys behind chair)

Keep your eyes closed tight
(Close eyes)

Until I say, "NOW, LOOK!"
(Cup eyes with hands and open wide)

164

Name _____   **Elves and Tree Finger Puppets**

Complete these finger puppets to use with the finger play poem on p. 164.

1. Color and cut out the finger puppets.
2. Glue or tape the tabs together so that the puppet fits around your finger.

© Carson-Dellosa Publ. CD-0946

Name _____   **Christmas Play**

A Party for Santa

This play can be performed by as many children as you wish. It requires a minimum of three players, but you may increase the number by casting more children as elves.

Characters: Mrs. Claus, Elves (two or more)

Mrs. Claus: Have you elves ever thought what it's like for Santa on Christmas morning? He comes back to a quiet North Pole having worked all night. People are waking up all over the world opening presents and having a wonderful time.

Elves: Think about it.
It's almost shocking!
He won't even have
A Christmas stocking.

Is it too late
For us to plan
To celebrate
With that cheerful man?

Mrs. Claus: No, let's quickly think of some presents we can make!

Elves: Let's make him new gloves
And a hat, right away
So the cold won't get him
When he's out on his sleigh.

Mrs. Claus: How about some special refreshments?

Elves: We'll mix up a tasty brew.
Can you prepare his favorite stew?

Mrs. Claus: Yes, of course! It's 5:00 A.M. I wonder how much time we have?

Elves: We'll have to hurry
To get things done.
The computer shows
He's on his last run.

(Puppets run around busily working)
(Later)

Elves: Look out the window -
Aren't those his sleigh tracks
And there in the corner
His big empty sacks?

Mrs. Claus: I hear him. He's going into the bedroom. Let's turn out the lights and hide.

(Time passes, stage remains very quiet)

Mrs. Claus: I'd better go see what's happened to him. I don't hear anything.

(She leaves - returns immediately)

Mrs. Claus: Well, little elves,
You won't have to hide.
Santa's too tired
After his ride.
The party food
Will have to keep.
Dear old Santa
Is fast asleep.

Zzzzzzzzzzzz (snoring is heard off-stage)

Mrs. Claus Puppet

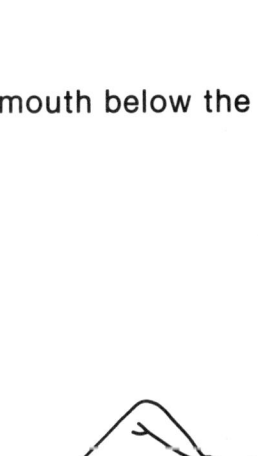

Materials: paper plate, crayons or markers, scissors, glue, stick or ruler, masking tape

(The pieces needed for this puppet can be found on page 168.)

Directions:
1. Color the ball on Mrs. Claus' hat green.
2. Color Mrs. Claus' hat red.
3. Color the small eye circles inside of Mrs. Claus' glasses blue.
4. Color the rims of Mrs. Claus' glasses black.
5. Cut out all of the pieces for the Mrs. Claus puppet. Make certain to cut out Mrs. Claus' eyes and glasses as one piece.
6. Glue the hat across the top of the paper plate (head).
7. Glue the hair just below the hat.
8. Glue the eyes and glasses below the hair.
9. Use a red crayon or marker to draw a nose below the glasses and a mouth below the nose.
10. Tape the end of a stick or ruler to the back of the head.

Elf Puppet

Materials: paper plate, crayons or markers, scissors, glue, stick or ruler, masking tape

(The pieces needed for this puppet can be found on page 168.)

Directions:
1. Color the ball on the elf's hat red.
2. Color the elf's hat green.
3. Color the elf's ears yellow
4. Cut out all of the pieces for the elf puppet.
5. Glue the hat across the top of the paper plate (head).
6. Glue the straight edge of each ear to the left and right sides of the paper plate by placing each ear behind the paper plate. Make sure the point of each ear points upward.
7. Use a black crayon or marker to draw two eyes below the hat.
8. Use a red crayon or marker to draw a nose below the eyes and a mouth below the nose.
9. Tape the end of a stick or ruler to the back of the head.

© Carson-Dellosa Publ. CD-0946

Name _____ **Mrs. Claus and Elf Puppets**

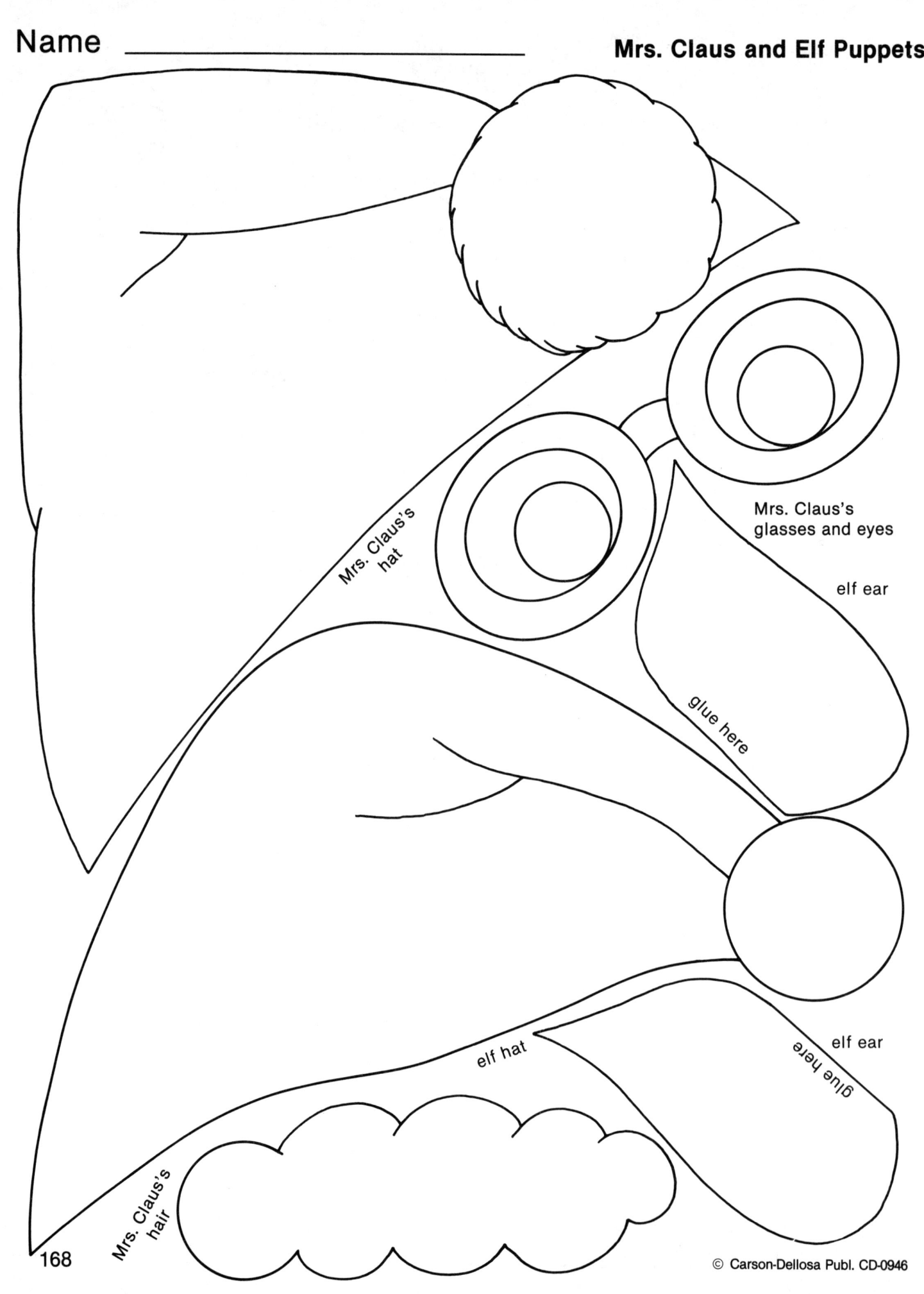

Name _____

Can you unscramble the words on the sled?

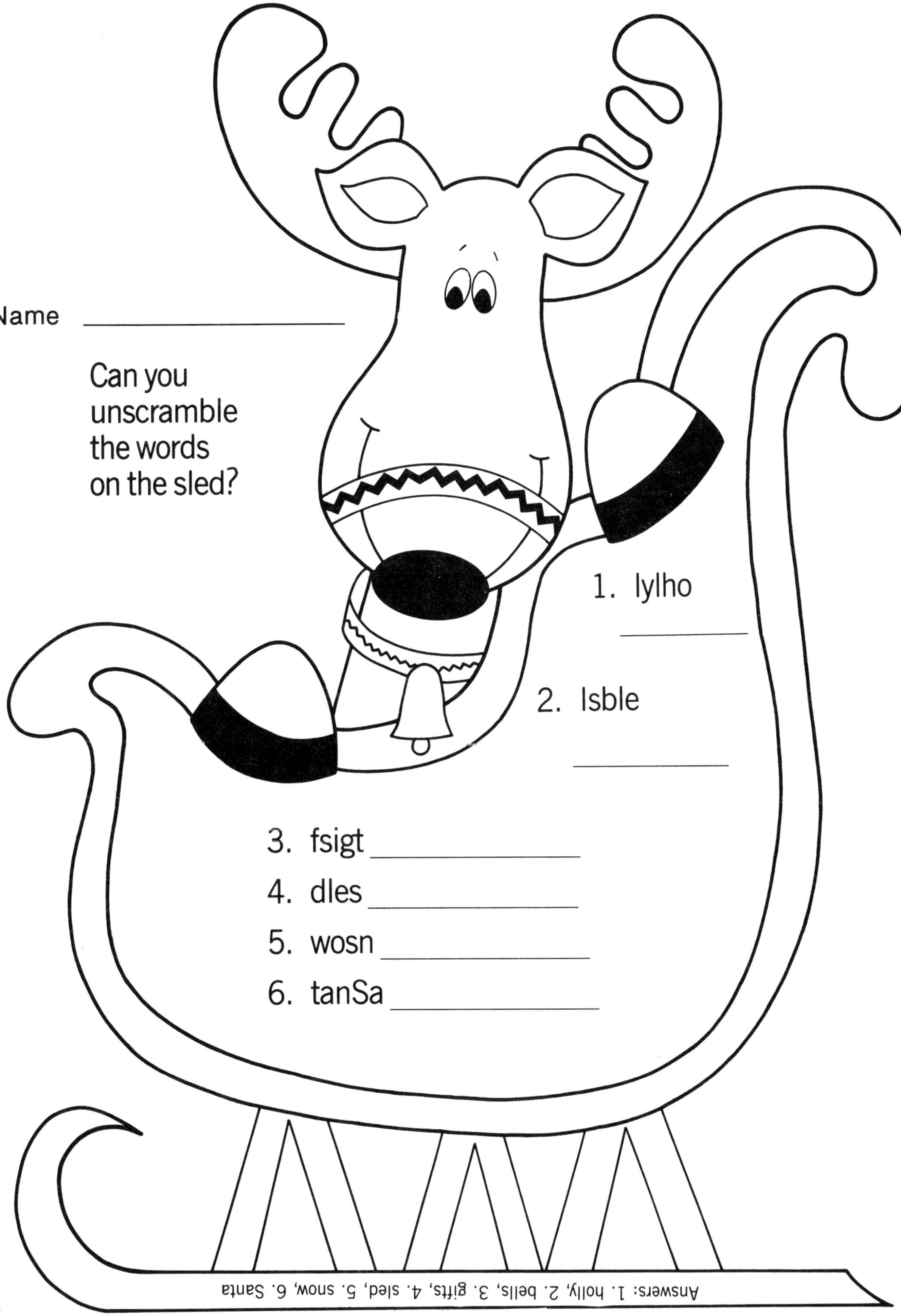

1. lylho _____

2. lsble _____

3. fsigt _____

4. dles _____

5. wosn _____

6. tanSa _____

Answers: 1. holly 2. bells 3. gifts 4. sled 5. snow 6. Santa

Name _____

Unscramble the words:

list
elves
Santa
Christmas

bells
mistletoe
cookies
ring
candy canes
surprises
decorate
toys
glitter
tree
angels

1. lsble _____
2. tsli _____
3. grni _____
4. syto _____
5. eter _____
6. seevl _____
7. sckooei _____
8. srsseiurp _____
9. slegna _____
10. shCtsrmia _____
11. slettmeoi _____
12. caderoet _____
13. aatnS _____
14. rltegit _____
15. ccaadnneys _____

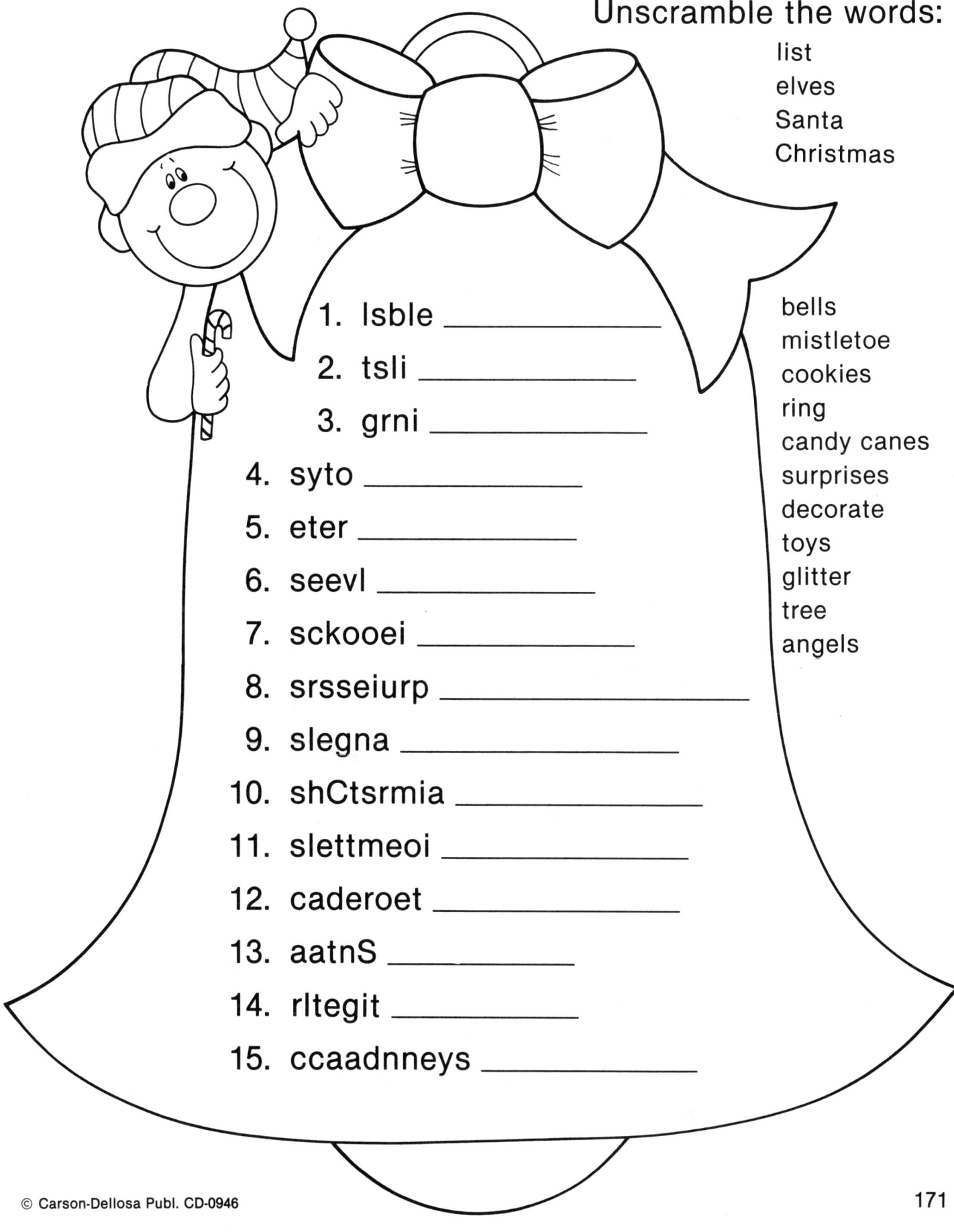

A CHRISTMAS OR HANUKKAH THANK YOU NOTE

Such fine holiday gifts!
    Now what should you do?
For the new books and toys,
    Write a great, big "Thank You!"

A Sample Christmas or Hanukkah Thank You Note

Dear Mom and Dad,
    I cannot thank you enough for all the great gifts. You gave me exactly what I needed and wanted.
    Thanks for making it a wonderful holiday.
               With love,
                  Sherri

Directions: Use the stationery provided to copy the sample Christmas or Hanukkah thank you notes. If you wish, write your own message. Color the picture and send the letter.

A CHRISTMAS OR HANUKKAH THANK YOU NOTE

The new year is here.
You have loads of toys!
It's time to say thank you,
Be good girls and boys.

A Sample Christmas or Hanukkah Thank You Note

Dear _____

The holidays were just wonderful. Thank you for the gift. I am enjoying it very much. Happy New Year.

With every good wish,

_____

Directions: Use the stationery provided to copy the sample Christmas or Hanukkah thank you notes. If you wish, write your own message. Color the picture and send the letter.

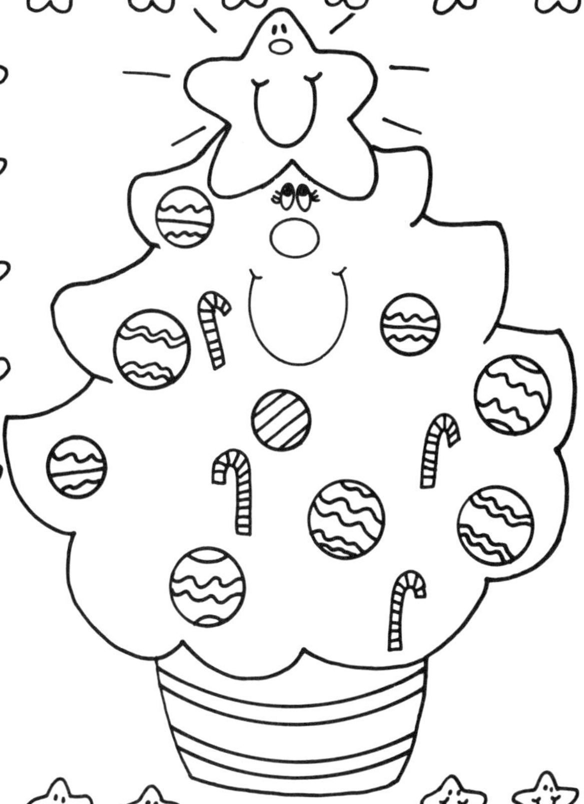

_____ is a shining star whose bright work belongs at the top of my Christmas tree!

_____
Signed

You can stuff my stocking with work like this anytime!

Happy Holidays!

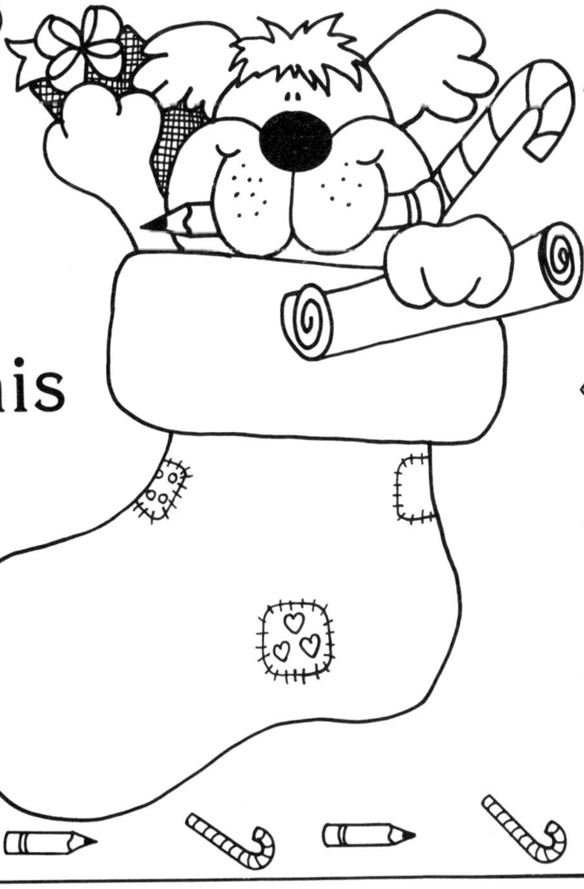

Name _____

Christmas Story Starter

Use some of the words below on the gingerbread man to write a holiday story.

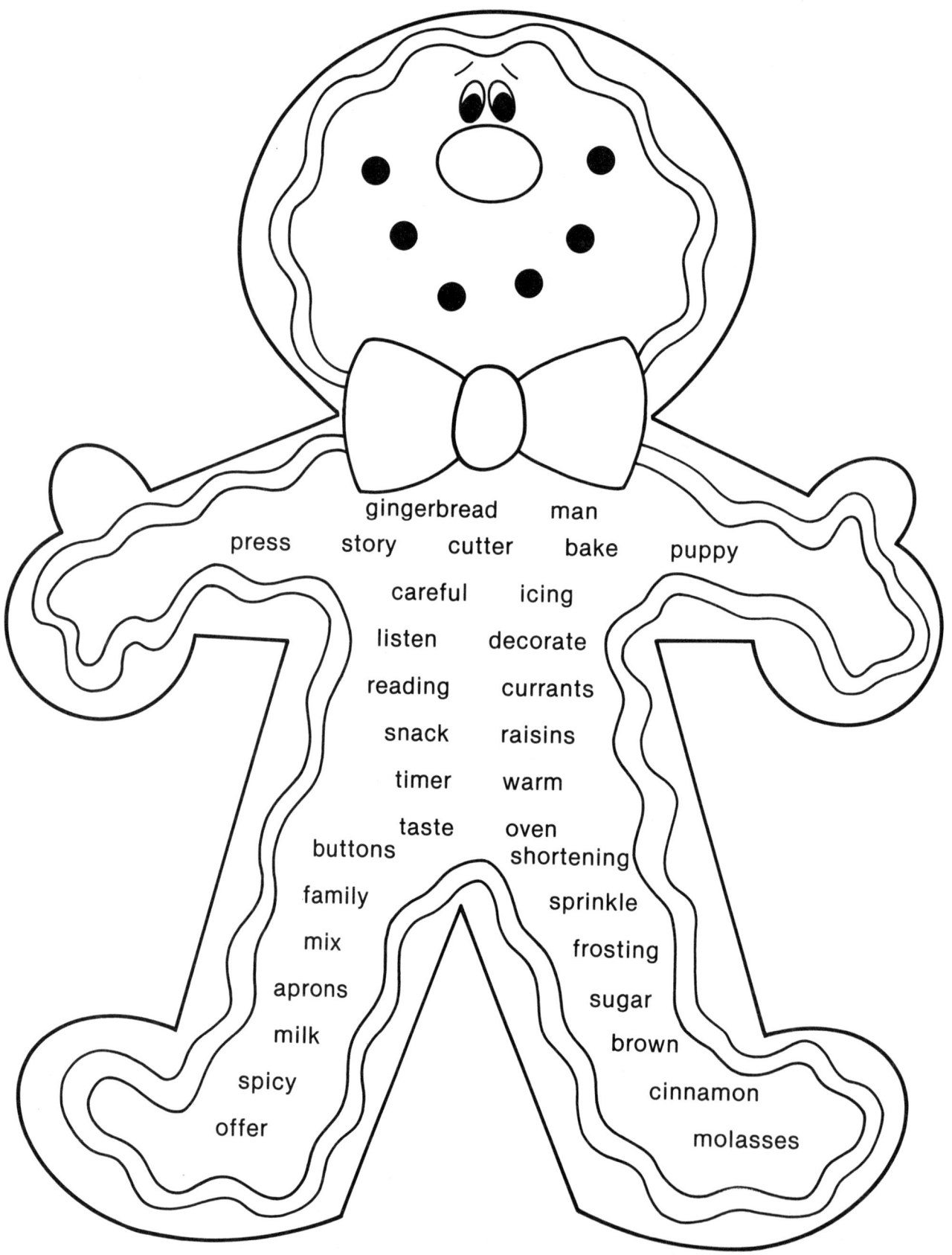

gingerbread man
press story cutter bake puppy
careful icing
listen decorate
reading currants
snack raisins
timer warm
taste oven
buttons shortening
family sprinkle
mix frosting
aprons sugar
milk brown
spicy cinnamon
offer molasses

176

Name _____

Christmas

How to Use

Related Poems
 Enlarge any of the patterns to use as the center of a bulletin board. Direct students to copy a related poem. Display the papers on the bulletin board.

Award Sayings
 Use an award saying with its related pattern to create student awards.

Related Poems

A beautiful box tied up with a bow -
What's in it? I don't know!
Could it be a shirt or a toy?
Whatever it is - I'm sure I'll enjoy!

Mom made a surprise the other day.
She gave it to me on a lovely tray.
A gingerbread cookie
  with buttons so neat -
But best of all he was good to eat!

An empty stocking hung by a chair -
Not a sign of Santa anywhere.
But comes Christmas - what a surprise
Filled to the top for bright little eyes.

A halo surrounding her lovely hair,
Wings that flutter as she floats in the air.
She never fails to fascinate me,
The angel high on the Christmas tree.

Award Sayings

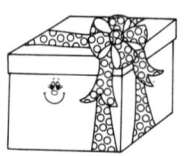

Gifted Student
Surprisingly Good!
I'm a pleasant present!

I add spice to my classroom!
I'm a cooperative cookie!
Sweet as Gingerbread!

I'm stuffed full of good working habits!
I'm "stocking" up good marks!

Heavenly Work
I am an angel!

Name _____ **Christmas**
(Instructions on previous page)

Name _____
Directions:

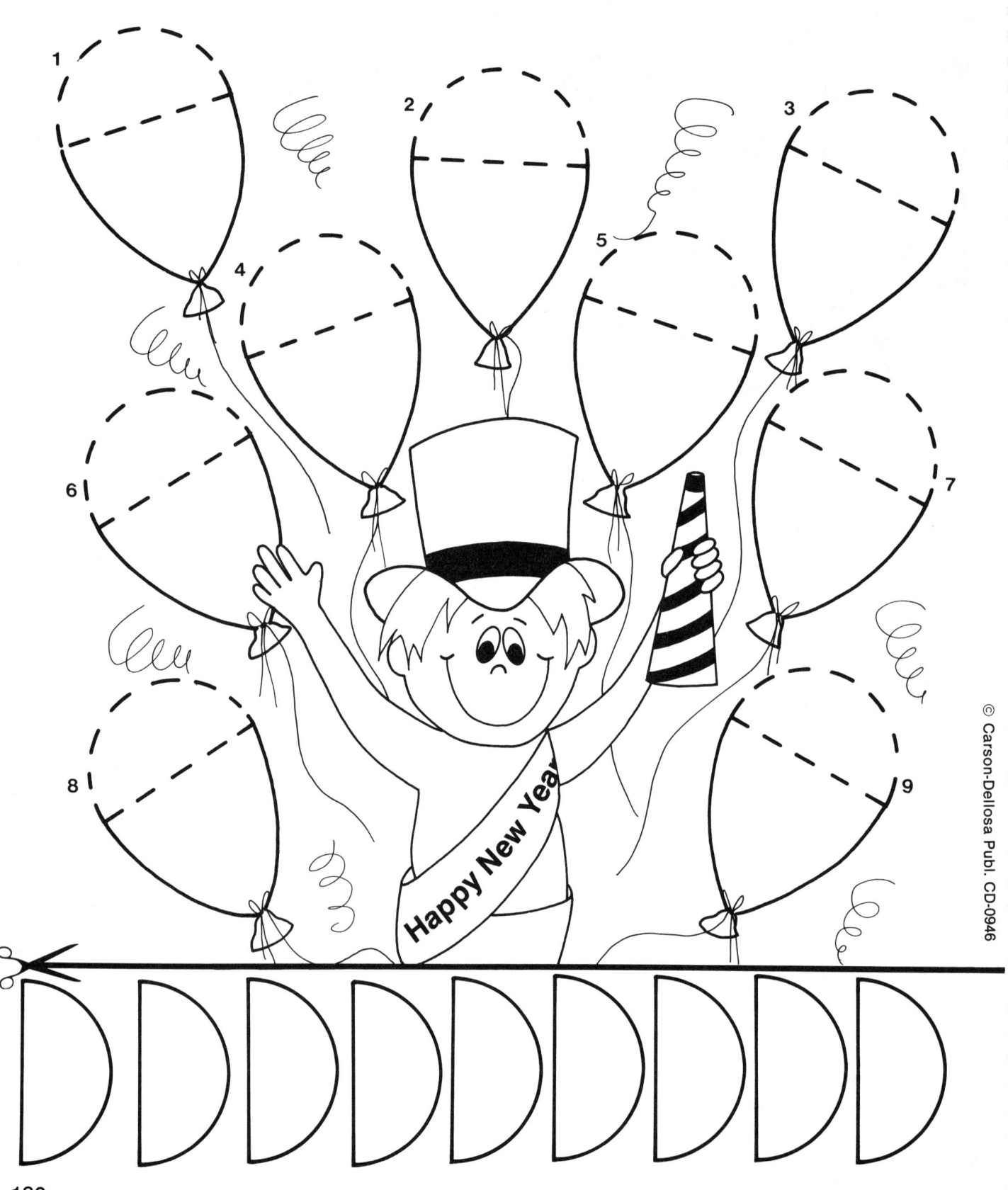

180

Name _____

Add or subtract to solve each problem and color:

8 - yellow
6 - orange
4 - red

Name _____

Make a Snowflake

Directions:

1. On a separate sheet of paper, use a compass or lid to make a circle a little larger in size than the size of the desired finished snowflake. Cut out the circle.

2. Fold the circle in half.

3. Fold the half circle into thirds.

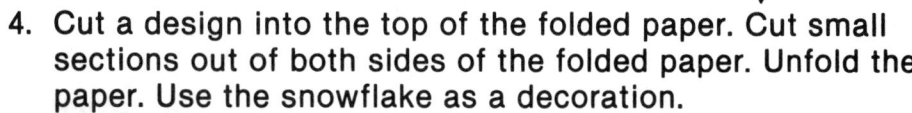

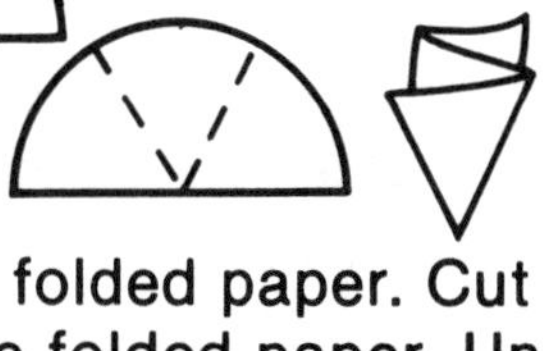

4. Cut a design into the top of the folded paper. Cut small sections out of both sides of the folded paper. Unfold the paper. Use the snowflake as a decoration.

Name _____

Maze

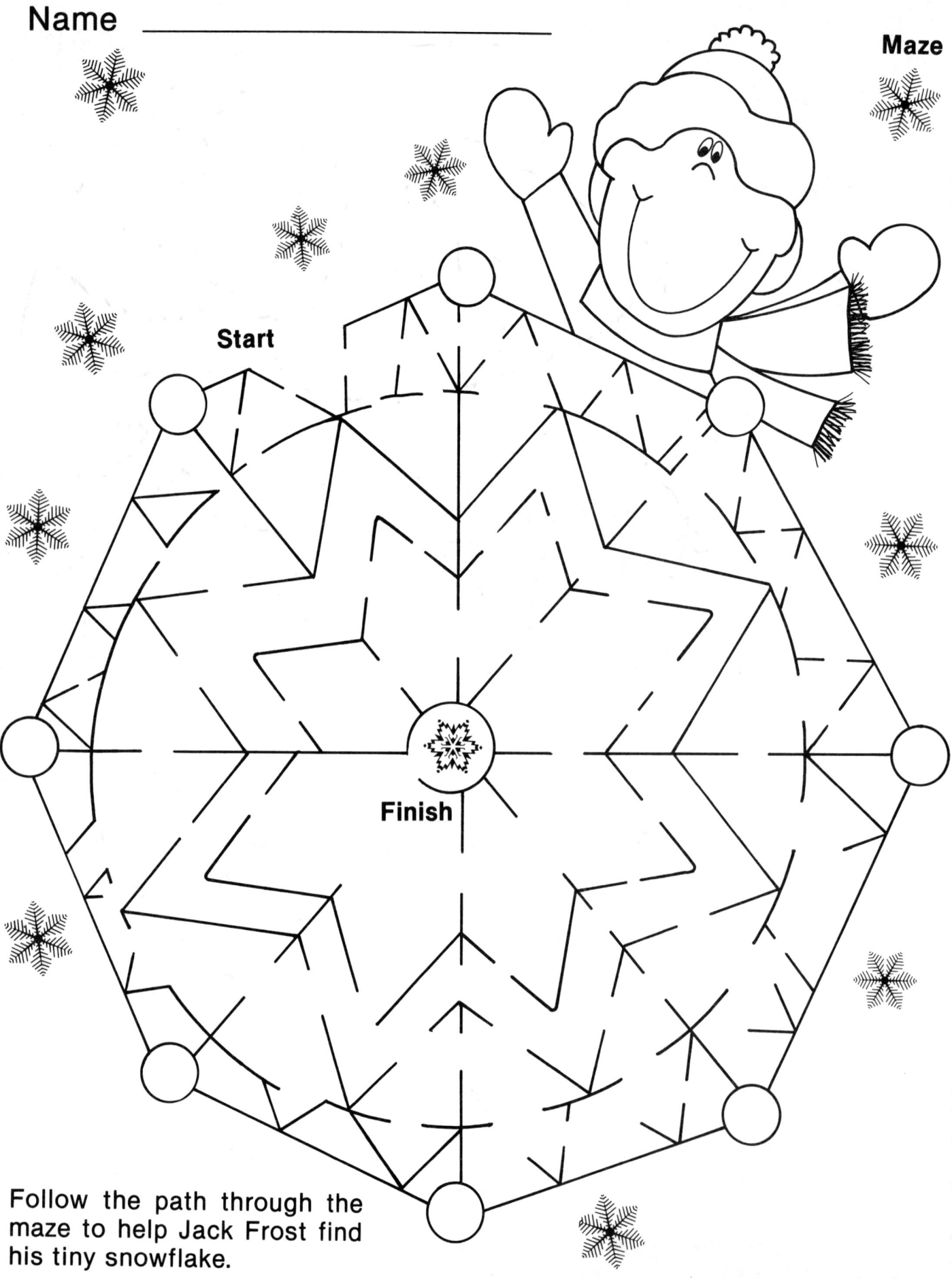

Start

Finish

Follow the path through the maze to help Jack Frost find his tiny snowflake.

Name _____   **Hidden Words**

```
A S D F G H J K I F A L L R E W Q U Y
V S K A T E H B G T S N O W M E N J K
D P R E W D C O L P I M I T T E N S C
T I S X I M O D F G H J C Y T O I U
N V B R J L H T L A K E V D W K
R G L I D E V C T L K J H G F
    B G T Y S C L A C E S
```

Circle the hidden words:

skate	spin	ice	snowmen
cold	twirl	mittens	hats
glide	fall	lake	laces

© Carson-Dellosa Publ. CD-0946

185

Name _____

Subtract to find the hidden combinations. Circle each hidden combination you find.

EXAMPLE:

16   7   9   16

8   5   3   15   9   6
14   7   7   10   5   5
1   17   9   8   12   7   5   6
5   13   7   6   17   10   7   8
9   6   3   12   1   11   5   6
6   4   2   16   8   8   1   7
     14   7   7   8   1   5
      1   5   3   2   4   6

186 © Carson-Dellosa Publ. CD-0946

Name _____   **Secret Message**

```
  1   4   3   5
 ___ ___ ___ ___

  8   2   6   5       2
 ___ ___ ___ ___     ___

 11   2   9   9
 ___ ___ ___ ___

  7  12  10   8
 ___ ___ ___ ___

 14  13 !
 ___ ___
```

Match the numbers to the letters. Find the message in the secret code.

1-C	4-O	7-W	10-T	13-S
2-A	5-E	8-H	11-B	14-U
3-M	6-V	9-L	12-I	

Snowman Crossword Puzzle

Across

1. Pile of wind-blown snow
2. Steep toboggan track
4. Type of white, cold-weather bear
5. One of two long runners for feet to travel on snow
8. _____ Man Winter
9. Long neckerchief for protection from cold
11. Slip and _____
15. Vehicles on runners for traveling over the snow.

Complete the crossword puzzle on the next page with the winter words that match these clues.

Down

1. Abbreviation for first winter month
3. _____ muffs
5. Shoe with blade on the bottom for travelling over ice
6. Dwelling built of ice blocks
7. Shape of snowball
9. Short stockings
10. It was so cold, he _____ in his tracks.
12. Outer garments to cover upper body
13. Mitten with fingers
14. Worn over shoes

Name _____

Name _____
Directions:

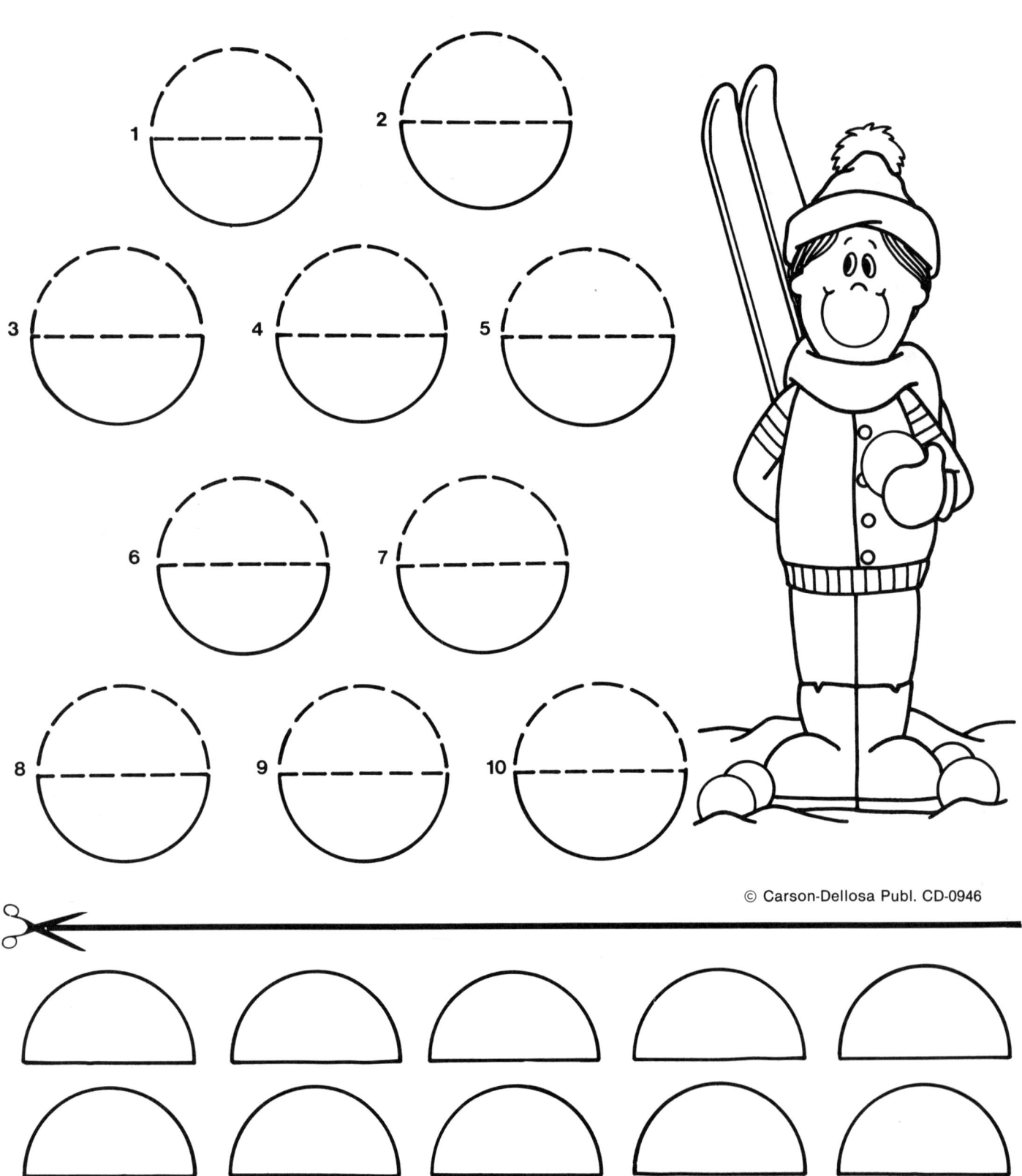

© Carson-Dellosa Publ. CD-0946

Name _____

Read the clues. Find the correct word in the word list to complete the sentence. Write the word in the crossword puzzle.

Down

1. Special shoes worn on ice are _____ .
2. The coldest season of the year is _____ .
4. The winter month that follows January is _____ .
7. On January first, friends will say, Happy New _____ .

Across

3. We shovel _____ in winter.
5. We celebrate Christmas in _____ .
6. The first month of the year is _____ .
8. We must walk carefully when sidewalks are _____ .

Word List

year   icy
January   skates
December
snow   winter
February

Name _____

**Winter
Story Starter**

Use some of the words on the snowman to write a winter story. Color the picture.

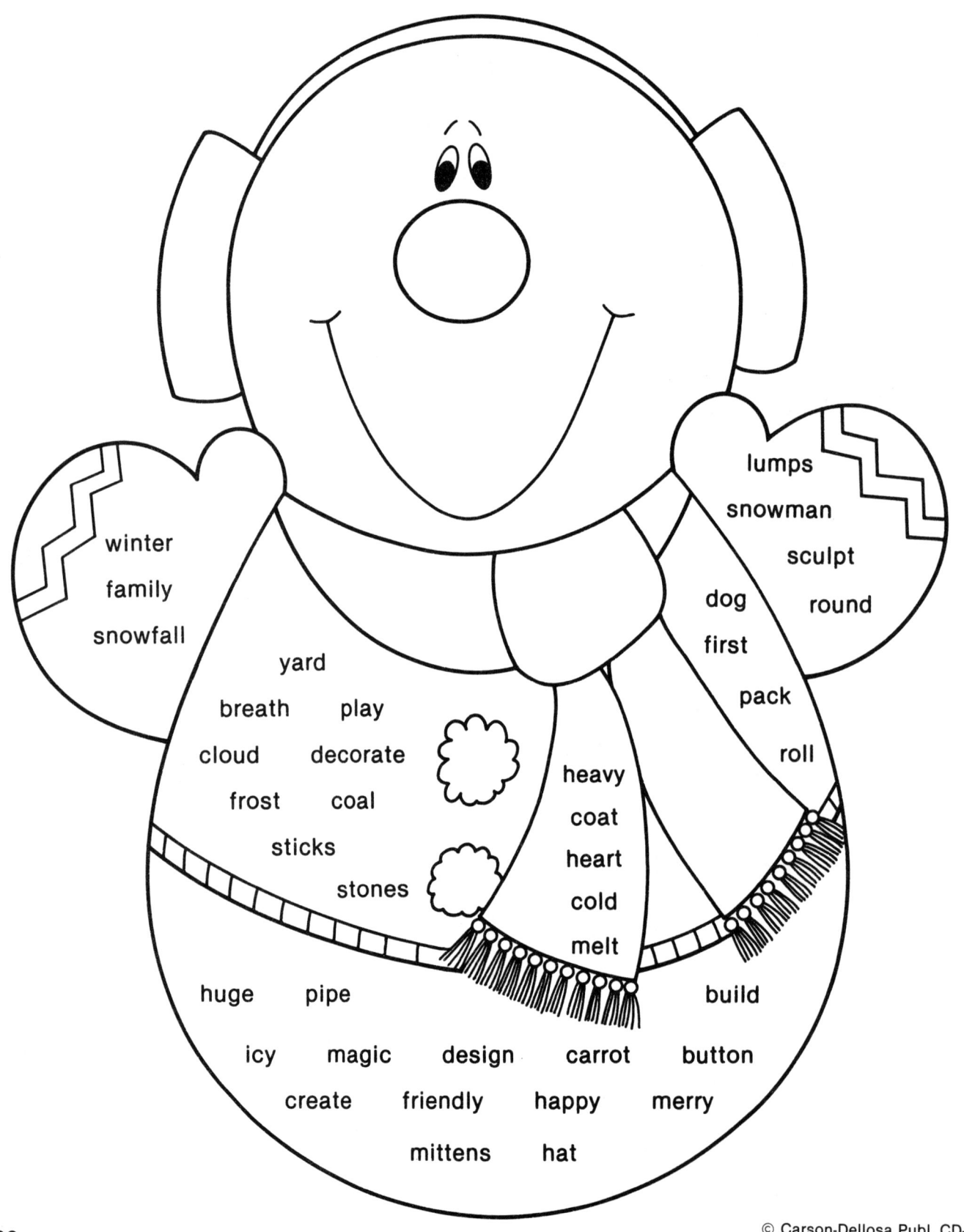

192

© Carson-Dellosa Publ. CD-0946

Name _____

Name _____   **Winter Story Starter**

Use some of the words on the mitten to write a winter story.
Color the pictures.

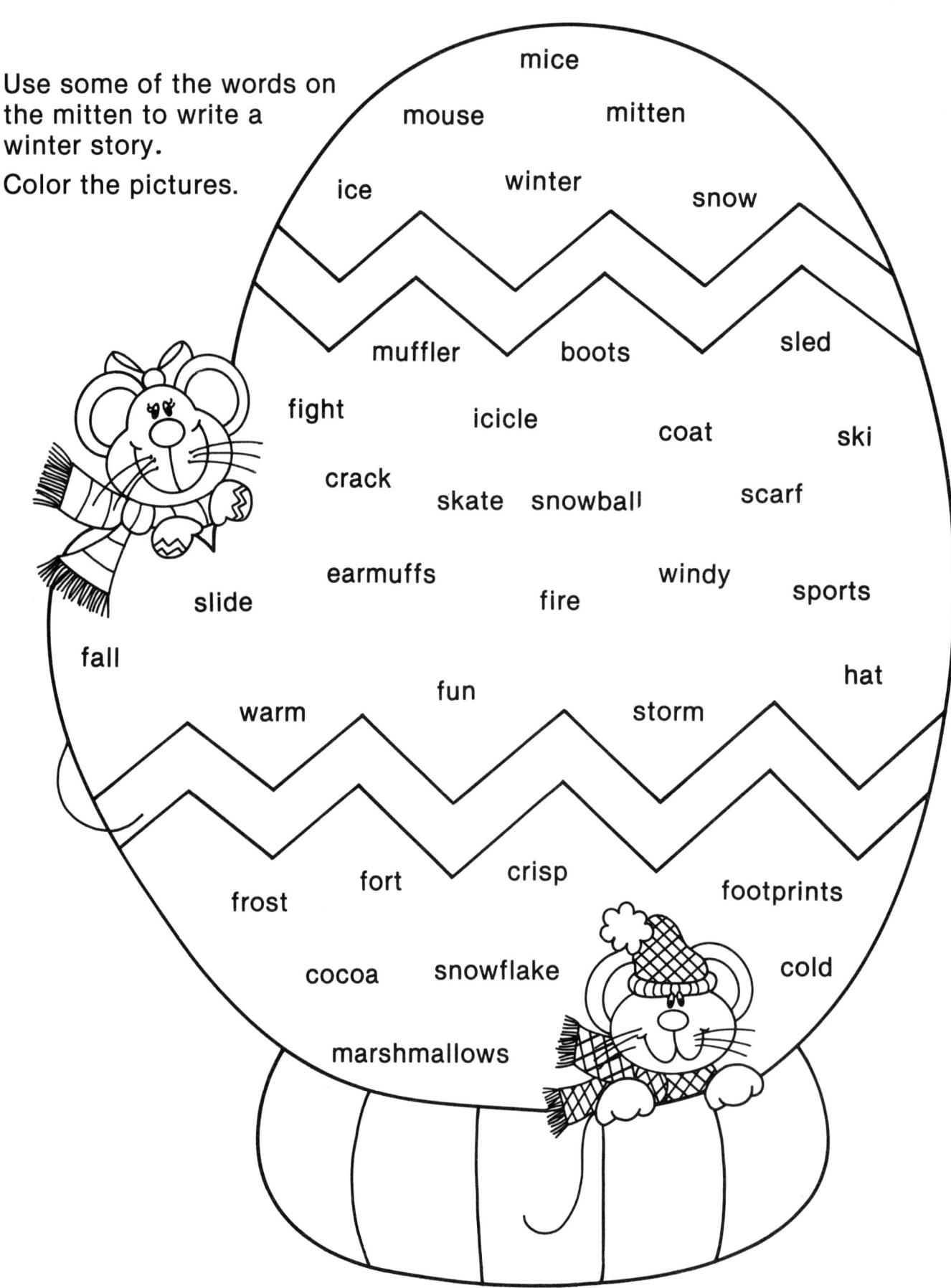

194

Name _____

Name _____

**Winter
Story Starter**

Use some of the words to write a winter story. Color the picture.

snowy tumble
laugh mittens shout knitted
saucer sunny hill sticks runner slope
play snowballs sledding fort steam
toboggan neighborhood fire January cocoa caps
gloves marshmallows scarf pond skating
shiver lace slick shouted crisp tingle
pair shovel angel imprint stamped
muffler sleigh icy windy
woolen kitten

Name _____

Winter

How to Use

Related Poems
Enlarge any of the patterns to use as the center of a bulletin board. Direct students to copy a related poem. Display the papers on the bulletin board.

Award Sayings
Use an award saying with its related pattern to create student awards.

Related Poems

No need to fear when I am near -
Your ears will never freeze.
Wear me when winter chills are here.
Your head you'll surely please.

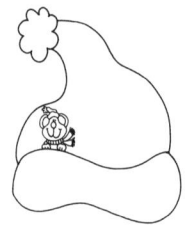

Award Sayings

Hats off to me!
"Cap"ital Work!

Made from wool of colors bright,
On our hands all snug and tight -
A pair of mittens - just the thing
To keep out winter's frosty sting.

I gave a helping hand!
I warm my teacher's heart!

A snowball when it's rolled through snow
Will rounder - rounder - rounder grow!
What can we do with this great ball?
Make a snowman towering tall!

"Snow" one is as nice as I am!
Perfect Snowman!

To make a snowlady
   you'll need ribbons and lace
And maybe eyelashes to go on her face.
For this lady you'll also need
   a scarf and hat
And maybe a coat if she's not too fat.

Frosty Friend
Icy good work

Name _____

Winter
(Instructions on previous page)

Name _____
Directions:

200
© Carson-Dellosa Publ. CD-0946

Name_____
Directions:

Name _____

Use the word list to unscramble the words on the skate.

Word List
- pond
- winter
- snowman
- glide
- cold
- mittens
- skate
- hat
- ice
- scarf

tksae _____

ligde _____

noswamn _____

timtnes _____

ath _____

opdn _____

cie _____

niwter _____

casrf _____

ocld _____

Name _____

Directions:

Winter Wonderland Worker Award

to _____

for

_____

_____

_____

_____

Signed

© Carson-Dellosa Publ. CD-0946

ICY...

**you do great work!
Congratulations!**

© Carson-Dellosa Publ. CD-0946

Name ____________________

C O
C P B A P
I D O I T X O
D O R U C E T S
B R A C C O O N S
D E E R O R Y B E U
F P A G D F E E R M
C O T T O N T A I L
O X S B I O S R N
Y B N E R N U K
O Y U P O S M
T P C O Y G R
E R O R A C O
D E F C N E X
C O U G A R
B C P I F T
R T I U O P S
U N A X T K
M E S N R U
T A M O Y N
S K O I K

DEER

COUGAR

OPOSSUM

COYOTE

COTTONTAIL

BEAR

FOX

PORCUPINE

RACCOON

SKUNK

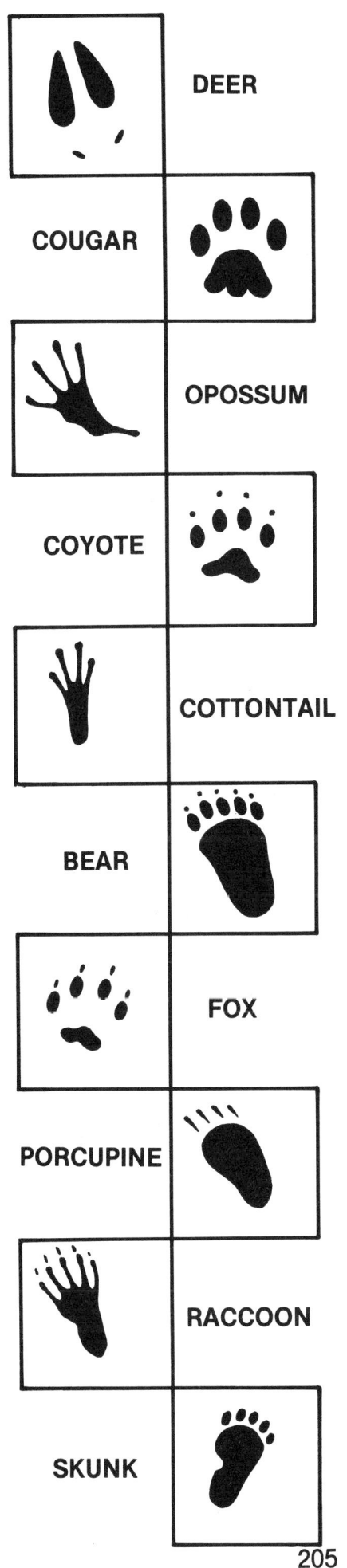

Name _____   Draw A Mouse

Follow the steps below to draw a mouse.

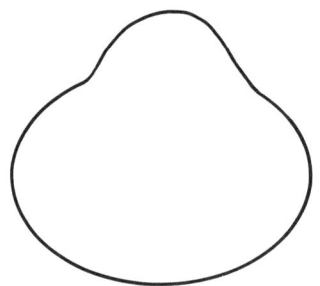
1. Draw a head.

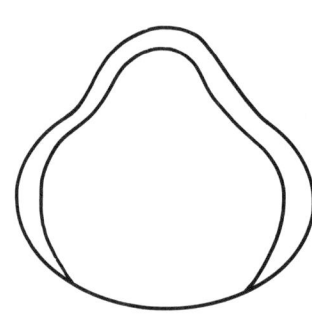
2. Draw a hat rim.

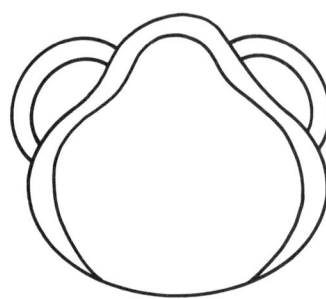
3. Draw the ears.

4. Draw a hat.

5. Draw a face.

6. Draw a scarf.

7. Decorate the hat or scarf any way you wish.

Draw your mouse here:

Name _____
Directions:

Name _____
Directions:

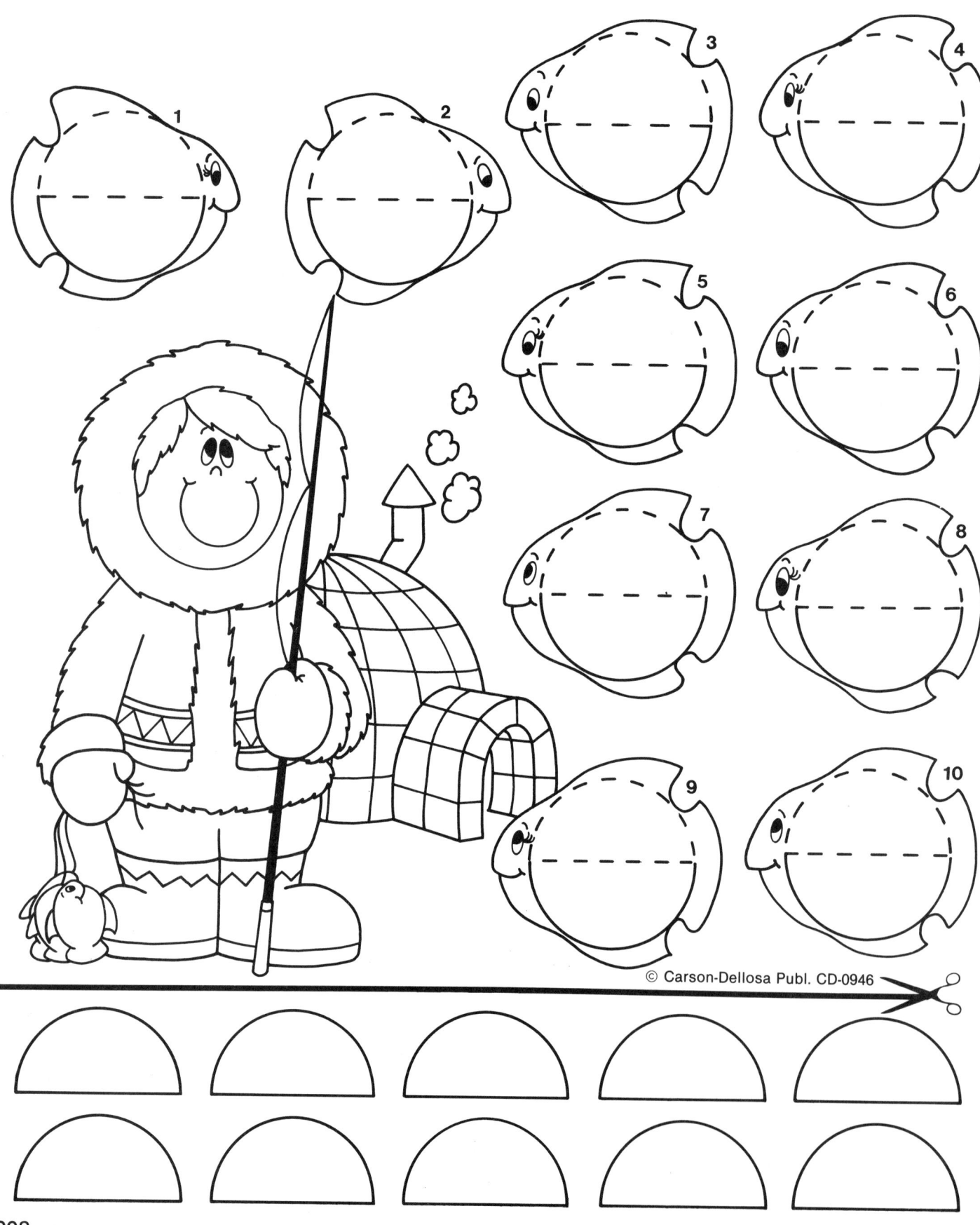

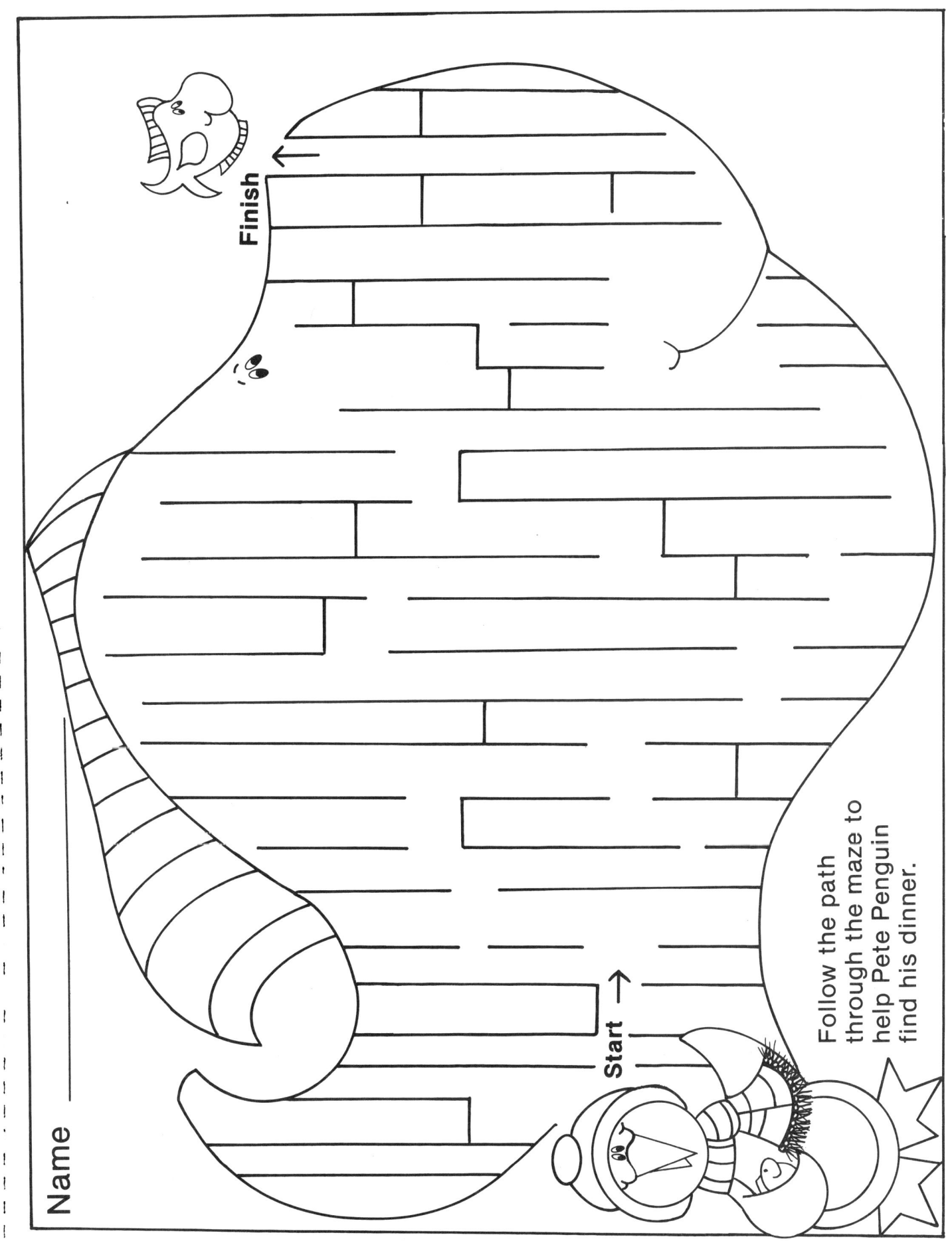

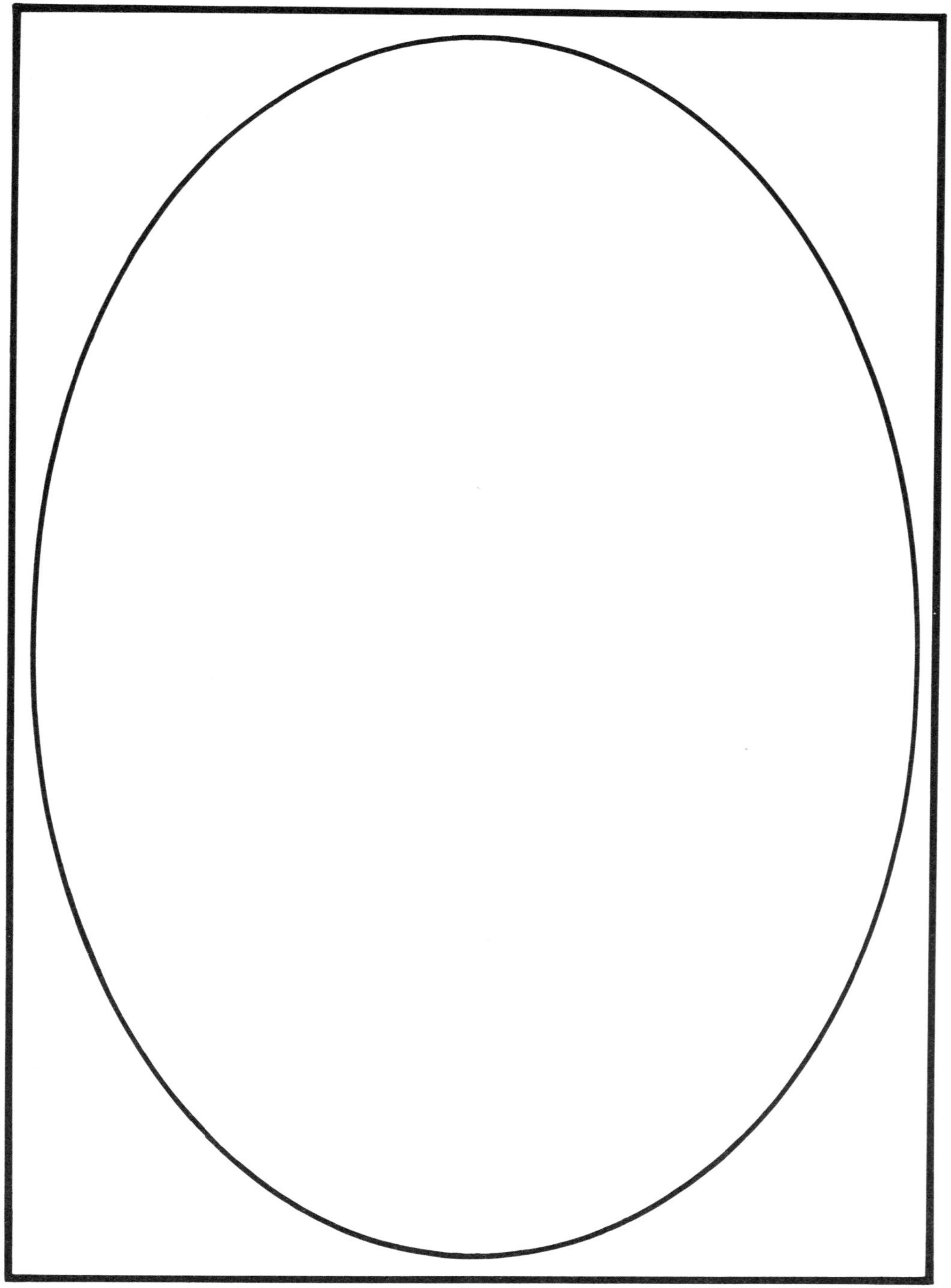

Name

Directions:
Note—For the entire project—deer, background and frame—only two colors are used, one light, one dark.
1. Color the deer a single dark color, adding no detail, or leave it white.
2. Cut out the deer and the snow it stands in.
3. Inside the oval frame, draw an appropriate background for the deer. It can be either dark or light, just so it is the opposite of the deer.
4. Decorate the frame.
5. Glue the deer so it fits inside the oval frame.
6. Cut out the entire frame.

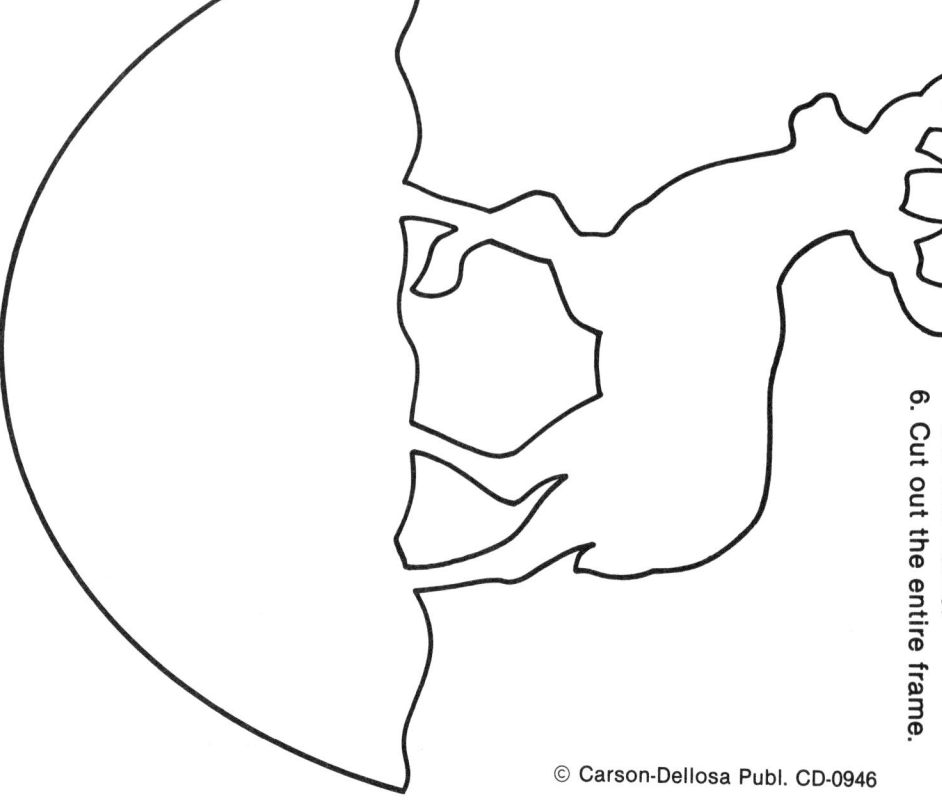

Name _____   **Winter Calendar Cover-Ups**

Color and cut out the calendar cover-ups. Glue each cover-up to an appropriate calendar date on the next page.

 --

Color the picture.

© Carson-Dellosa Publ. CD-0946

Name _____   **CALENDAR**

Fill in the month and dates on the calendar.
Glue the calendar cover-ups to the calendar.
Color the picture.

Sunday	Monday	Tuesday	Wednesday	Thursday	Friday	Saturday

Winter Puppet Play

Read and perform the puppet play. You may wish to complete the paper bag puppets on the next pages to use with the play.

The Penguin Follies
by Gail Aemmer

Narrator: Porter and Petunia Penguin are getting ready for the Penguin Follies. The Penguin Follies is an exciting, fun-filled stage show and the penguins are the players. They dance, sing, tell stories, roller skate and act out little plays. Tonight is the first night of the show. Petunia and Porter are practicing their act.

Porter: To be, or not to be . . It's no use, Petunia. I just can't go on tonight. I'm too scared. How can someone who is as scared as I am go on stage for the Penguin Follies? (hanging his head) I'm a failure, Petunia.

Petunia: Don't be silly, Porter. You've just got a simple case of stage fright. Come on. Let's practice our dance. (Petunia moves toward Porter as if to dance)

Porter: (jumping back away from Petunia, shouting) It's really worse than you think, Petunia! Oh, what am I going to do? (sobbing loudly)

Petunia: Porter, I may have something that just might help you, if you're really that nervous. It's a poem that my aunt Paula Penguin taught me when I was first learning to roller skate. It goes like this:

> When you get scared and you don't know just why,
> Chase away those fears with a blink of your eye.

Then you blink your eyes once, really tight and when you're done, you won't be scared anymore!

Porter: Gosh! Do you think it really would work for me?

Petunia: Of course it will, Porter. It worked for me. You would never have believed how frightened I was to roller skate. Then when I said those words, all of a sudden, I wasn't afraid anymore! You try it!

Porter: Well, all right, I'll try it.
> When you get scared and you don't know why,
> Chase away those fears with a blink of your eye.

(after a short pause) Hey! You know, I do feel pretty brave! I'm not nervous, or scared at all! Petunia, you're wonderful! Thanks! (gives Petunia a hug)

Petunia: Now, let's practice for the Penguin Follies!

Porter: Oh, yes! Let's do!

Narrator: The Penguin Follies was a smashing success. Everyone said that the very best penguins in the show were Porter and Petunia. Porter, everyone said, was very relaxed and did his part so well. Petunia never told anyone about Porter's secret, and don't you tell either!

Name _____

Porter Penguin Paper Bag Puppet

Materials: lunch bag, crayons or markers, scissors, glue

1. Color and cut out the head and body.
2. Glue the body to a lunch bag under the flap.
3. Glue the head to the lunch bag flap.
4. Put your hand into the bag to move the head of the penguin.

Name _____

Petunia Penguin Paper Bag Puppet

Materials: lunch bag, crayons or markers, glue, scissors

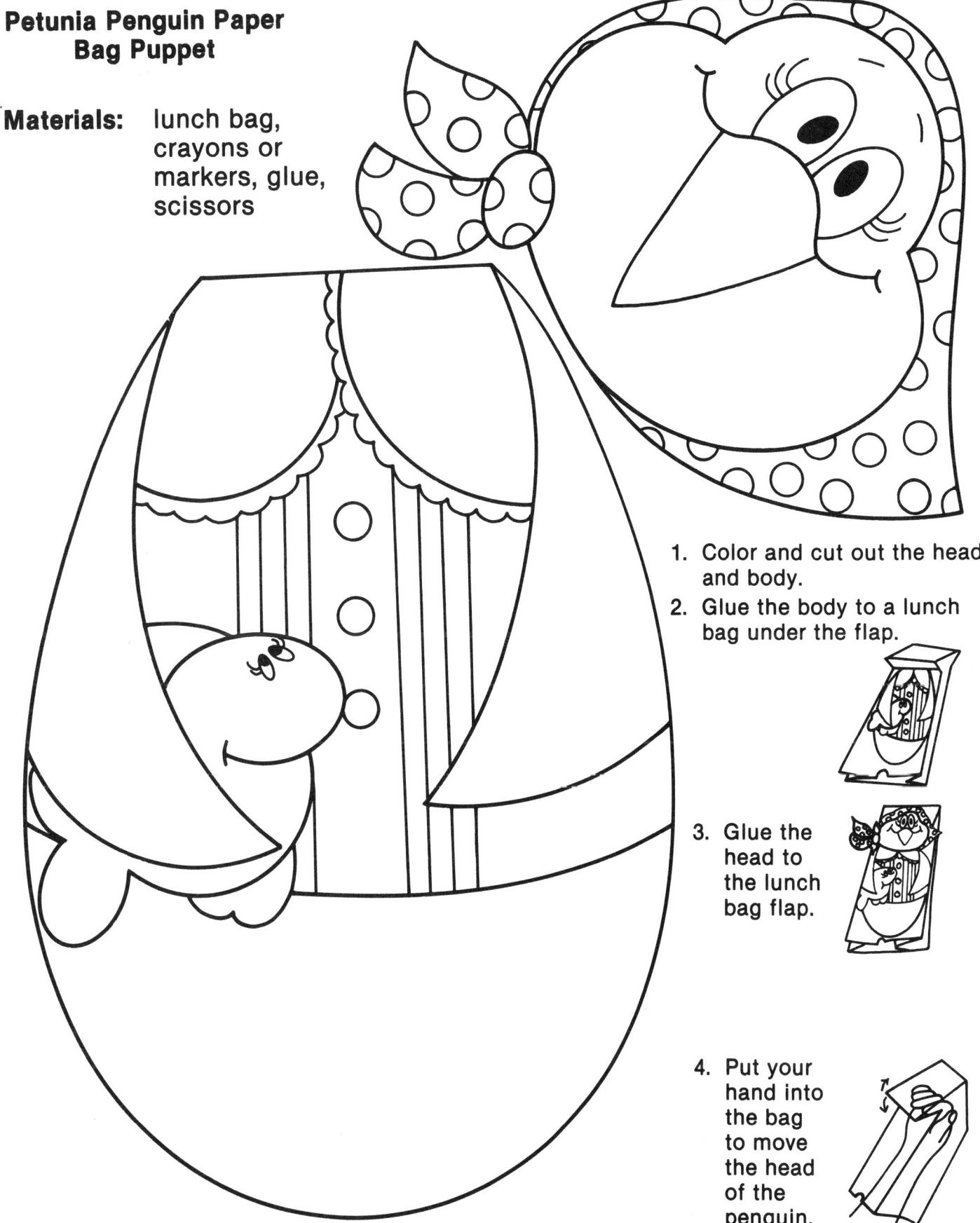

1. Color and cut out the head and body.
2. Glue the body to a lunch bag under the flap.
3. Glue the head to the lunch bag flap.
4. Put your hand into the bag to move the head of the penguin.

Name _____

Manuscript Letter

ome manuscript letters are letters and pictures or decorations all in one. When creating your own manuscript letter for a story, keep these pointers in mind:

1. Know the first word of your story so you can choose a letter to use.
2. Start your drawing with the letter itself. The letter you use must be drawn so it is easily readable.
3. The picture that you create around your letter should have something to do with the subject of the story.
4. The picture should blend with the letter. Notice how the skater in this letter is in front of the "S" but does not hide it.
5. You may wish to put a border around your manuscript letter to frame it.

© Carson-Dellosa Publ. CD-0946

Directions:

1. On the following page write a winter story or poem. Be sure to leave out the first letter of the the first word.
2. Following the pointers given above, create your own manuscript letter in this space, using the first letter of the first word of your story.
3. When the picture-letter is complete, cut it out and paste it to the space provided on your story page.

Here are some words that could be used to start your story:

cold, skis, steep, pine trees, faster, white, stars

216

Name

Paste Manuscript Letter Drawing Here.

Name _____

What's Wrong With This Winter Scene?
Circle the things that are wrong in this picture.

Name _____   **February Finger Play Poem**

Read the finger play poem. Perform the finger movements as you read the poem again. You may wish to complete the finger puppets on the next page to use with the poem. Color the picture.

Groundhogs
by Gail Aemmer

Groundhog Day is coming; the groundhogs are getting ready. Let's look in on May, Thomas, Fran and Eddie.

May is cleaning up the house; it's looking spic and span.
(Hold up 1 finger)

Thomas is telling all his friends, as many as he can.
(Hold up 2 fingers)

Fran is picking flowers so their house looks nice and fresh.
(Hold up 3 fingers)

Eddie's brushing his smooth brown fur to look his very best.
(Hold up 4 fingers)

Groundhog Day is finally here; they all pop up together.
(All 4 fingers pop up)

And if they run (They've seen the sun!) we'll have more wintery weather!

Name _____   **Instant Ground Hog Finger Puppets**

These puppets may be used in the play, "Groundhogs", or in your own February play.

Materials: crayons, scissors, pencil
Directions: Color and cut out each puppet on the dotted line. Use a pencil to punch a hole through the center of each of the circles at the bottom of the puppet. Use scissors to cut out the remaining portion of the circles. Place your first two fingers through the holes of the puppet to form the legs. Make the puppet move by moving your fingers.

221

Name _____
Directions:

Name _____
Directions:

Name ____________________

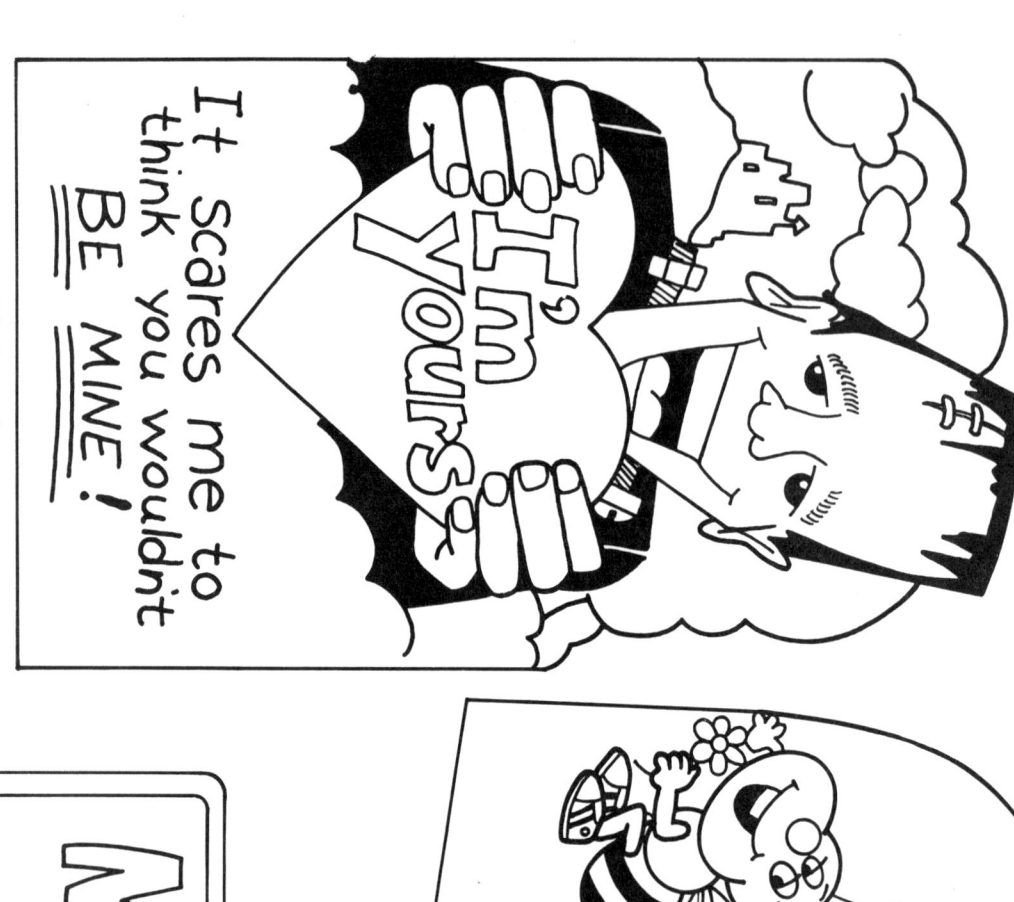

I'm yours
It scares me to think you wouldn't BE MINE!

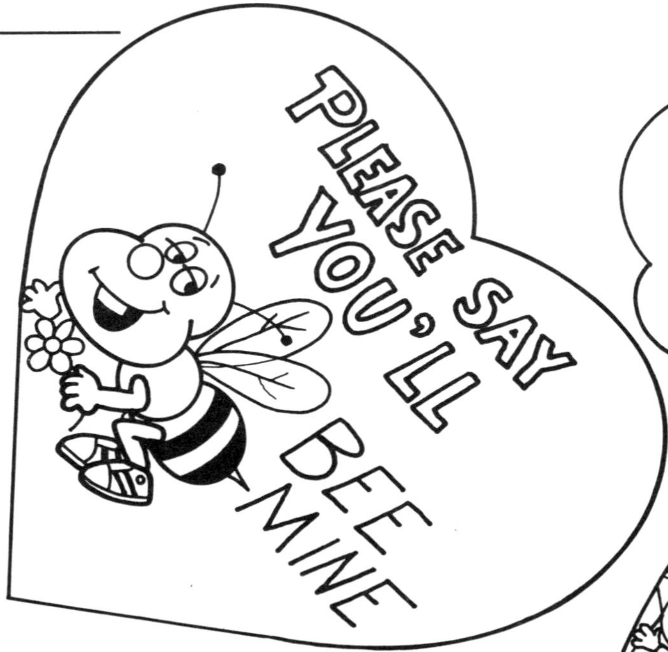

PLEASE SAY YOU'LL BEE MINE

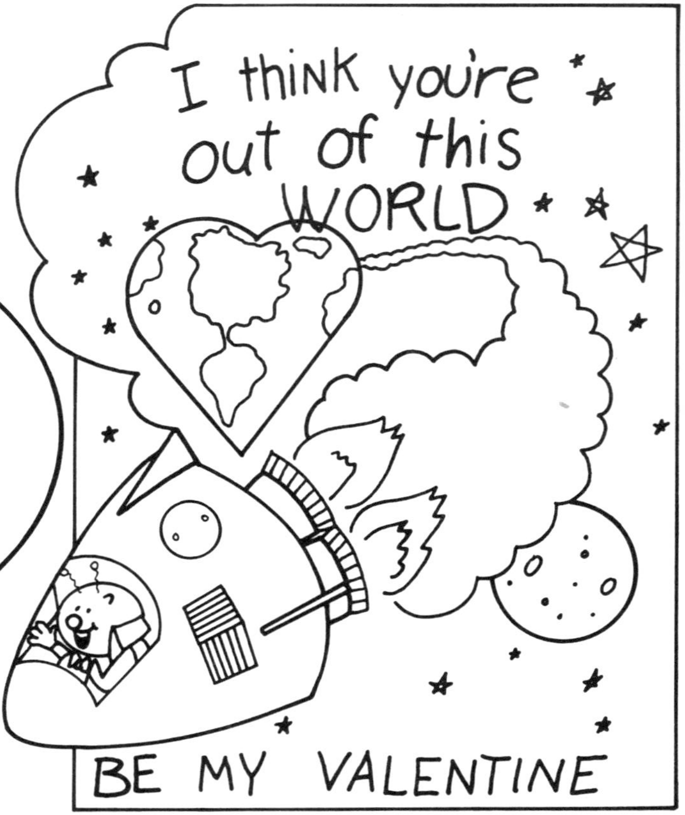

I think you're out of this WORLD
BE MY VALENTINE

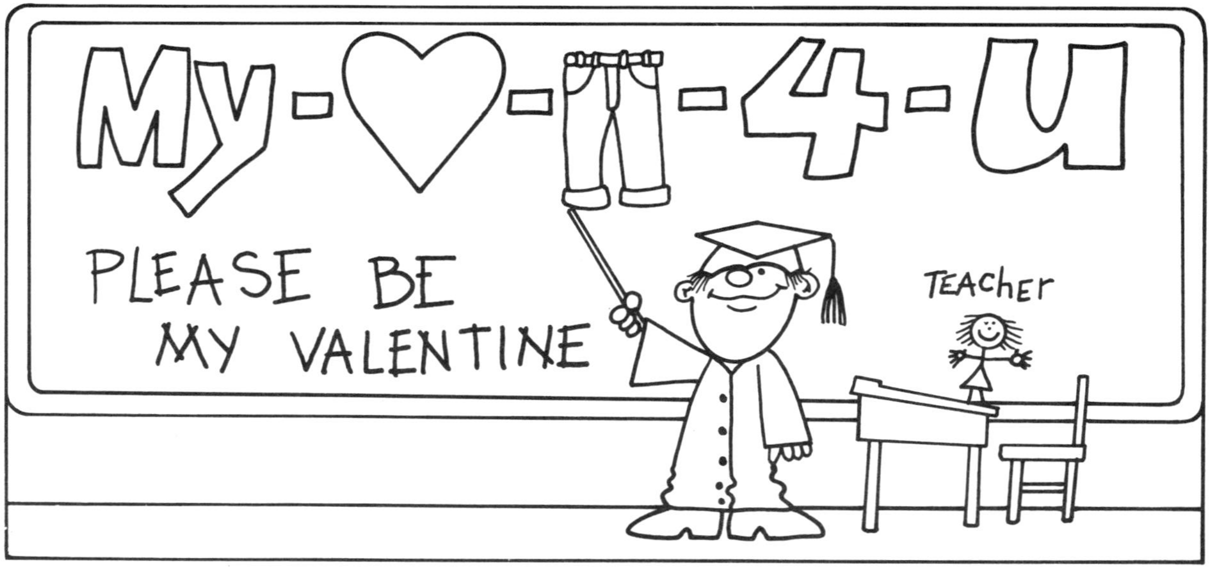

My-♥-π-4-u
PLEASE BE MY VALENTINE
TEACHER

Valentines

Directions:

1. Color and cut out all of the valentines.
2. Write the name of the person you are giving the card to, along with your name, on the back of each valentine.
3. Give the valentines to your friends and family.

Name_____
Directions:

Cupid's Arrow Maze

Clarence Cupid and his buddy Peter Pond are getting ready to go visit their friends Angelica and Lily. Help them find their way through the maze to Lily's pad.

START HERE

FINISH HERE

Name _____   **Secret Code**

Use the code key to find the secret message.

Code Key
33 = D   83 = H   7 = A
77 = L   79 = N   69 = T
19 = I   56 = O   17 = U
51 = S   8 = E   26 = R
42 = Y   66 = V   2 = P

__ __ __ __ __ __ __ __ __
19   83 8   7 26 69 19 77 42

__ __ __ __   __ __ __   __ __ __ __
83 56 2   8   42 56 17   83   7 66   8

__   __ __ __ __ __ ,
7   83 7   2   2 42

__ __ __ __ __ __ __ __ __
66   7 77   8 79 69 19 79   8 51

__ __ __ !
33   7 42

Name _____

Use the word list on the heart to unscramble these words.

Word list: hearts, cupid, valentine, arrow, present, admire, candy, friend, red, card

1. epsnret _____
2. upcdi _____
3. ancyd _____
4. levniaten _____
5. ahters _____
6. maidre _____
7. iferdn _____
8. edr _____
9. orwar _____
10. rdca _____

Name _____

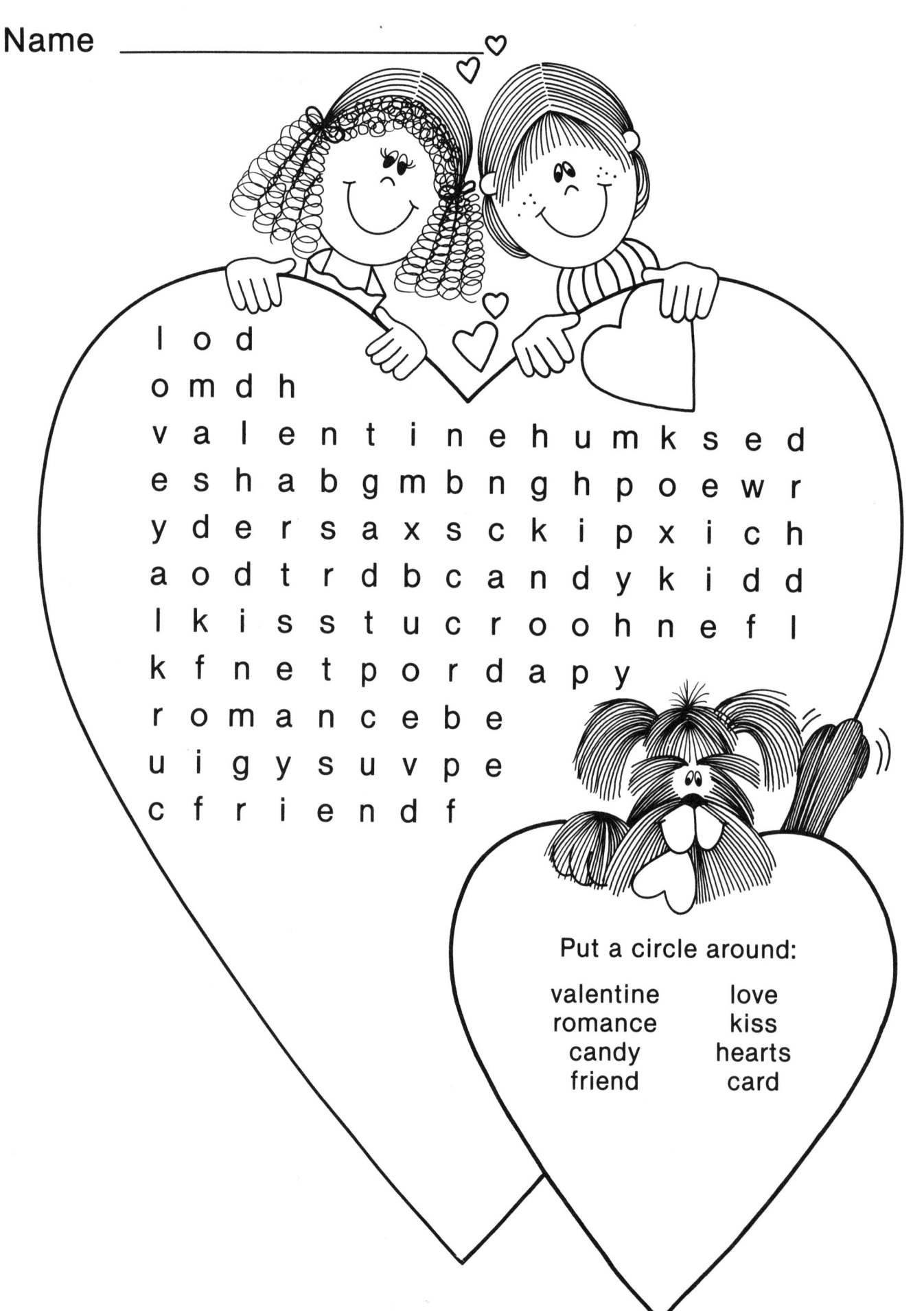

```
l o d
o m d h
v a l e n t i n e h u m k s e d
e s h a b g m b n g h p o e w r
y d e r s a x s c k i p x i c h
a o d t r d b c a n d y k i d d
l k i s s t u c r o o h n e f l
k f n e t p o r d a p y
r o m a n c e b e
u i g y s u v p e
c f r i e n d f
```

Put a circle around:

valentine   love
romance   kiss
candy   hearts
friend   card

Name _____

Cut and paste the number that comes <u>after</u> the number in each heart.

Name _____

Secret Message

Solve the problems to find the message in the secret code. Match the letters beside the answers to the matching numbers below.

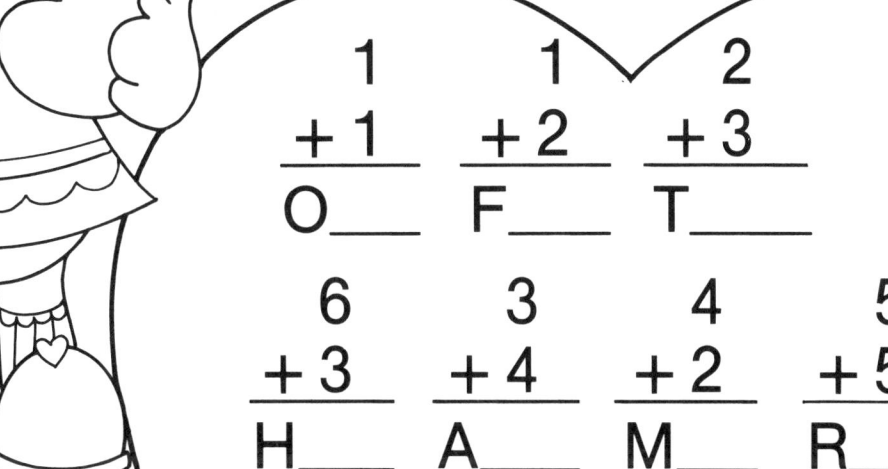

```
  1      1      2
 +1     +2     +3
 ――     ――     ――
 O__    F__    T__

  6      3      4      5
 +3     +4     +2     +5
 ――     ――     ――     ――
 H__    A__    M__    R__

  2      1      1
 +6     +3     +0
 ――     ――     ――
 E__    S__    Y__
```

__ __ __ __ __ __
9 8 7 10 5 4

__ __ __ __   __ __
3 10 2 6   6 1

__ __ __ __ __
9 8 7 10 5

Name _____

START

Can you find the path on the maze to help deliver this valentine?

Name _____

Put a circle around:
tail shaggy thump
nose send deliver
wag heart red
trick

Name _____

Circle the hidden words: dog cat bird friends gift share candy exchange presents heart valentine

236

Name _____   **Valentine Wristbands**

Directions:
1. Color and cut out all of the pieces.
2. Follow the steps shown to make the springs. Glue the ends of the springs down.

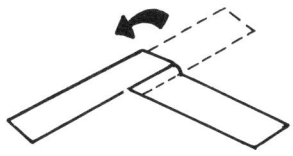 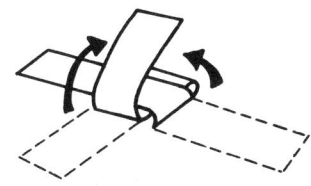 

3. Glue one spring to each dotted line box on the wristbands.

4. Glue the Love Bug to the spring on the flowered wristband.

5. Glue the cupid to the spring on the other wristband.

6. Tape the ends together so that each wristband fits around your wrist.

FOLD TO MAKE SPRING

FOLD TO MAKE SPRING

READ DIRECTIONS CAREFULLY

READ DIRECTIONS CAREFULLY

  Glue spring here.

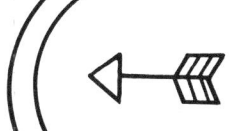 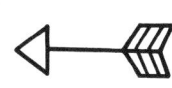 Glue spring here.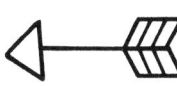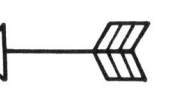

Name _____

Valentine Stick-on Seals

Directions:
1. Color the seals.
2. Mix an equal amount of Lepages® glue and water together in a small container, like a paper cup.
3. Use a paintbrush to apply the glue mixture to the back of this page.
4. Let the page dry completely, glue side up.
5. Cut out all of the seals.
6. When you are ready to use a seal, moisten the back of it with a damp sponge and press it onto the surface of an item.

238

© Carson-Dellosa Publ. CD-0946

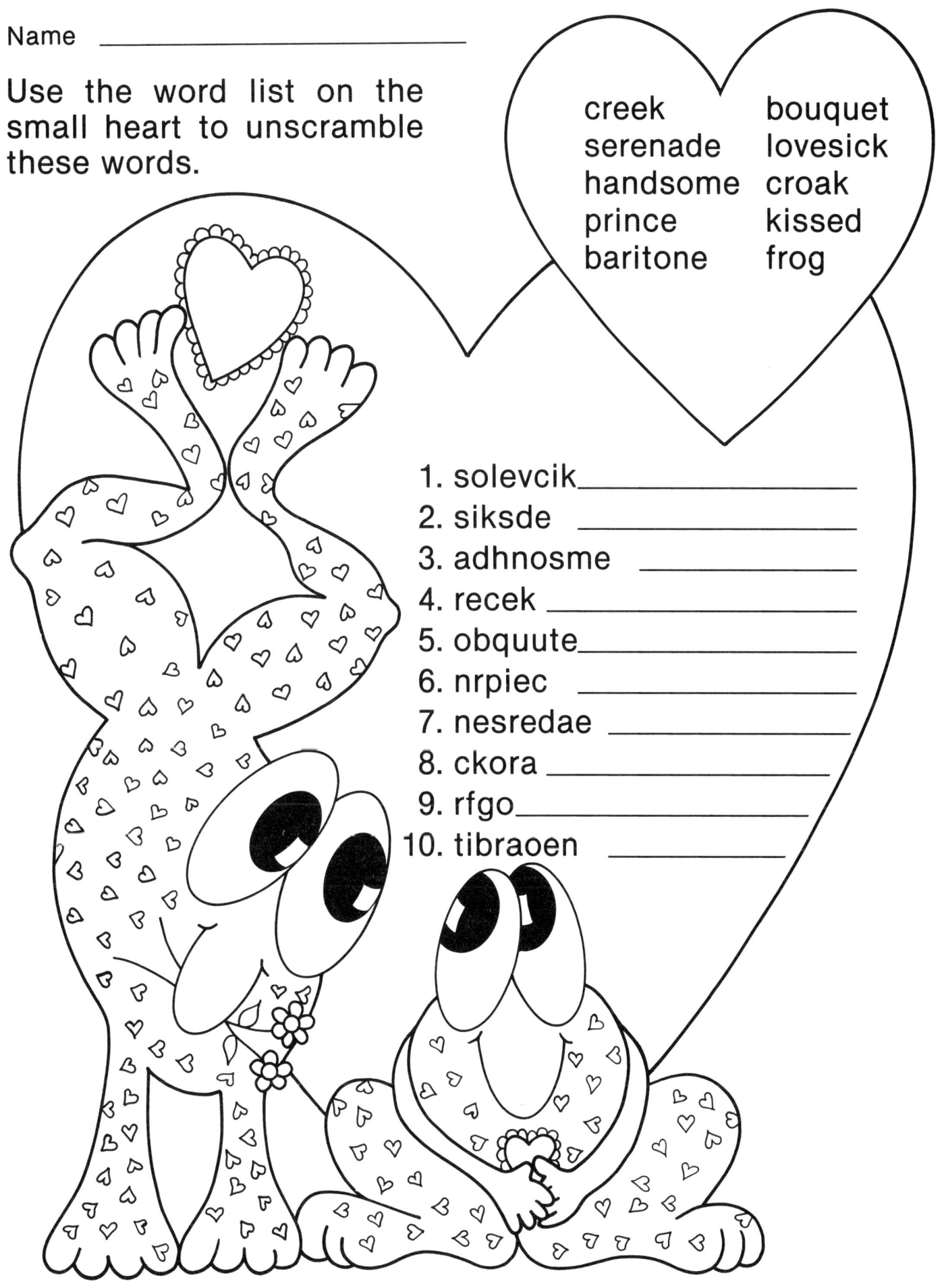

A VALENTINE'S DAY THANK YOU NOTE

You got a pretty valentine
    From a special friend, so true.
You want to write your special friend,
    And make your friend glad, too!

A Sample Valentine's Day Thank You

Dear Dave,
    Your valentine was the nicest one of all. I was very happy to receive it.
    You made my Valentine's Day a really special one.
        Your pal,
        Lisa

You received a special gift.
    It came on Valentine's Day.
What a fine surprise it was!
    What should you write and say?

A Sample Valentine's Day Thank You

Dear _____,
    You made my Valentine's Day very special. You're such a nice person.
    Thank you for being so thoughtful.
        Best ever,
        _____

Directions: Use the stationery provided to copy one of the sample Valentine's Day notes. If you wish, write your own message. Color the picture and send the letter.

_____,

Name _____

Valentine Story Starter

Use some of the words on the valentine to write a Valentine story.

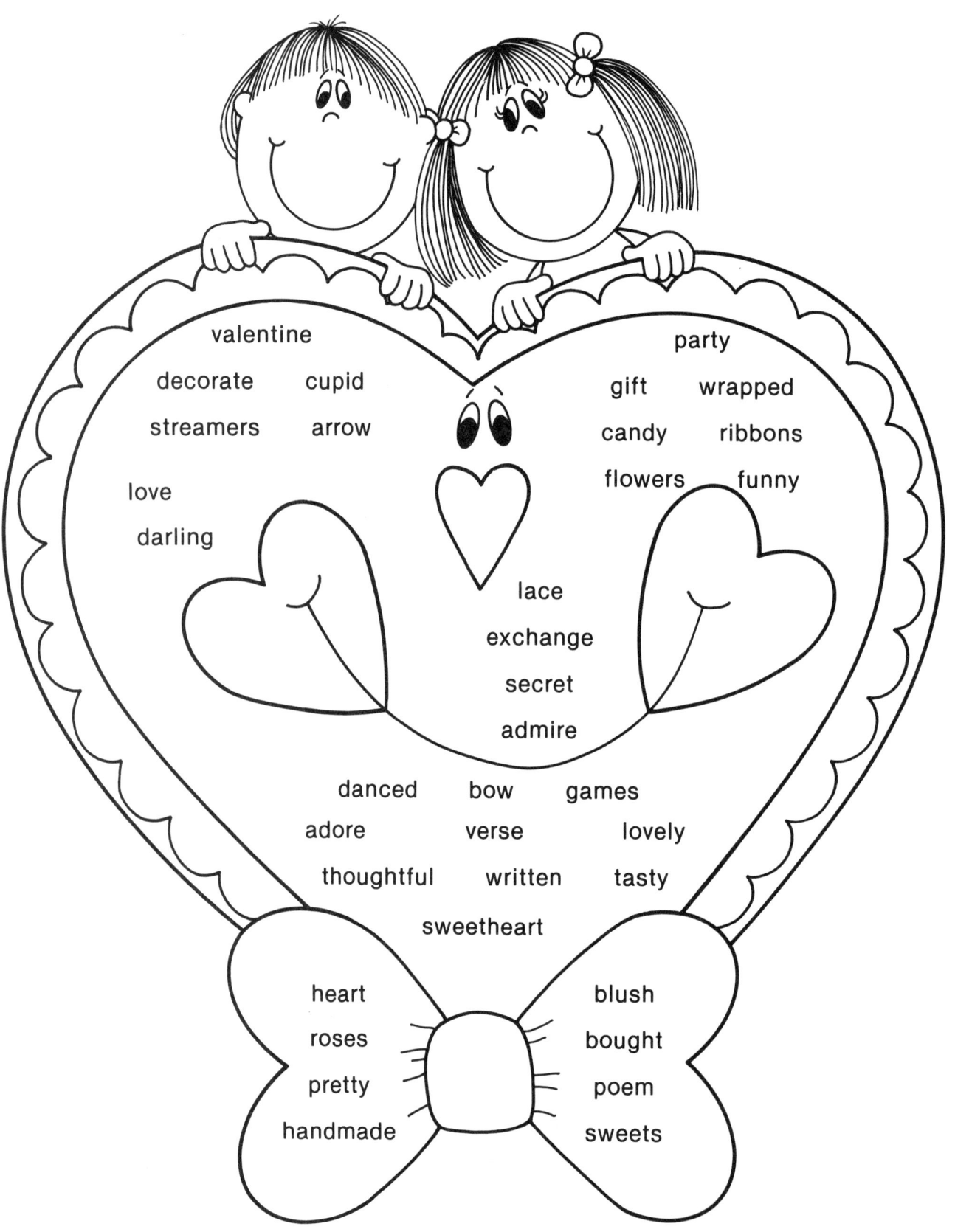

Name _____

Name _____

1. soume _____
2. erpesnt _____
3. figt _____
4. erd _____

9. alce _____
10. rhaet _____
11. vloe _____

5. ncayd _____
6. aveelntni _____
7. naormce _____
8. pucdi _____

Unscramble the words:

love   lace
heart   valentine
red   mouse   present
gift   candy   romance
cupid

Use some of the words to write a mouse's Valentine story.

Name_____

_____,

You stole my heart with your great work!

_____
Signed

© Carson-Dellosa Publ. CD-0946

Every "birdie" loves great work, and _____ does great work!

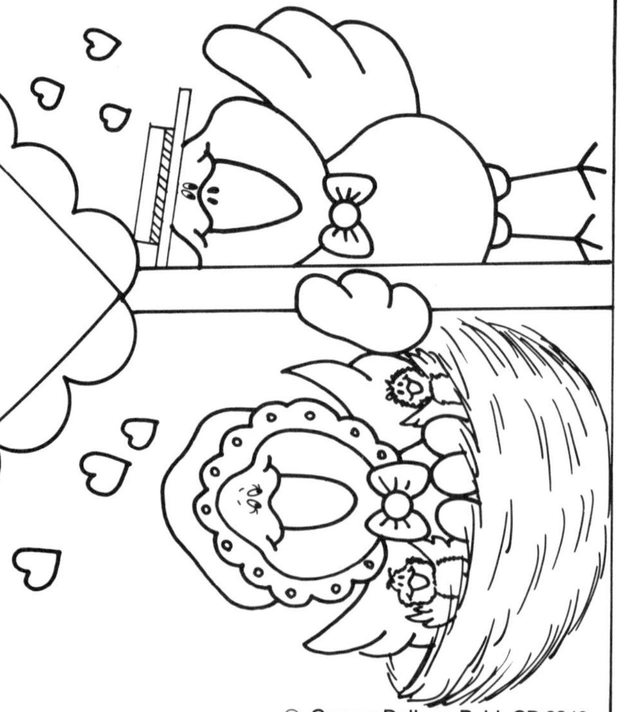

© Carson-Dellosa Publ. CD-0946

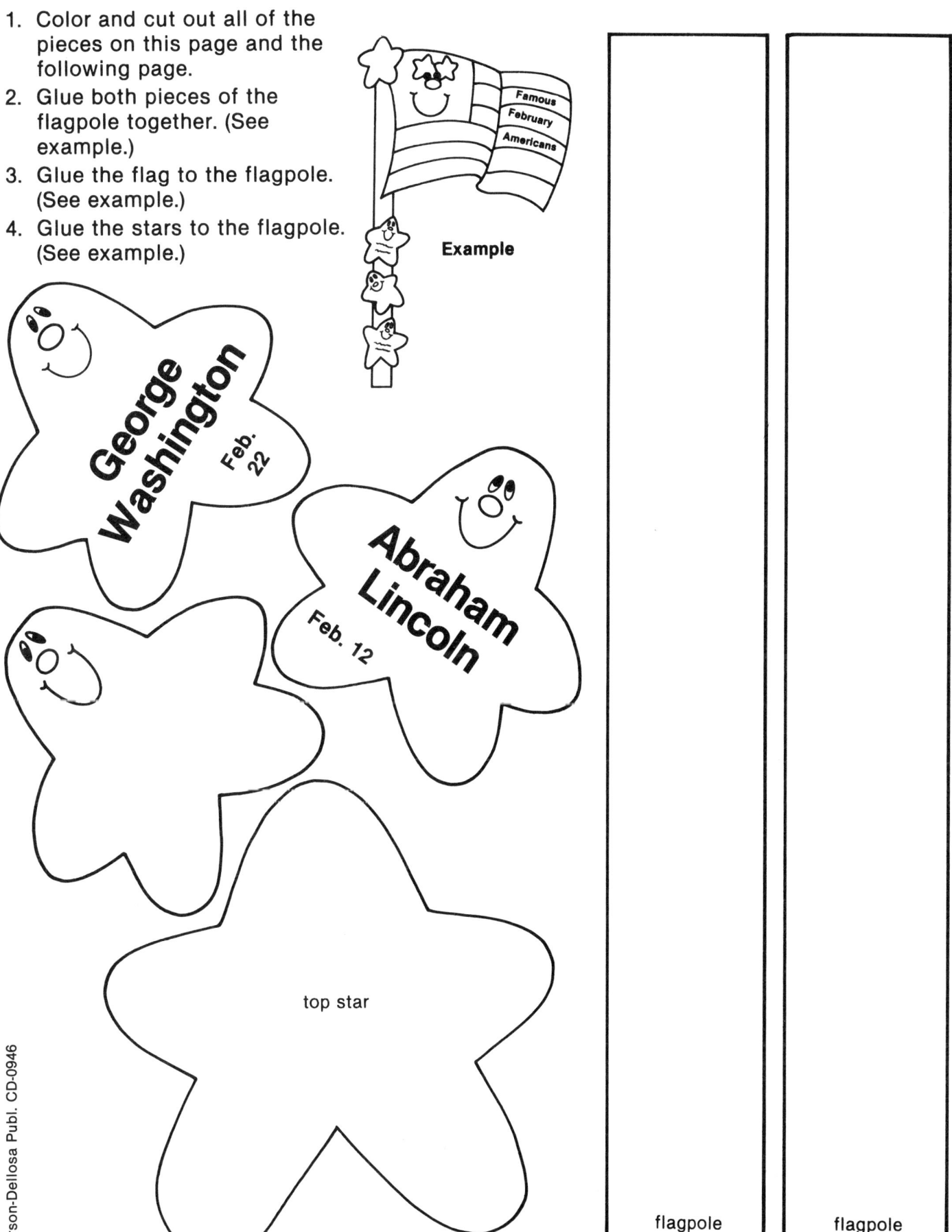

Name _____   Flag Art Project

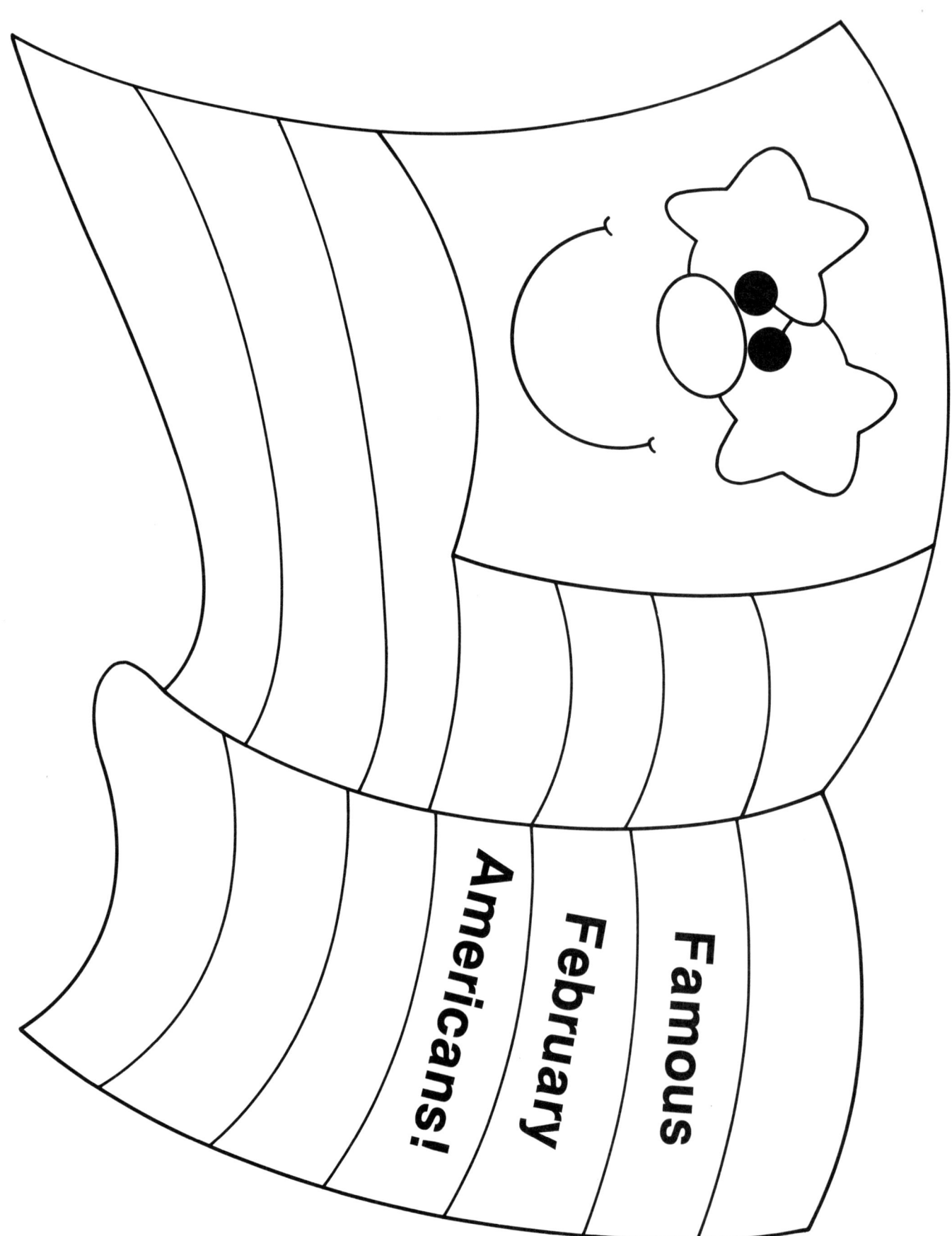

248
© Carson-Dellosa Publ. CD-0946

Name _____   **February Story Starter**

Use some of the words below to write a story about George Washington. Color the pictures.

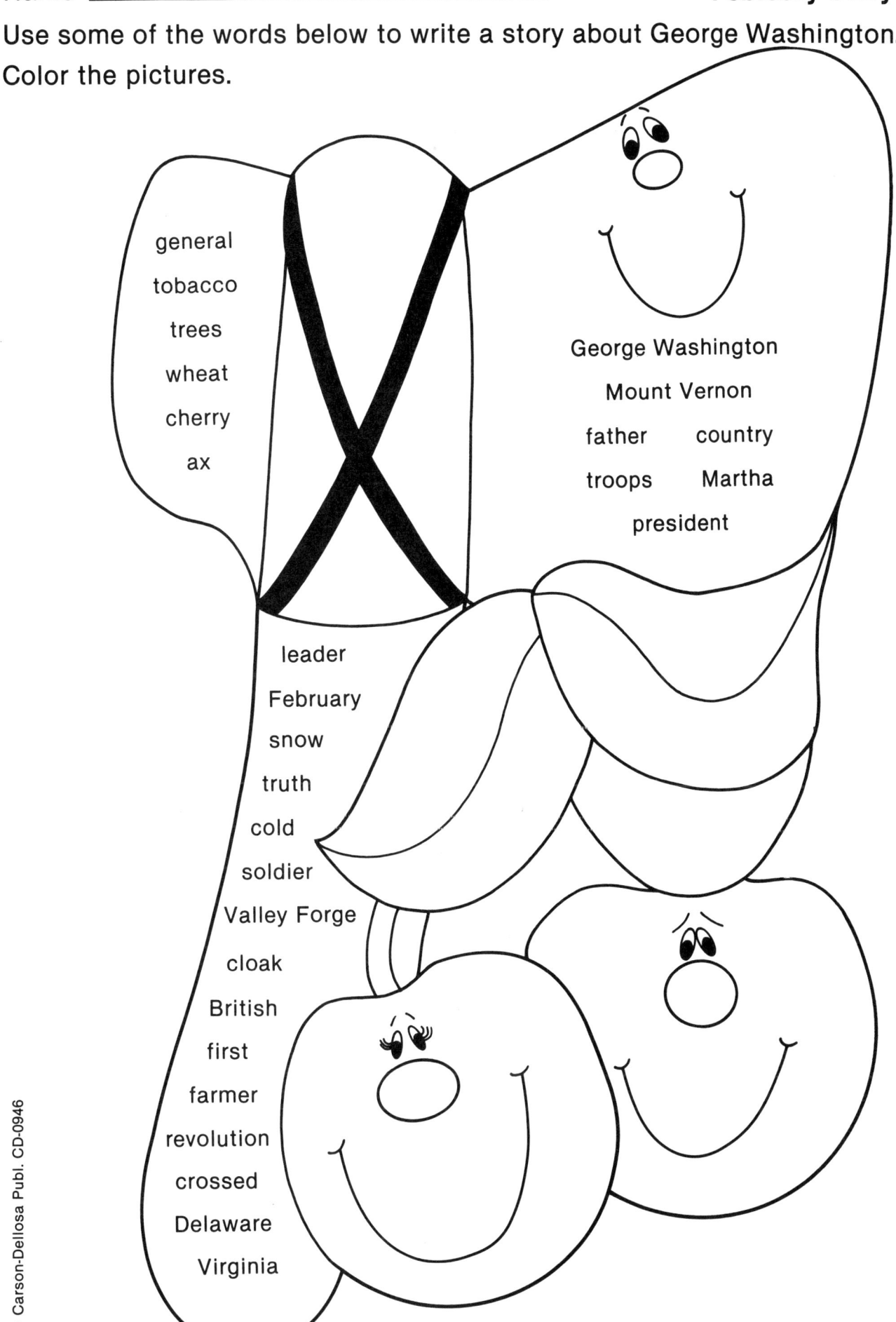

general
tobacco
trees
wheat
cherry
ax

George Washington
Mount Vernon
father   country
troops   Martha
president

leader
February
snow
truth
cold
soldier
Valley Forge
cloak
British
first
farmer
revolution
crossed
Delaware
Virginia

Name_____

Cut out the cherries. Count by 2's and paste the cherries in the correct order.

2 6
10 14 18
22 26 30
34 38
42 46 50

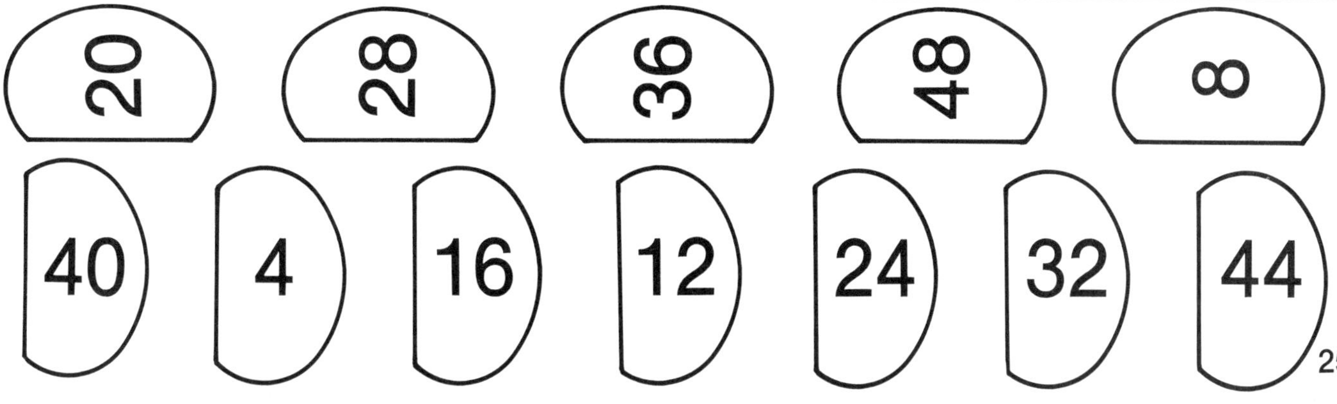

20 28 36 48 8
40 4 16 12 24 32 44

Name_____

Count by 2's to connect the dots.

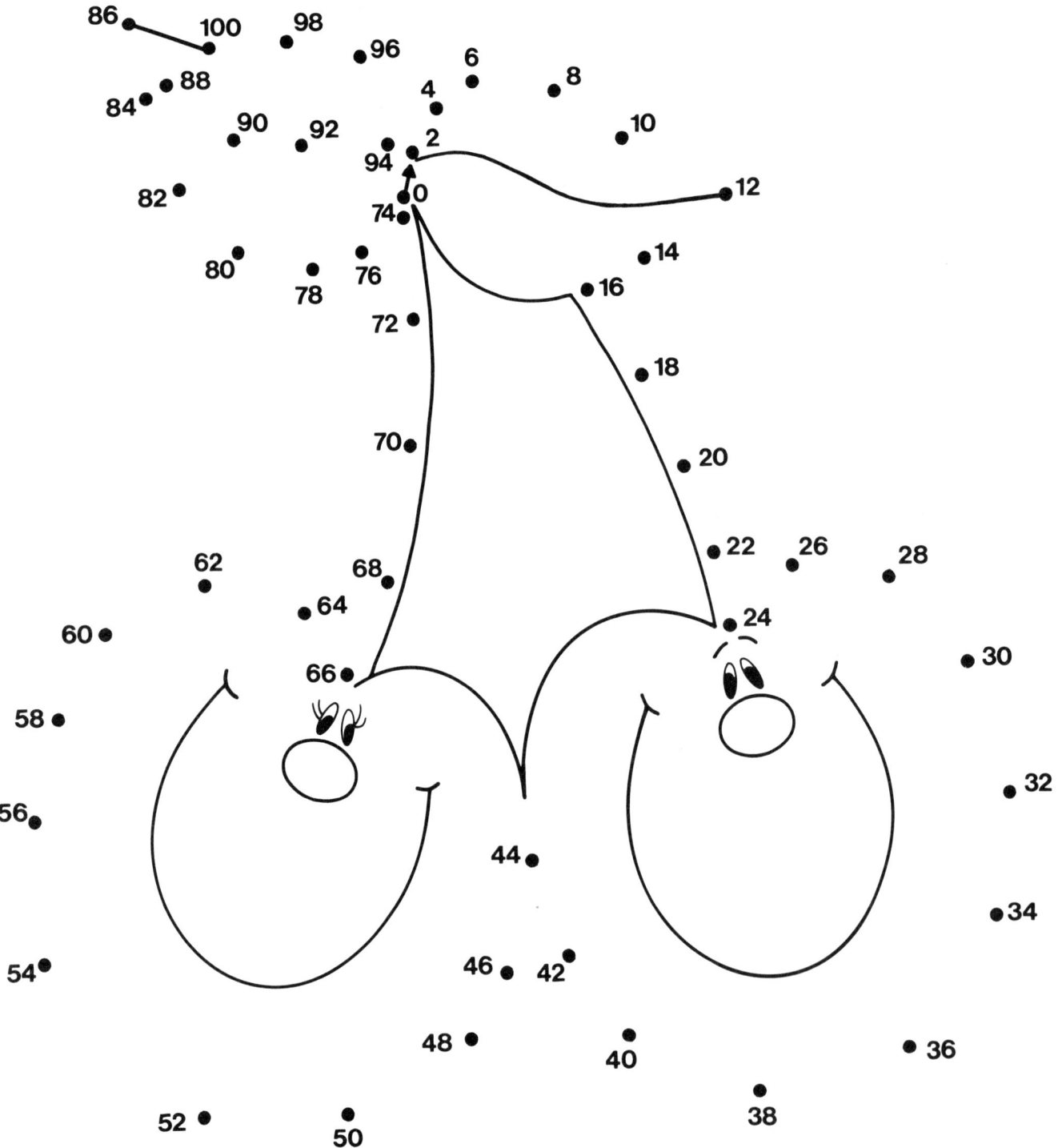

Name_____

Count by 2's to connect the dots.

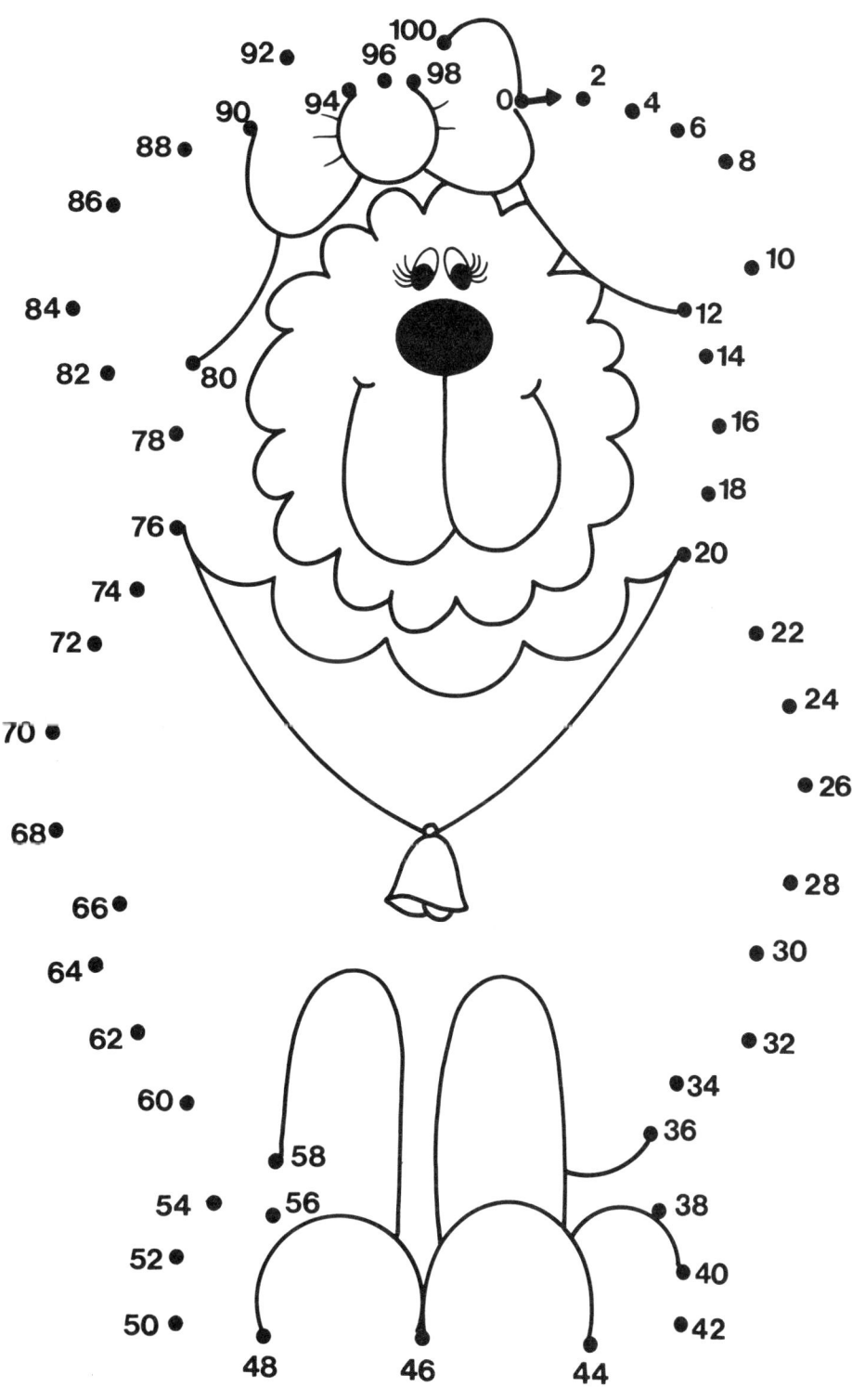

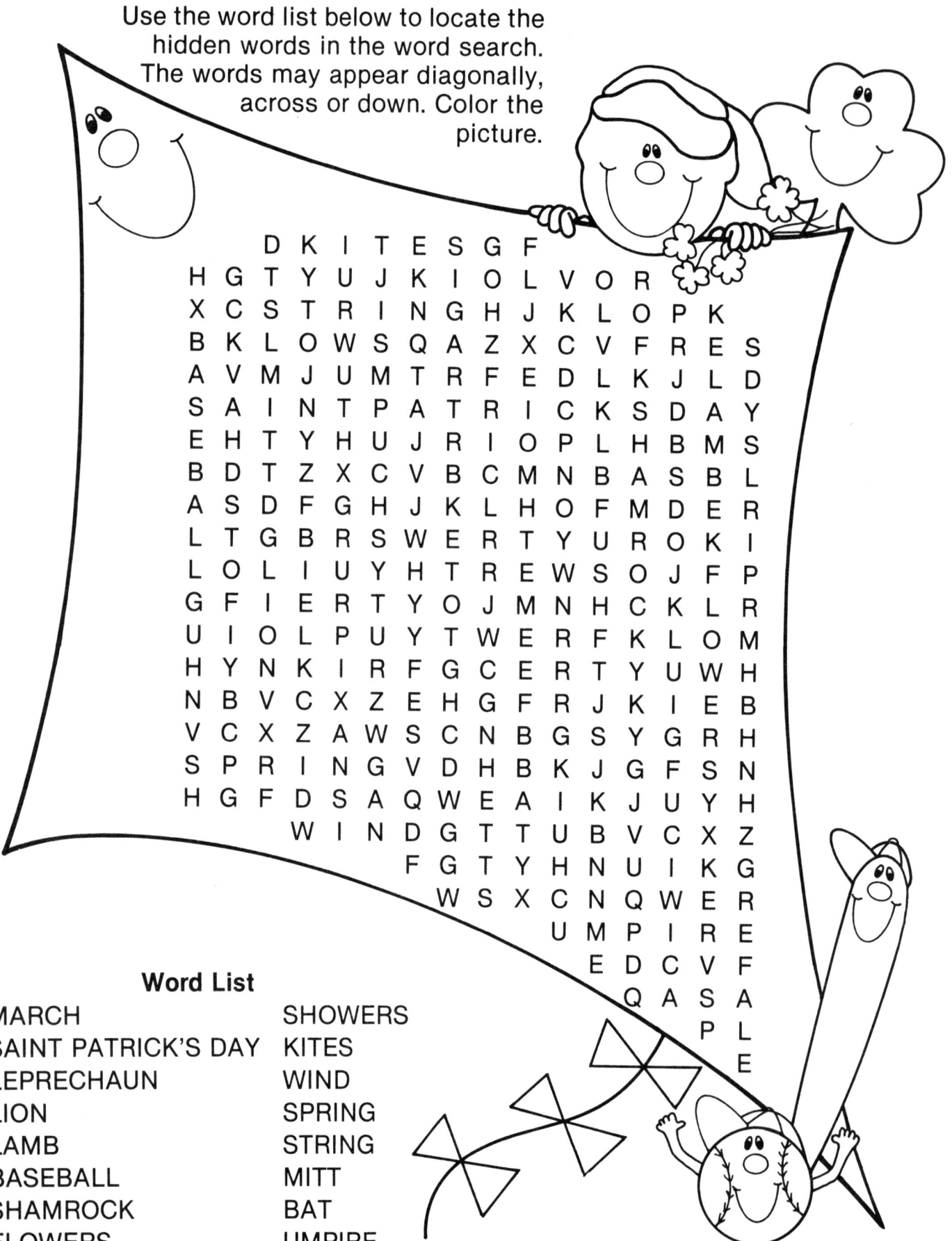

Spring Gambols: Hide-and-Seek Pictures

Find and circle the objects hidden in this picture: moon, ghost, snake, mug, screwdriver, old lady's face, heart, spoon, sundae, jack-in-the-box, cork, fish.

Name _____

Name _____

Look-Alike Lions and Lambs

Circle the pictures in each row that look the same. Color the pictures.

256

Name _____

Use the word list below to unscramble the words on the sheep. Have fun coloring the picture.

Word List
sheep   eggs
lamb   jelly beans
Easter   wool
basket   chocolate

1. aetsEr _____
2. nbaeseljly _____
3. tooleahcc _____
4. ekbsat _____
5. mbla _____
6. ephes _____
7. gesg _____
8. lowo _____

© Carson-Dellosa Publ. CD-0946

Name _____   **Spring Calendar Cover-Ups**

Color and cut out the calendar cover-ups. Glue each cover-up to an appropriate calendar date on the next page.

Hidden Words

Circle the hidden words:
MONDAY, WEDNESDAY, FRIDAY, SUNDAY, APRIL, SPRING, DAYS, DATE, TUESDAY, THURSDAY, SATURDAY, MARCH, MAY, EASTER, MONTHS, CALENDAR

M	O	N	D	A	Y	G	F	H	J	K	S	U	N	D	A	Y	J	U	C	E	D
O	L	H	G	J	X	Z	F	R	I	D	A	Y	T	R	E	W	Q	D	A	Y	S
N	M	J	K	T	G	F	R	D	S	C	T	D	C	H	O	L	S	A	L	Y	R
T	U	E	S	D	A	Y	H	G	T	H	U	R	S	D	A	Y	I	T	E	K	M
H	U	Y	T	R	P	B	V	D	H	I	R	F	G	I	L	S	W	E	N	M	Z
S	F	G	J	O	R	I	O	E	F	G	D	I	O	P	Y	R	V	C	D	O	L
Y	H	N	B	G	I	R	F	A	L	M	A	R	C	H	I	K	M	L	A	E	D
A	Q	Z	X	S	L	C	D	S	E	G	Y	X	L	I	K	M	G	T	R	I	M
T	G	B	V	F	R	E	D	T	T	G	B	N	H	J	I	K	O	L	P	Q	A
S	P	R	I	N	G	Y	H	E	D	F	G	H	W	E	D	N	E	S	D	A	Y
G	F	D	S	A	H	J	K	R	N	B	V	C	X	Z	A	S	D	F	G	H	K

Name _____

Fill in the month and the dates on the calendar. Glue the calendar cover-ups to the calendar. Color the picture.

Sunday	Monday	Tuesday	Wednesday	Thursday	Friday	Saturday

Name _____

**BULLETIN BOARD IDEA
SAINT PATRICK'S DAY**

"Top of the Morning to You!"

260

© Carson-Dellosa Publ. CD-0946

Name _____

TIME OF YEAR: Saint Patrick's Day

MATERIALS: heavy paper of any color (5" by 4"), yellow paper, orange and green crayons, pencils and scissors

DIRECTIONS: Fold heavy paper in half. Place shamrock on fold of paper. Trace pattern. Cut out shamrock to create a stencil.

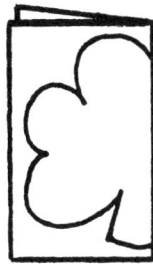  

trace shamrock cut out shamrock stencil of shamrock on heavy paper

Place stencil over yellow paper. Use crayon to stroke lines inward across outline of shamrock onto yellow paper.

yellow paper
shamrock stencil

Repeat this procedure several times alternating the use of orange and green crayons to create an allover pattern on yellow paper.

 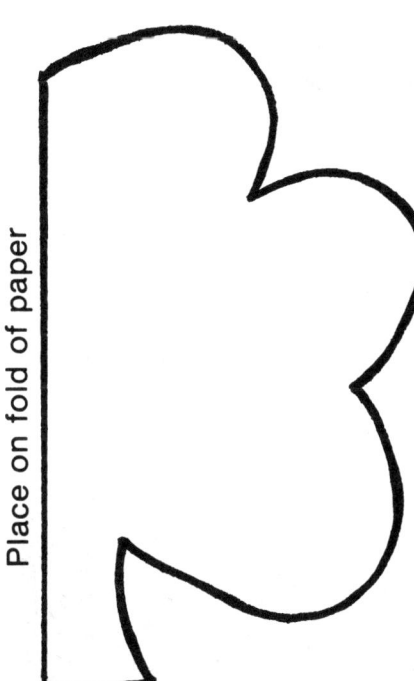

Place on fold of paper

shamrocks

Name _____

Leprechaun Logic—What's Wrong Here?

Circle the things that are wrong in this picture.

Name _____

Spring Fever Funnies

Make your own cartoon! Write in each square what you think this character is saying.

© Carson-Dellosa Publ. CD-0946

263

Name_____
Directions:

Name _____

Put a circle around:

leprechaun　　shamrock　　green
emerald　　Irish　　charms
　　　　　　　　luck

```
                    e   k
                    m   c
      y   l   d   k   e   p
      a   e   r   u   r   m
      r   p   t   g   a   d
      d   r   e   c   l   o   f
      t   e   d   p   d   o   l
  l   s   c   x   e   y   b   u
  a   o   h   r   g   m   a   c
  s   h   a   m   r   o   c   k
  d   r   u   x   e   u   h   t
  b   n   e   e   i   a   l
      a   t   n   y   r   a
      c   g   h   j   m   i
          l   r   i   s   h
```

Name _____

Name _____

St. Patrick's Day Story Starter

Use some of the words to write a leprechaun story. Color the pictures.

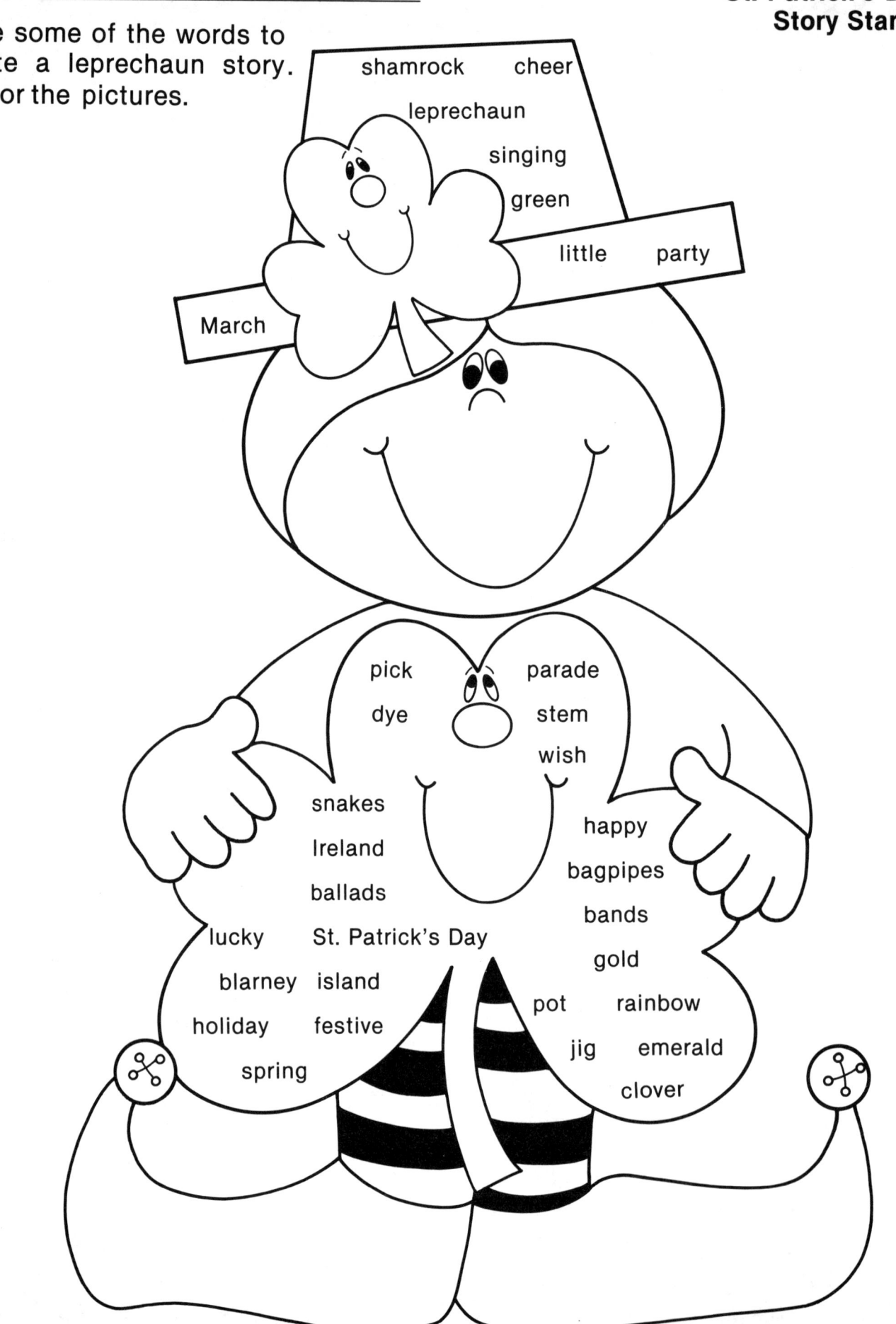

shamrock cheer
leprechaun
singing
green
little party
March

pick parade
dye stem
wish
snakes happy
Ireland bagpipes
ballads bands
lucky St. Patrick's Day gold
blarney island pot rainbow
holiday festive jig emerald
spring clover

268

© Carson-Dellosa Publ. CD-0946

Name

Name _____

1. tpo _____
2. rlihs _____
3. mrahcs _____
4. kchsmaor _____
5. ercanlpehu _____
6. ntfroeu _____
7. tSikrcatP _____
8. neger _____
9. ldaeemr _____
10. aaepdr _____

Unscramble the words:

St. Patrick   green
fortune   emerald
leprechaun   charms
shamrock   Irish
pot   parade

Name _____
Directions:

It's the
"Luck of the Irish"
to have a
good worker
like you!

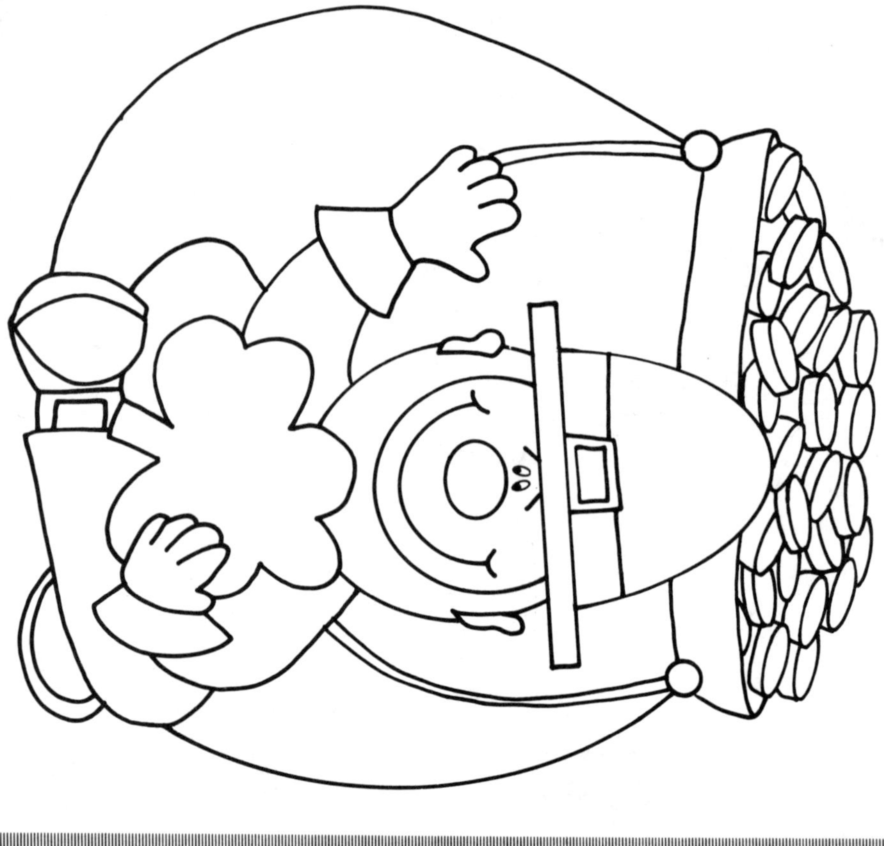

You've done great work....
You're worth your weight
in gold!

Name _____ Greet-the-season Greeting Cards

Directions:
1. Look at the holiday greetings below. Choose two to send for spring holiday cards. Color and cut out the appropriate greetings.
2. On the following page, draw and color two card covers (in the bordered, right-hand spaces). Cut out each card pattern on the solid outside lines.
3. Fold each pattern back on the dotted line so the picture faces out.
4. Cut out the four tab strips on this page. Make two pop-ups for the holiday greetings by following the diagrams below. Use two strips for each pop-up. Tape the ends of each pair of strips together so the pop-up stays in place.
5. Tape or glue one end of each pop-up to the back of the holiday greeting and the other end to the inside back panel of the card.
6. Sign and close each card, and give it to someone special.

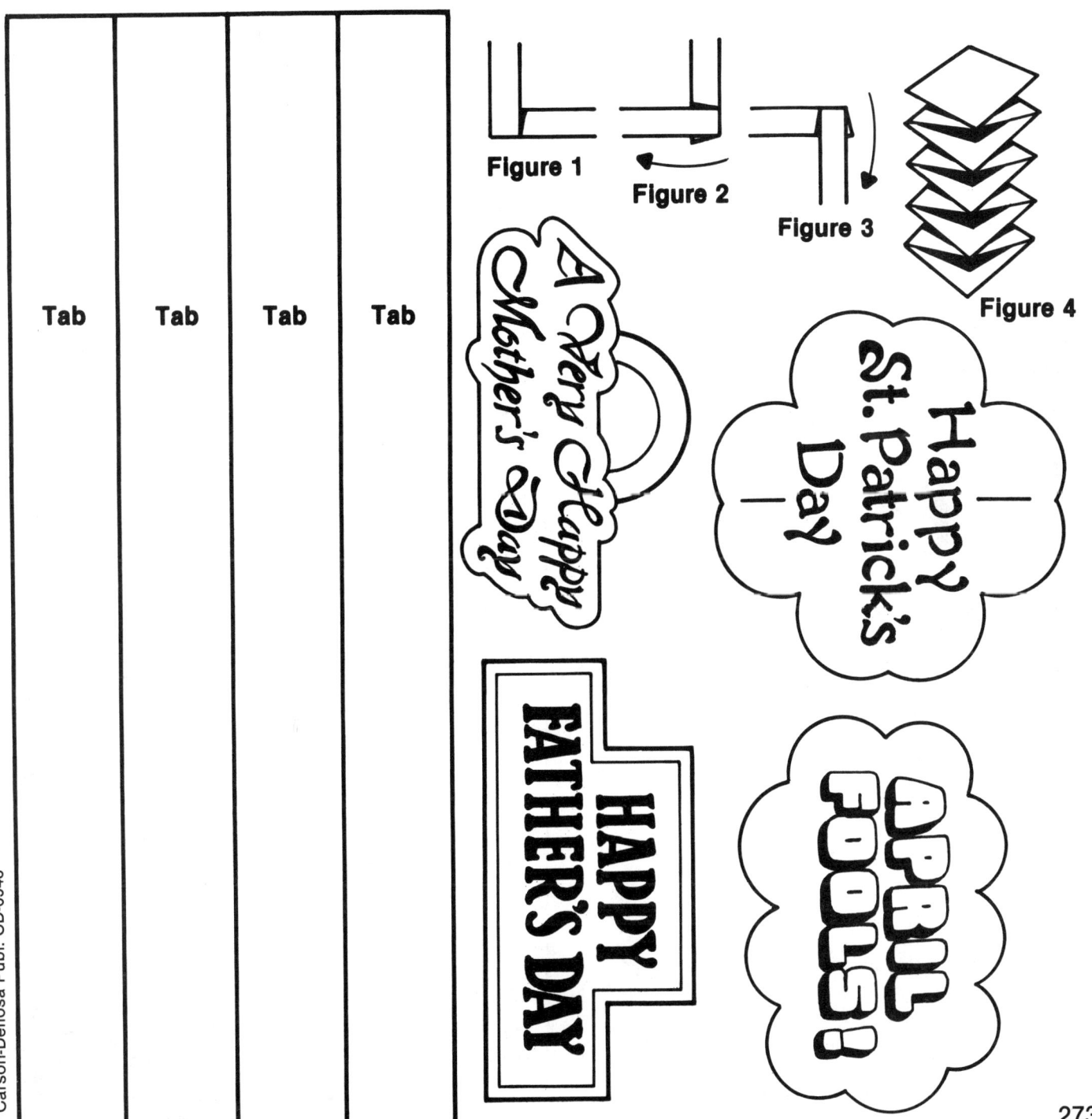

273

Spring

How to Use

Related Poems
 Enlarge any of the patterns to use as the center of a bulletin board. Direct students to copy a related poem. Display the papers on the bulletin board.

Award Sayings
 Use an award saying with its related pattern to create student awards.

Related Poems

St. Patrick's Day means wearing green.
Shamrocks all around are seen.
Leprechauns in Irish tales
Say, if you wear shamrocks, nothing fails!

The pitcher and I have a lot of fun
Trying to keep someone from getting a run.
But when they do the joke's on me
'Cause I get smacked really hard, you see.

I'm strong and straight and made of wood.
I'd smash a baseball if I could.
Swing me level and swing your best.
I promise you I'll do the rest.

How wonderful to fly so high,
To look on the world and wonder why
The hand holding me must take me down
Just when I feel I own the town!

Award Sayings

Shining Shamrock
Witty and "Clover" Student
Lucky me!

I am a top scorer!
I'm on the ball!

I'm batting 1000!
I never strike out!
I've got the bases covered!

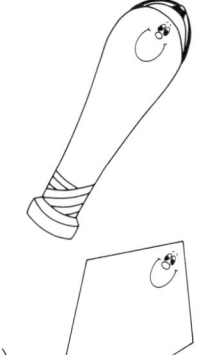

Soaring Grades
Flying High!
Soaring to the top of the class!

Name _____

Spring

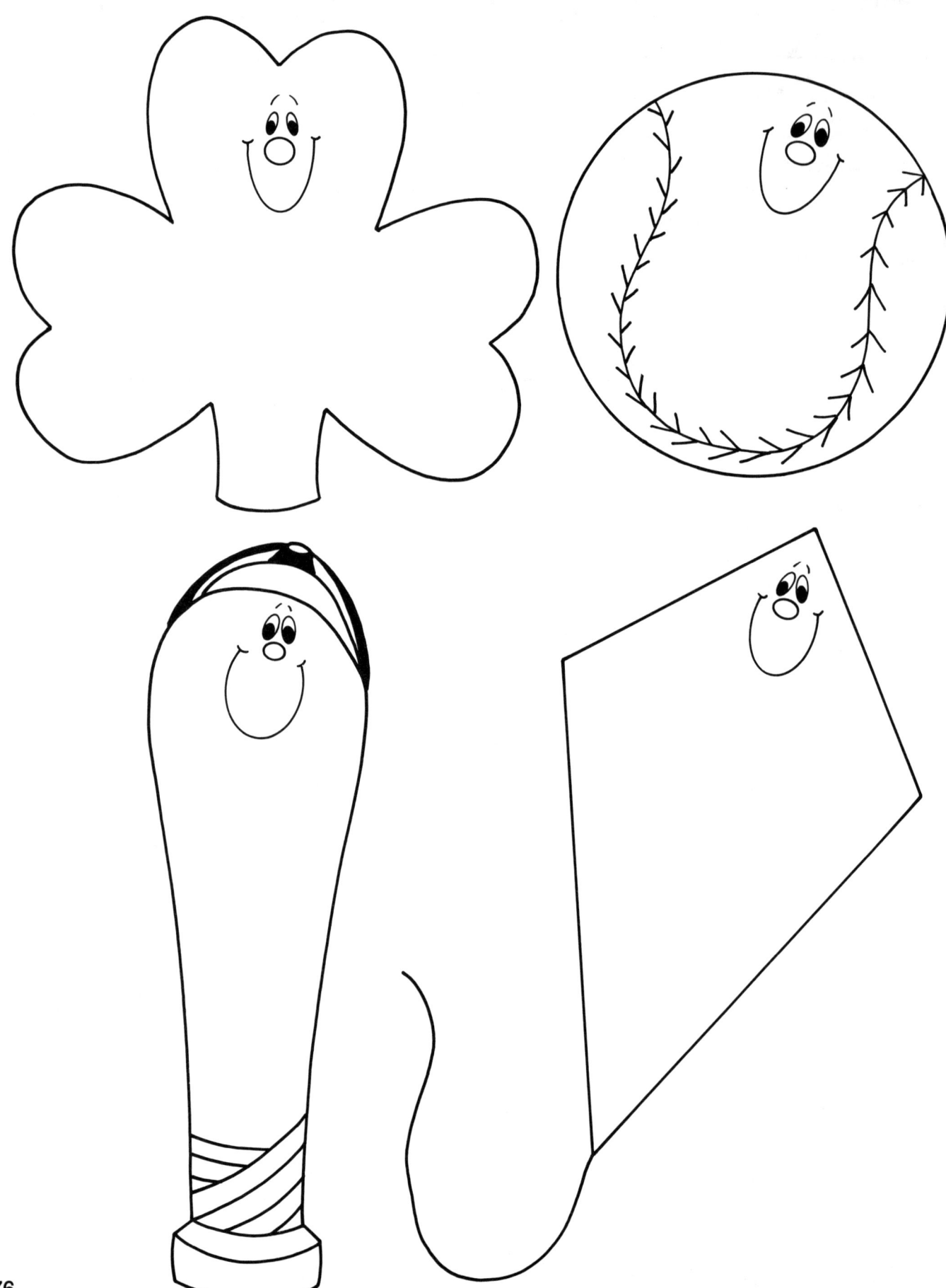

Name _____

Use the word list below to unscramble the words on the duck's feathers. Have fun coloring the picture.

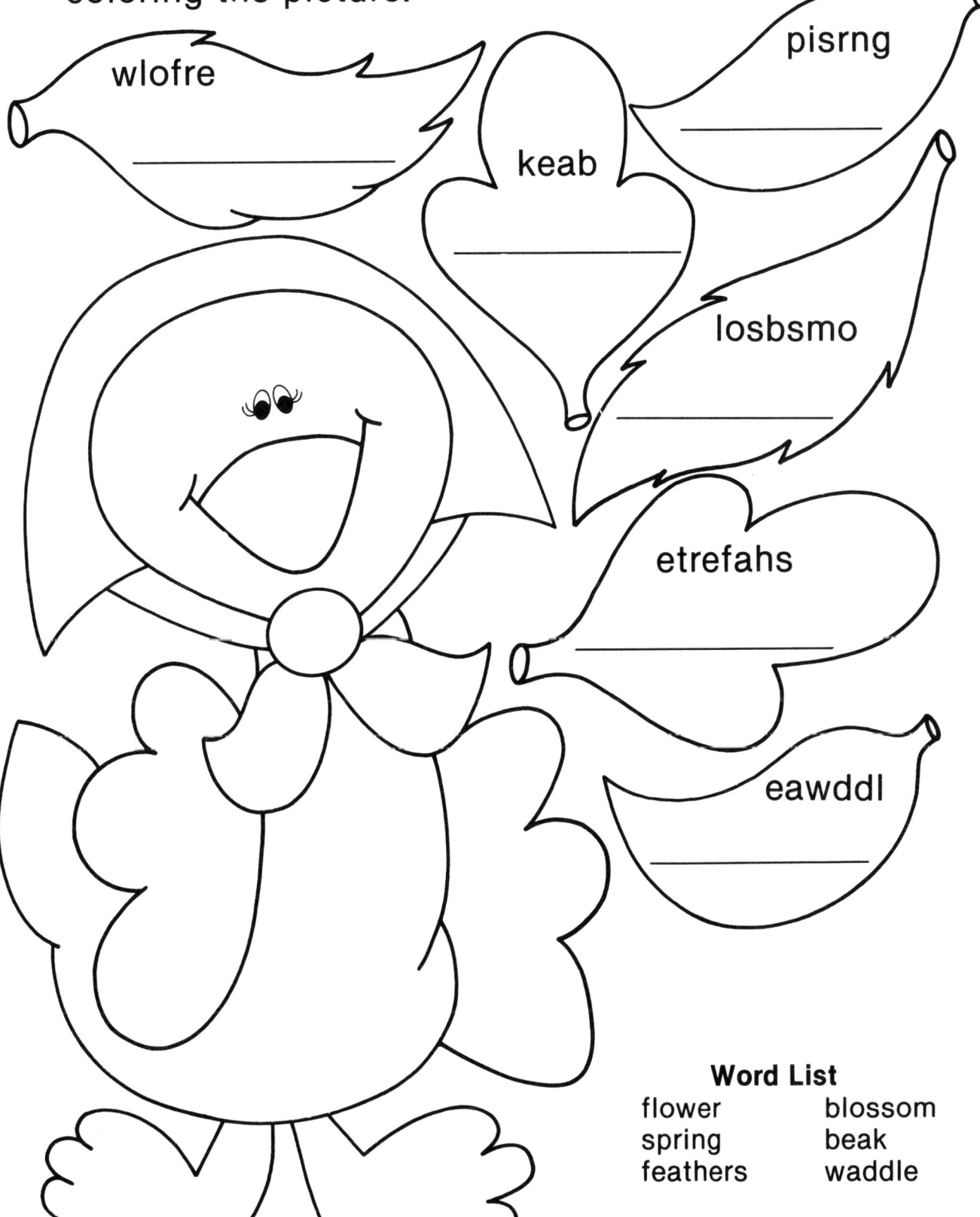

Word List
flower   blossom
spring   beak
feathers waddle

277

Name _____
Directions:

Name _____
Directions:

279

Name _____
Directions:

280

Name _____   **Rainbow Art Project**

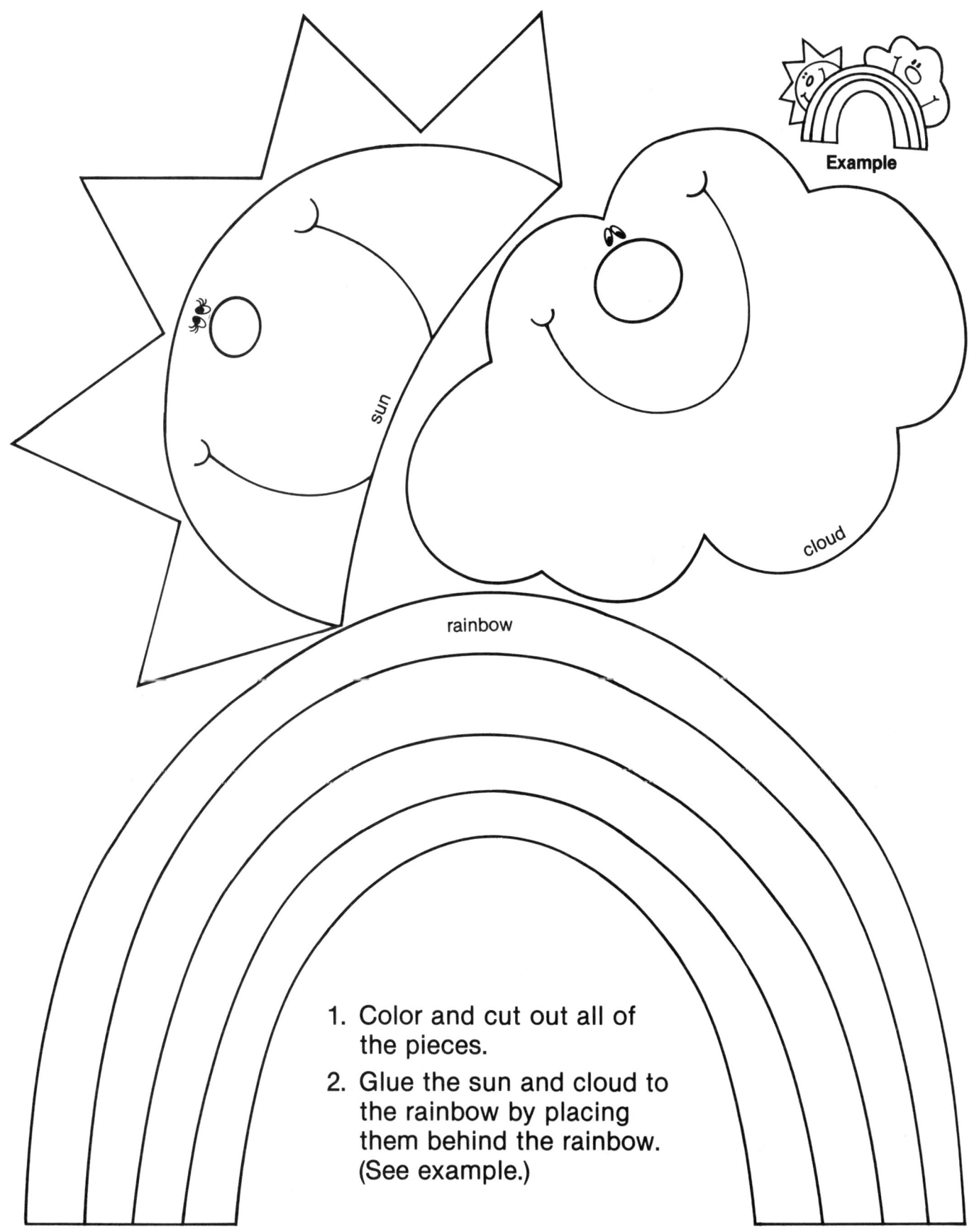

Example

sun

cloud

rainbow

1. Color and cut out all of the pieces.
2. Glue the sun and cloud to the rainbow by placing them behind the rainbow. (See example.)

Name _____

Name _____ Directions:

284

Name _____   Directions:

1
2
3
4
5
6
7
8
9
10
11

© Carson-Dellosa Publ. CD-0946

285

Get Into the Picture

Put a little of yourself into a spring picture! In the space below, print your own initials in any position in the center of the space. Then create your picture so that the initials are part of the characters or scenery. In the example provided, can you see the P by the frog's foot and the S in its eyes?

Name_____

Name _____

BUG'S EYE VIEW

Do you know what is pictured in the first two squares? They're familiar items, but maybe the water faucet and mushroom stem seem unfamiliar when seen from a bug's viewpoint.

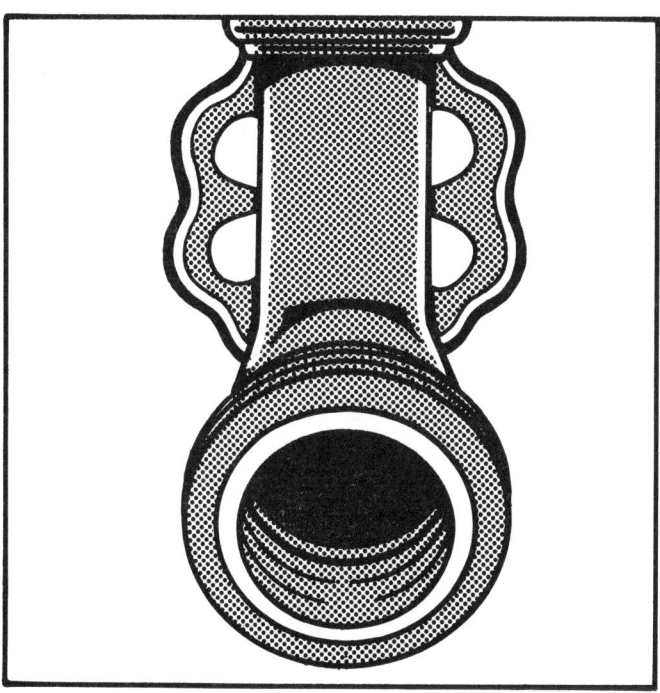
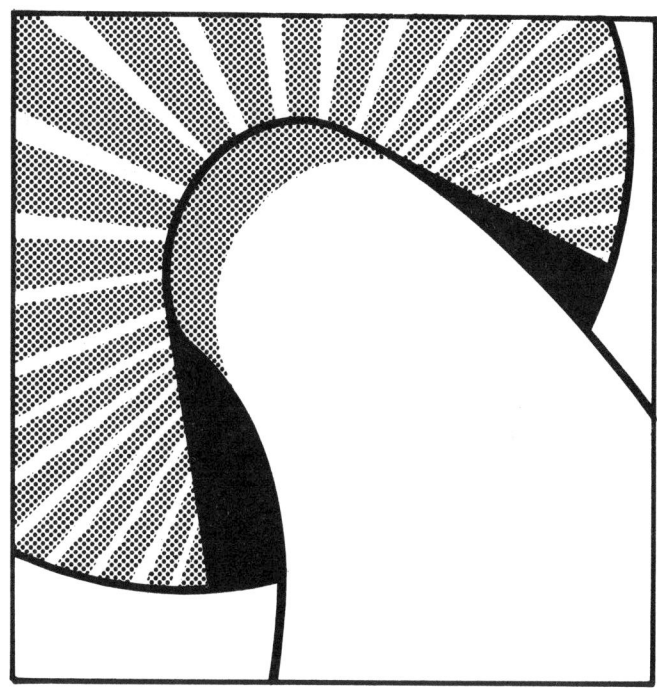

Try drawing bug's eye views in the two squares provided. Suggested things to draw: hungry bird, golf ball on a tee, shovel or other garden tool, car tire. Remember: Things look big when seen by a bug.

Name _____ **Buzzing Bonnie**

Follow these directions to make Buzzing Bonnie. (pp. 288-289).

1. Color the nose black.
2. Color each antenna black.
3. Color the flower center yellow.
4. Color each of the flower petals red.
5. Color the bee's head yellow.
6. Color every other stripe on the bee's body yellow.
7. Color the rest of the stripes black.
8. Cut out all of the patterns.
9. Roll each antenna around a pencil to make it curl.
10. Paste one antenna at the top of each side of the head.
11. Paste the nose on the X below the eyes.
12. Paste the flower just below the bee's chin.
13. Cut the dotted line on each wing.
14. Fold cut lines on each wing inward and paste X on top of O.
15. Paste the pointed end of each wing behind each side of the body.

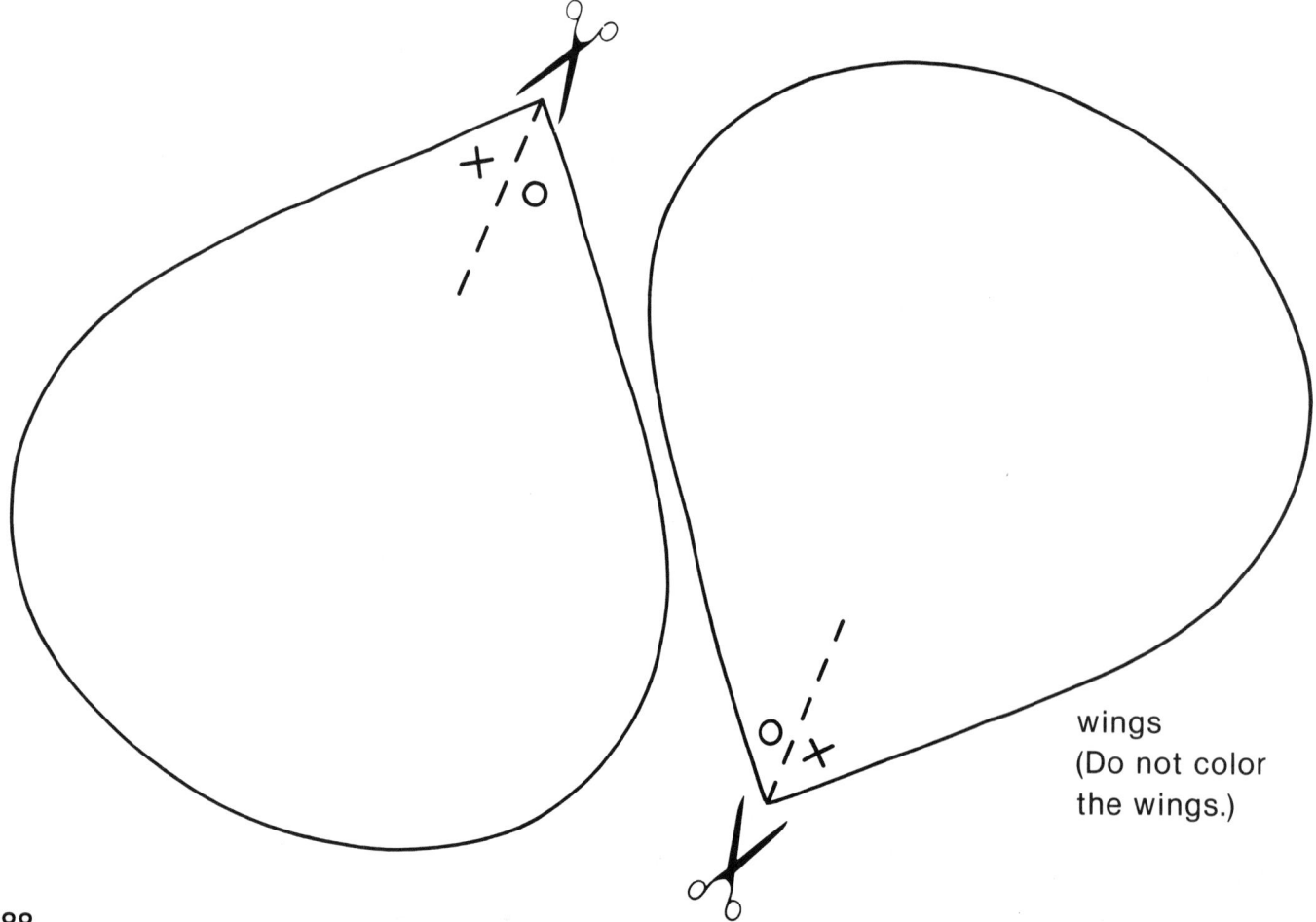

wings
(Do not color the wings.)

Name _____ **Buzzing Bonnie**

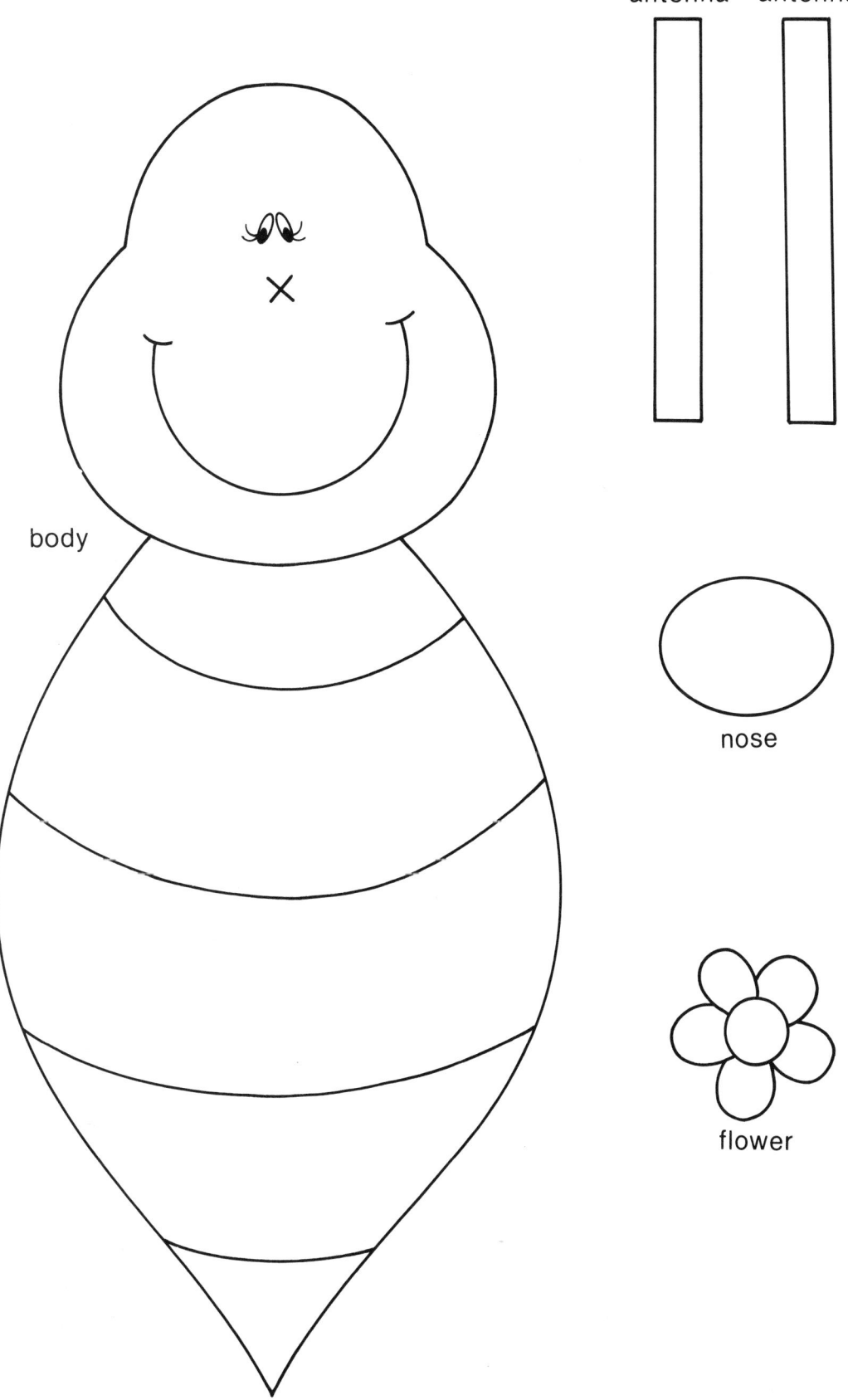

Name _____

Directions:

Name _____   Fanciful Figures

With a little imagination, people and scenery can be made from straight lines and basic shapes - squares, circles and triangles. In the spring scene below, those shapes are used to make a kite, person, dog, trees, flowers, and background.

On the following page, color and cut out some or all of the shapes provided. Arrange them in the large rectangle so they form a spring scene. Glue the pieces in place. Add straight lines where needed.

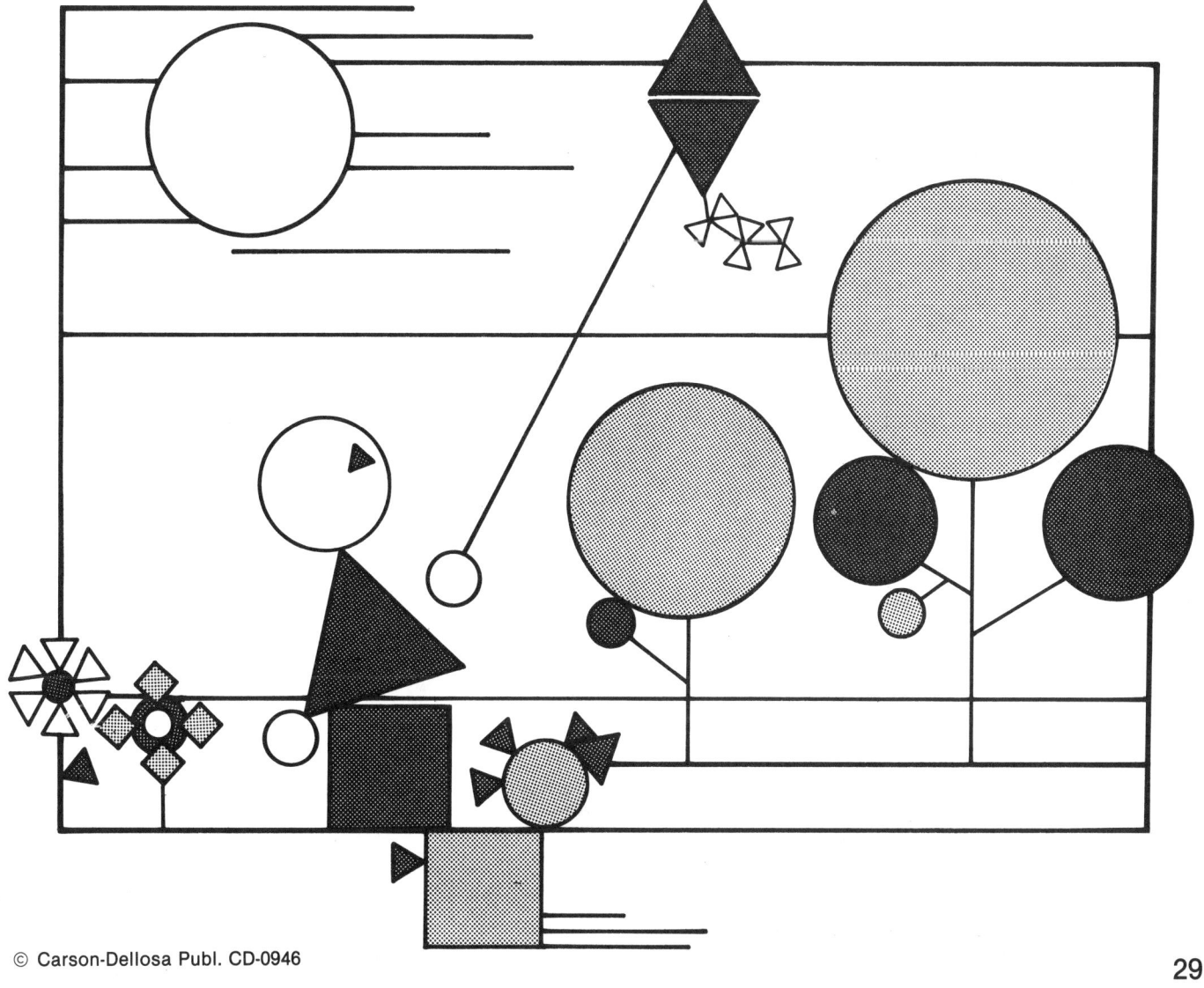

Name _____

Name_____
Directions:

Name _____ BULLETIN BOARD IDEA

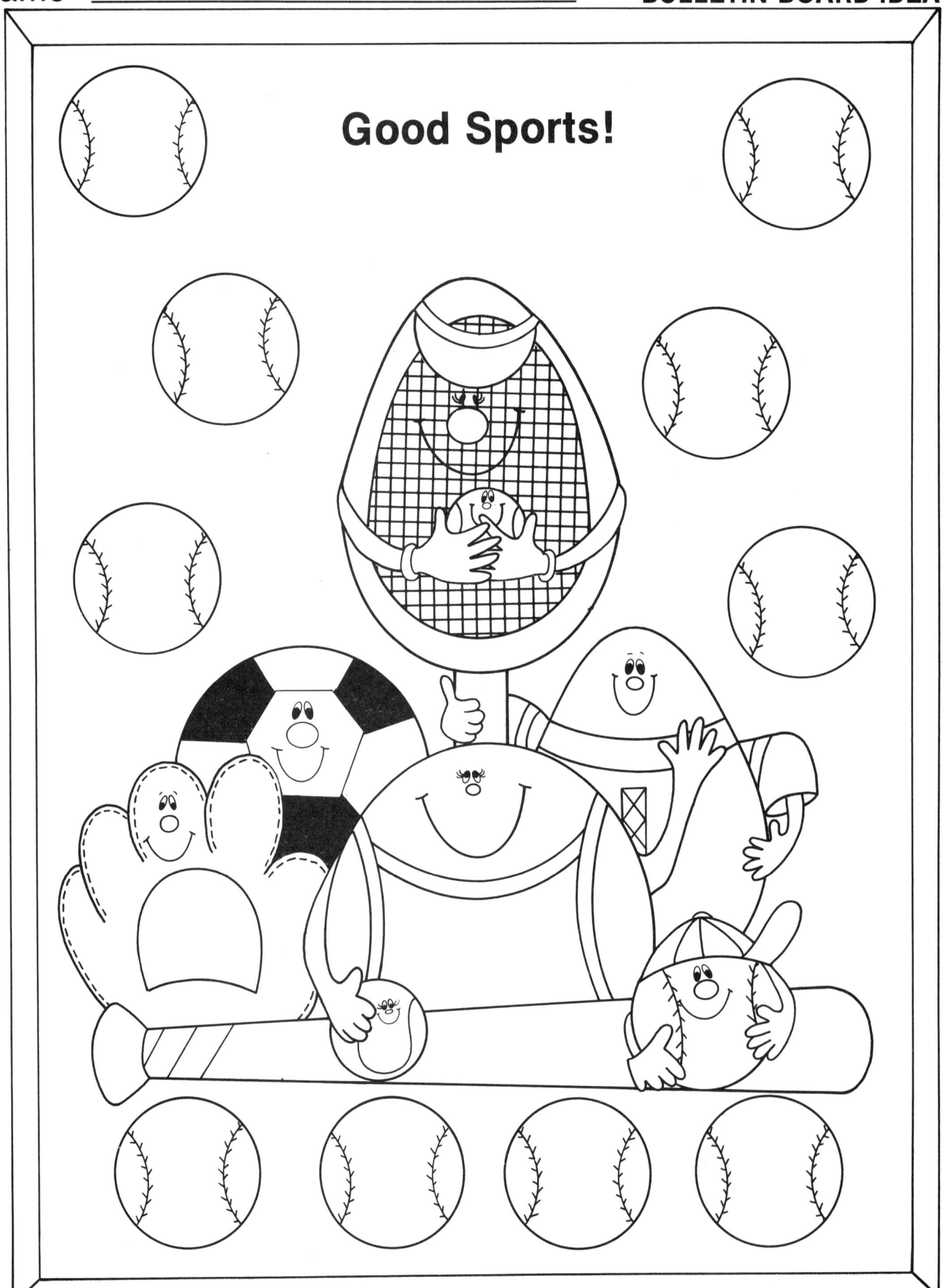

294 © Carson-Dellosa Publ. CD-0946

Name _____

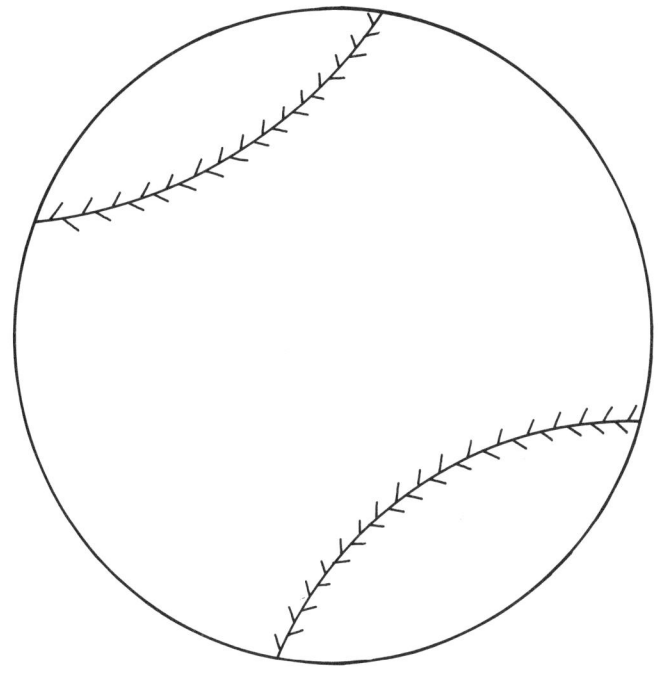

Name Tag Pattern for Bulletin Board

The following groups of students could be rewarded using the "Good Sport" theme:

1. Students who show good sportsmanship in the classroom, on the playground and during physical education class.
   (Teachers have the option of writing each student's specific deed or quality on the name tag along with the student's name.)
2. Students who show a positive attitude despite unusual circumstances: disappointments, difficult tasks, etc.
3. By changing the title of the bulletin board to "Students on the Ball in Math" or "Students on the Ball in Spelling", etc., the reward bulletin board can relate to any skill the teacher selects.

Name _____ **Fluttering Florence**

Follow these directions to make Fluttering Florence. (pp. 296, 297, 298).

1. Color the outside border of each wing blue.
2. Color the inside of each wing orange.
3. Color the nose black.
4. Color the shirt red.
5. Color the face, arms and body yellow.
6. Color the bow orange.
7. Color each antenna black.
8. Color the flower center yellow.
9. Color the flower petals orange.
10. Color the flower stem and leaves green.
11. Cut out all of the patterns.
12. Paste the right wing behind the right side of the body.
13. Paste the left wing behind the left side of the body.
14. Roll each antenna around a pencil to make it curl.
15. Paste one antenna behind each side of the top of the head.
16. Paste the bow on top of the head or under the chin.

body

antenna

antenna

Name _____ **Fluttering Florence**

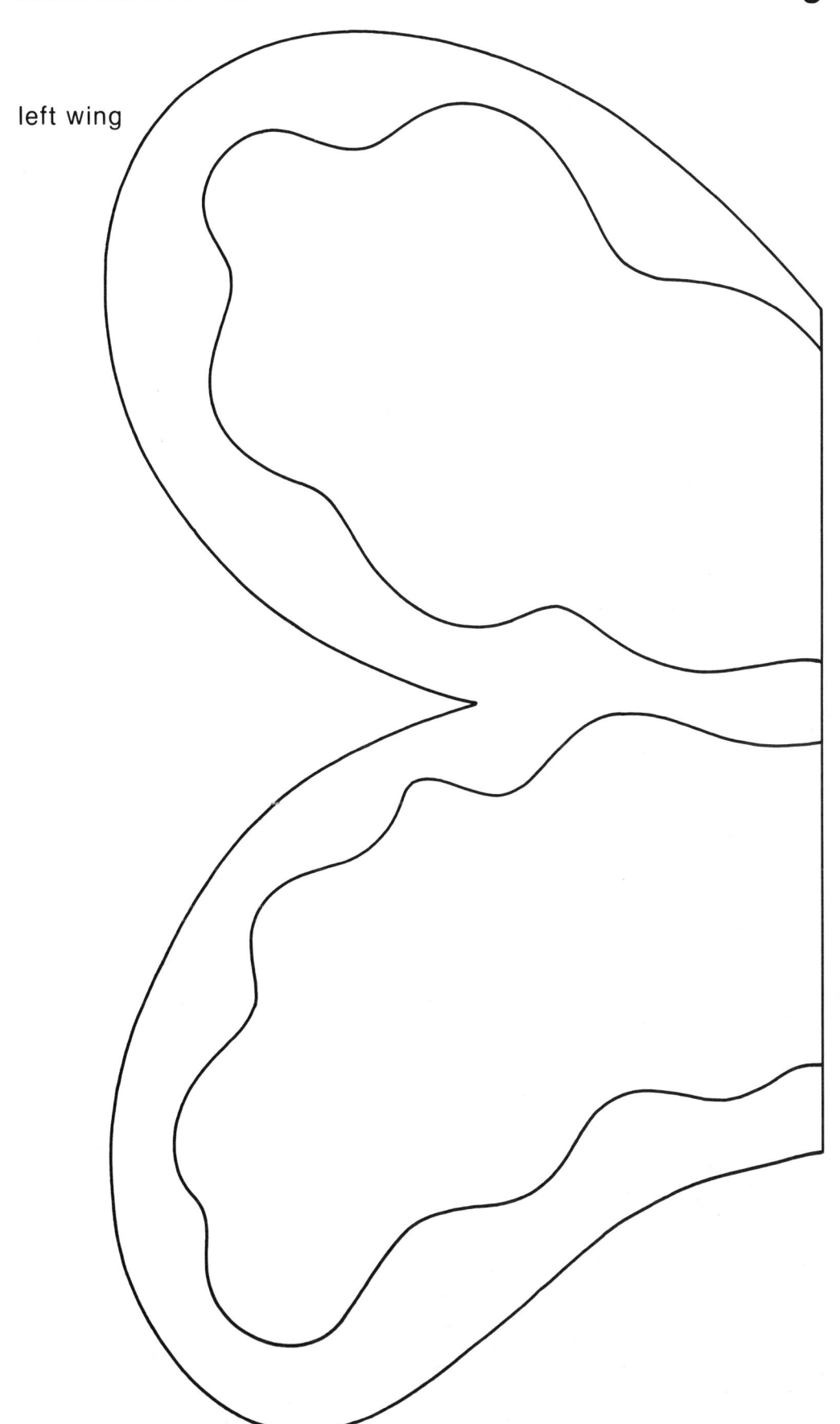

left wing

Name _____ **Fluttering Florence**

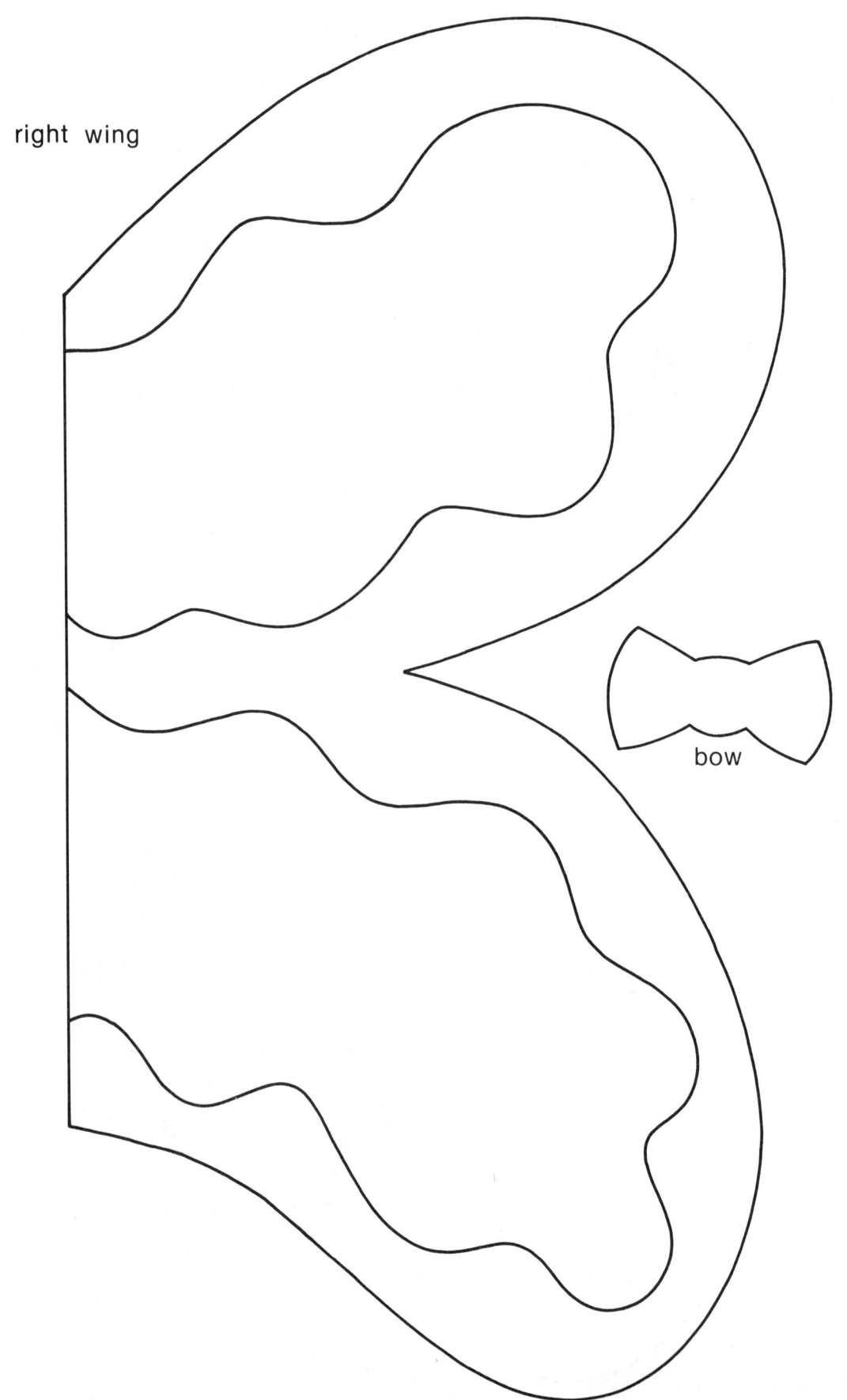

right wing

bow

298 © Carson-Dellosa Publ. CD-0946

Name _____   **Frog Puppet**

Materials: paper plate, crayons, scissors, glue, tape or stapler
Directions:
1. Color the bottom of the paper plate and the hand strap green.
2. Color the top center of the plate red.
3. Color the top rim of the plate green.
4. Color the eyelids yellow.
5. Color the legs and arms green.
6. Color the tongue red.
7. Cut out all of the pieces.
8. Fold the paper plate in the middle so that the red side doesn't show.
9. Fold the tongue back on the dotted line and glue it to the middle of the red circle.
10. With the red side open, glue the arms to the plate by placing them between the two halves of the plate.
11. With the red side open, glue the legs to the plate by placing them beneath the bottom of the plate.
12. Fold the eyes back on the dotted lines and glue them to the plate by placing them behind the top of the plate.
13. Staple or tape the hand strap to the plate by placing the strap several inches behind the eyes.
14. Slide your fingers under the strap and put your thumb below the fold to work the puppet.

eye leg
leg eye
hand strap
arm arm tongue
glue here glue here glue here

© Carson-Dellosa Publ. CD-0946

Butterfly Crossword Puzzle

Find the answers to these clues, and put them in the butterfly on the following page.

ACROSS

1. Seasonal tidying-up: spring _____
8. April Fool's prank
9. Precipitation
10. Golfer's cry
11. Metal of Oz's woodsman
13. Baseball's four-base hit: Home _____
14. Leprechaun lore: You'll _____ a pot of gold at the end of the rainbow.
15. _____ Redbreast
17. Our natural heat and light source
18. Rabbit
20. Spring holiday that falls on different dates each year.
22. A flowerless spore plant
23. A type of alcohol
26. _____. Patrick's Day (abbreviation)
28. First spring month with 30 days (abbreviation)
29. Last spring month with 30 days
31. Honored on Mother's Day
33. When spring has come, winter has _____.
35. Tall marsh weeds, or bulrushes
36. 11:32 a.m., 9:56 p.m.
38. Footwear

DOWN

1. Bird noises
2. Behold!
3. To receive for work accomplished
4. Wood-chopping tool
5. St. Patrick's Day color
6. Against (prefix)
7. Mother's Day, Father's Day and Easter have this day in common.
10. "April showers bring May _____."
12. "March comes _____ like a lion and goes out like a lamb."
14. Flag Day is June _____.
16. No _____, ands, or buts about it - spring is here!
18. Honey _____
19. Old-fashioned word for "no"
21. Picnic bug
22. May Day is May _____.
24. Spring tree buds become these.
25. Month of first official spring day
27. Insects
30. A negative answer
32. Memorial Day month
34. "Old MacDonald had a farm, E-I-_____"
37. Not you

Name _____

Name _____
Directions:

Name _____

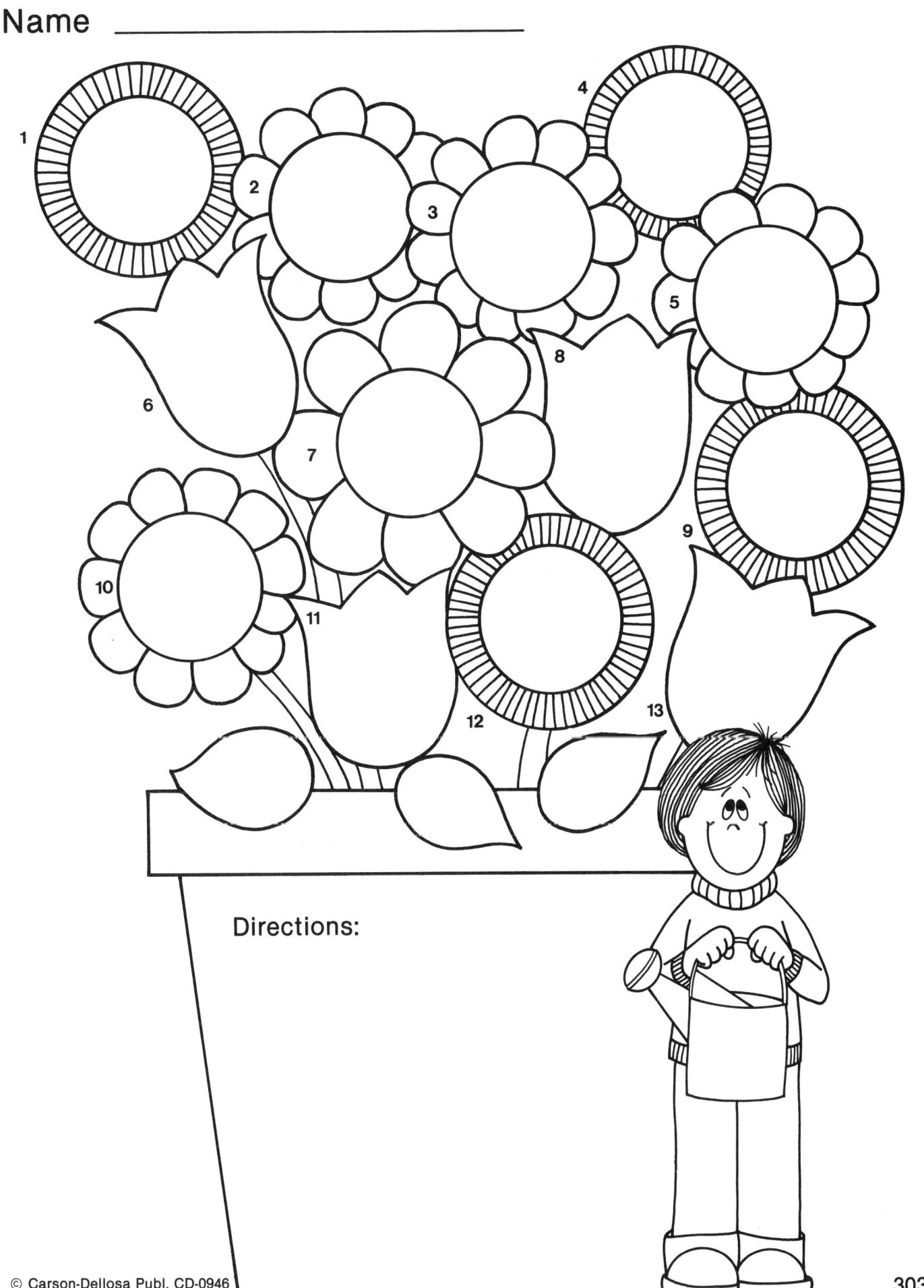

Directions:

© Carson-Dellosa Publ. CD-0946 303

Name_____

Directions:

304

Name _____

1. D A F F O D I L

2. _ _ _ _ _ _ _ _

3. _ _ _ _ _ _

4. _ _ _ _ _

5. _ _ _ _ _ _ _

6. _ _ _ _ _ _

7. _ _ _ _ _ _ _

8. _ _ _ _ _ _

9. _ _ _ _ _ _ _ _ _

Flower Scramble

Unscramble the names of these flowers and write each in the proper space. Each flower head also counts as one letter space. An example has been done for you.

Flowers:
1. LFADFODI
2. MUGANIRE
3. SNYAP
4. RIIS
5. AEIUNPT
6. LOEVIST
7. ESOPPPI
8. PULSIT
9. RETPUUBCT

Now take all nine letters that appear in the flower heads, and unscramble them to find out a flower's favorite kind of people.

© Carson-Dellosa Publ. CD-0946   305

Name _____

Seasons - Spring

Read the clues. Find the correct word in the word list to complete each sentence. Write the word in the crossword puzzle.

Across

3. We _____ kites in spring.
4. The month after March is _____.
6. We plant tomato _____ in spring.
7. The wind _____ our hats off.
8. The season after winter is _____.

Word List

spring, fly, robins, March, blows, April, seeds, May, flowers

Down

1. The first month of spring is _____.
2. April showers bring _____ flowers.
3. _____ bloom in spring.
5. _____ build their nests in spring.

Name _____

Connect the dots.

Name _____

Gardern Grower's Seed Scrambles

The names of the seeds listed below can be found horizontally, vertically, or diagonally in the word scramble. Find and circle each name.

```
W D A I N I A P C M R G R
M A R I G O L D U A P E C
E Y T P E L O N C U E M U
T S N E S U N Z U N P A R
Z U C G R O Z I M K P I M
I N E C A M R N B L E G K
D F B W C F E D E B R L D
M L Y P M D A L R P E D A
C O R E C U T M O T Z C I
E W A Z U C C H I N I B S
W E C U I K S D W C A E Y
A R T N P N I C Z R F L W
P U M P K I N B P F E K N
E D A D Y C M I N D S M O
P E D A S T O M A T O A S
```

Seed List

SUNFLOWER CUCUMBER
MARIGOLD   PUMPKIN
ZINNIA   PEPPER
DAISY   WATERMELON
TOMATO   ZUCCHINI

_____ does work that's worth chirping about!

Signed _____

© Carson-Dellosa Publ. CD-0946

Your work makes me leap for joy!

© Carson-Dellosa Publ. CD-0946

Name _____

Directions:

1.
2.
3.
4.
5.
6.

Name _____

Egg Hunt

Mrs. Hen has lost her egg in the depths of a giant Easter basket. There are so many chicken footprints around, she can't remember how to get to the bottom of the basket. Can you help?

HELP ME! I'M SO CONFUSED!

START HERE

The chicken footprints are actually arrows, pointing the ways you are allowed to travel. For example, ↓ means you must proceed to the square directly below and follow its direction. Half of the squares offer you a choice of two directions.

MAMA!
FINISH

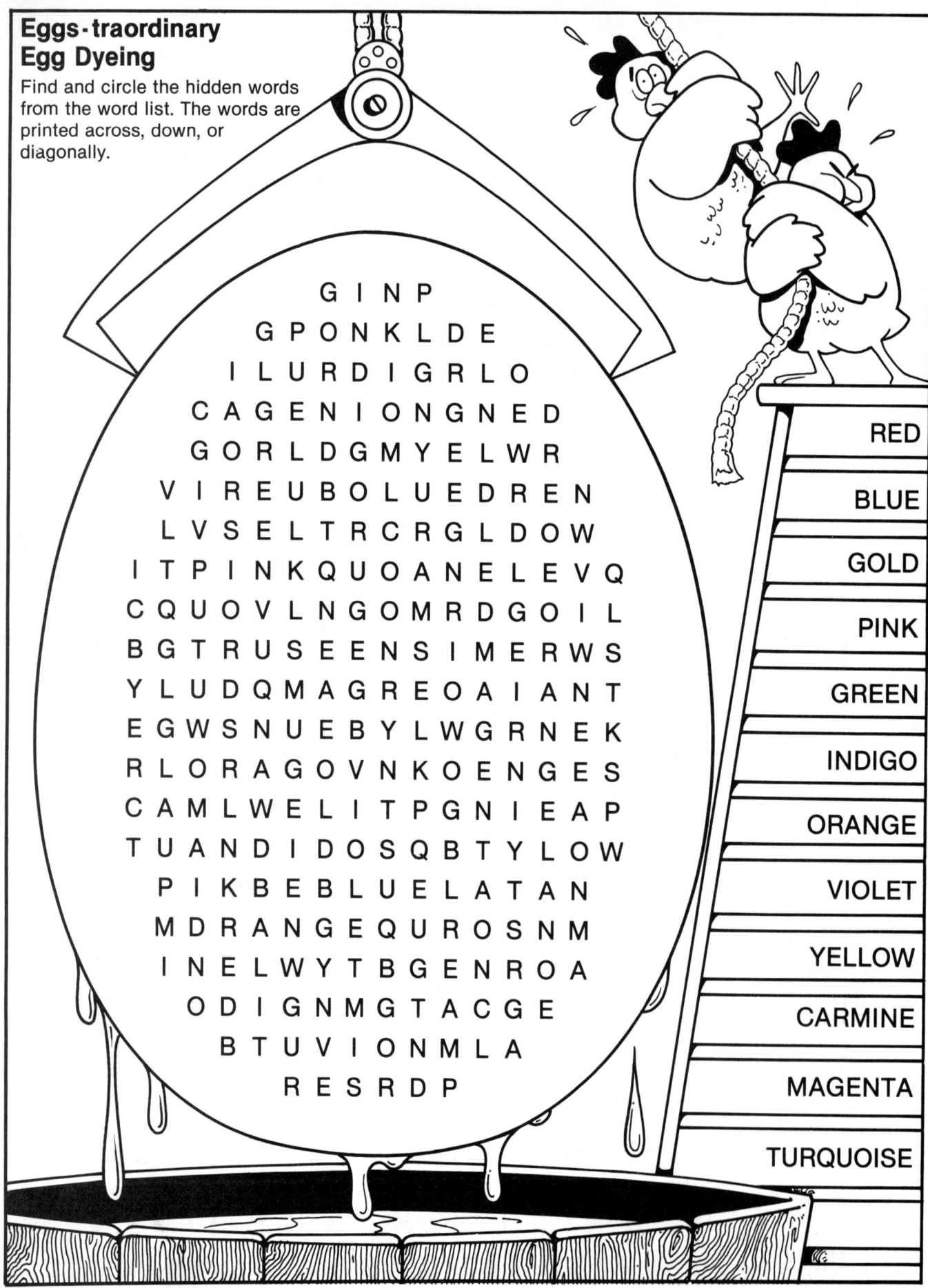

AN EASTER THANK YOU NOTE

Your Easter was fun!
    Such a grand day!
A nice little thank you
    Should be sent right away!

A Sample Easter Thank You Note

Dear Aunt Jackie,
    The Easter basket was just wonderful.
    Thank you. Your kindness made it such a fun Easter Day!
    With love,
    Tommy

A Sample Easter Thank You Note

Dear _____,
    I don't know when I have enjoyed Easter so much.
    Thank you for helping to make it such a fine day!
    Sincerely,

Directions: Use the stationery provided to copy the sample Easter notes. If you wish, write your own message. Color the picture and send the letter.

Name _____

Directions:

Name _____
Directions:

Name _____
Directions:

317

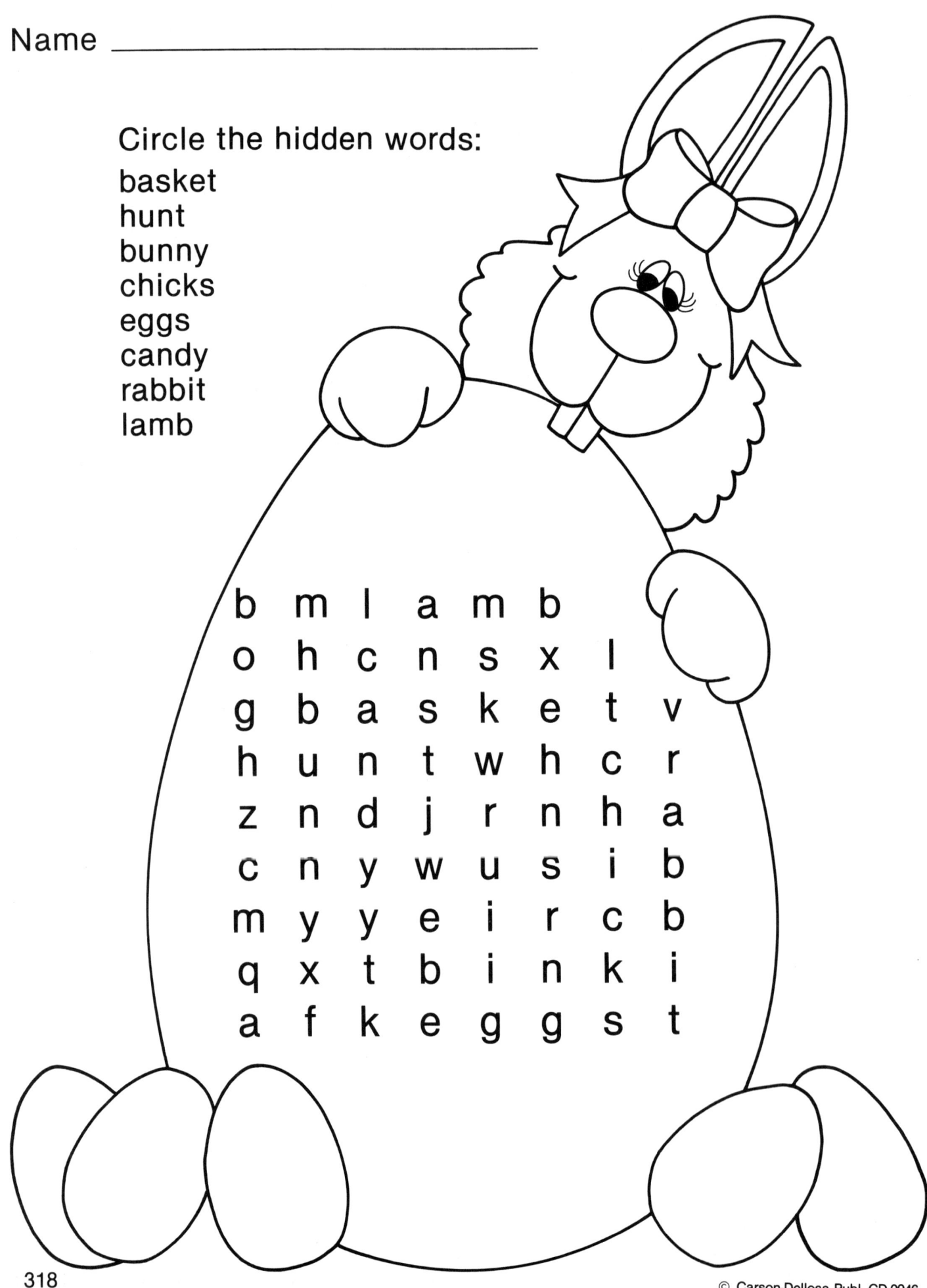

Name _____

Illuminated Easter Letter

uite popular in the Middle Ages, illuminated letters were designed and drawn primarily by monks. The first letter of a page or paragraph was decorated with ornate designs or pictures, often relating to the text. When creating your own illuminated letter for a story, keep these points in mind:

1. Know the first word of your story so you can choose a letter to use.
2. Start your drawing with the letter itself. The letter you use must be drawn so it is easily readable.
3. The picture that you create around your letter should have something to do with the subject of the story.
4. The picture should blend with the letter. Notice how the Easter lily in this letter is in front of the "Q" but does not hide it.
5. You may wish to put a border around your illuminated letter to frame it.

Directions:

1. On the following page, write an Easter story or poem. Be sure to leave out the first letter of the first word.

2. Following the pointers given above, create your own illuminated letter in the space to the right, using the first letter of the first word of your story.

3. When the picture-letter is complete, cut it out and glue it to the space provided on your story page.

Here are some words that could be used to start your story:

warm
eggs
purple
grass
morning
chicks
basket
chocolate

© Carson-Dellosa Publ. CD-0946

319

Name _____

Name_____
Directions:

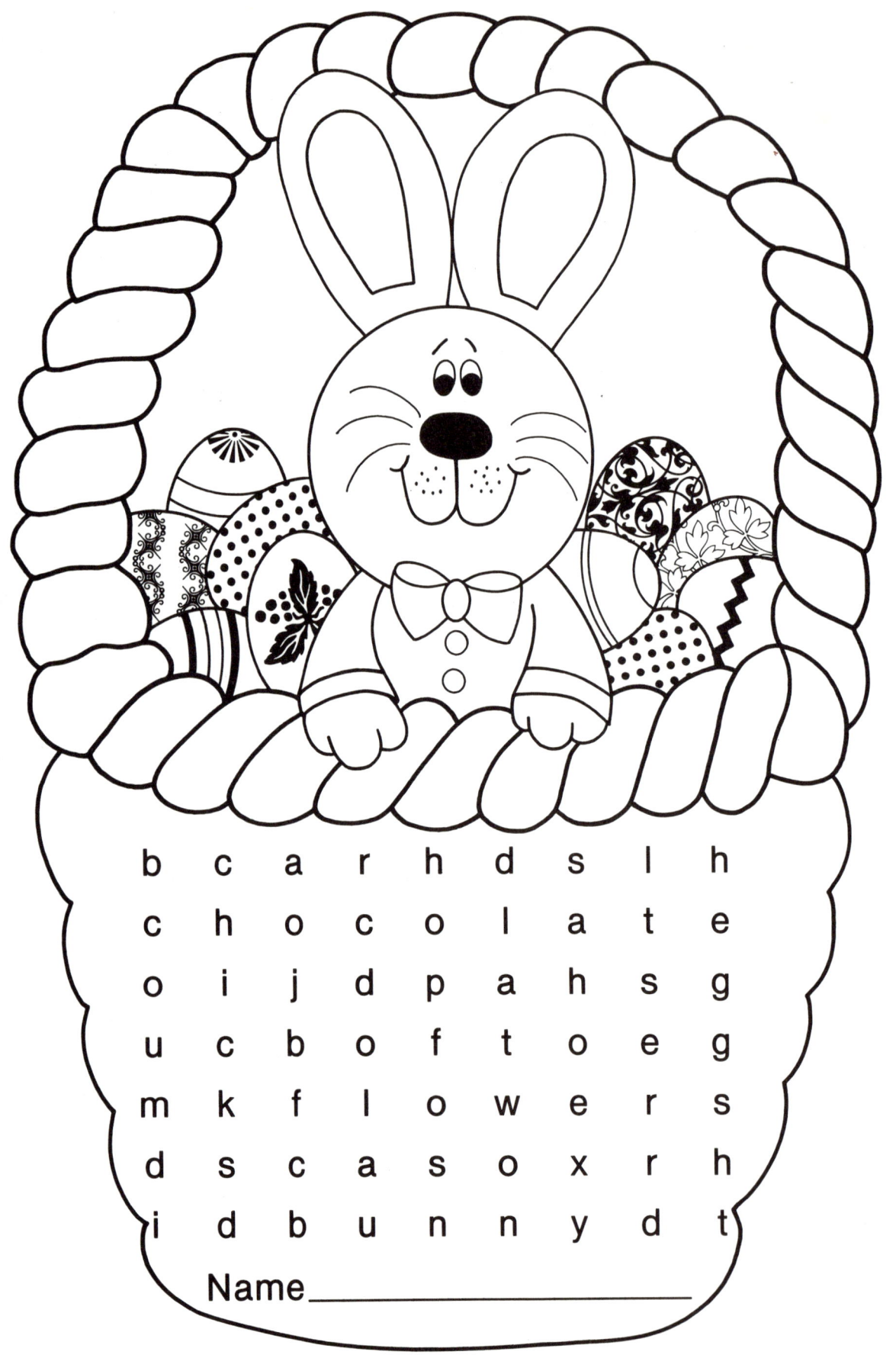

Put a circle around: chocolate, chicks, hop, eggs, flowers, bunny

Name _____

Fancy Rabbits

Color all of the pieces. Cut out the pictures on the right and decorate the rabbits below.

© Carson-Dellosa Publ. CD-0946

323

Name _____

Betsy Bunny

Follow these directions to make Betsy Bunny. (pp. 324-325).

1. Color the nose black.
2. Color the inside of both ears pink.
3. Color the bow orange.
4. Cut out all of the patterns.
5. Paste the nose on the X.
6. Paste the ears behind the top of the head.
7. Paste the bow on the top of the head or on the chin.

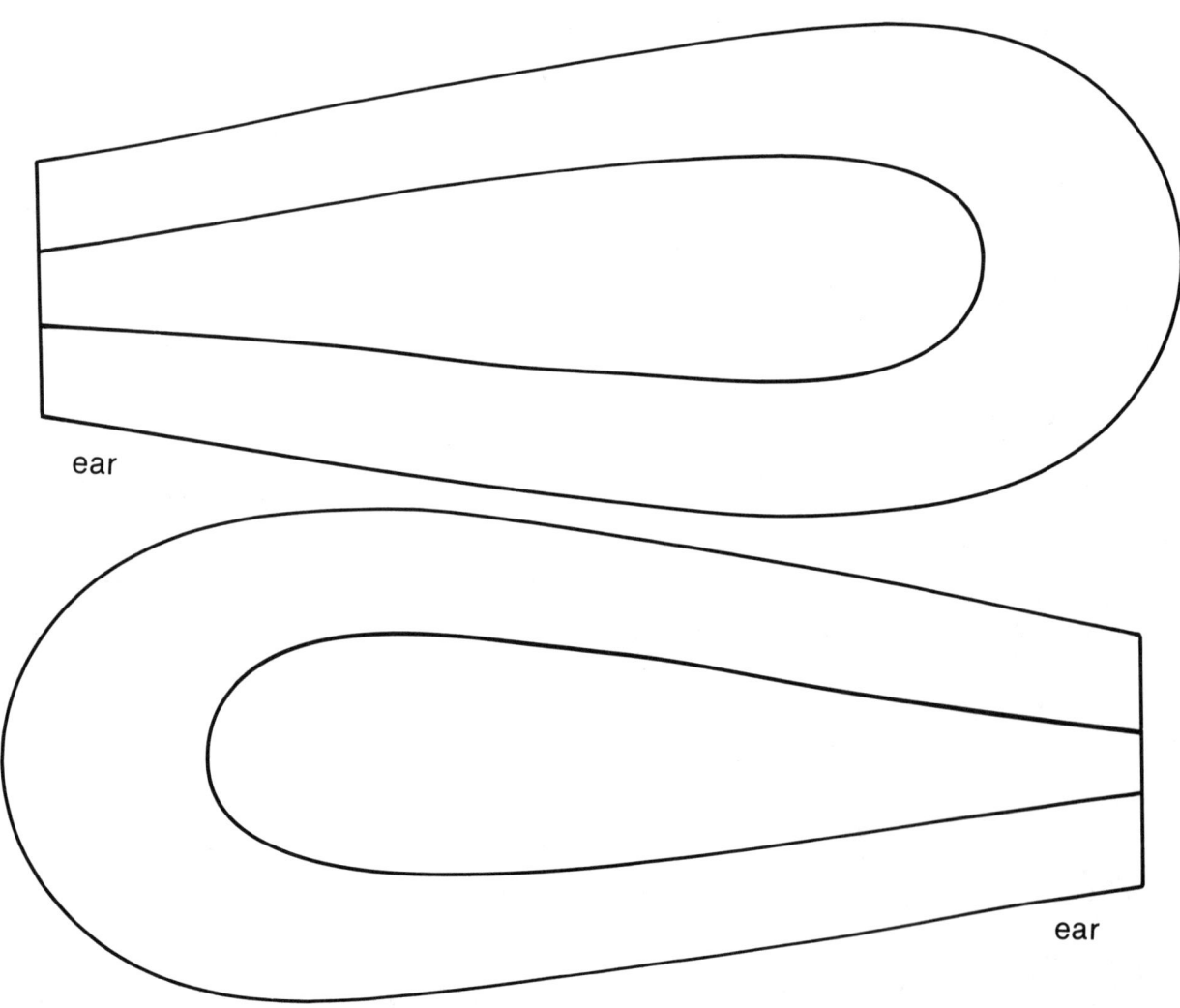

Name _____ **Betsy Bunny**

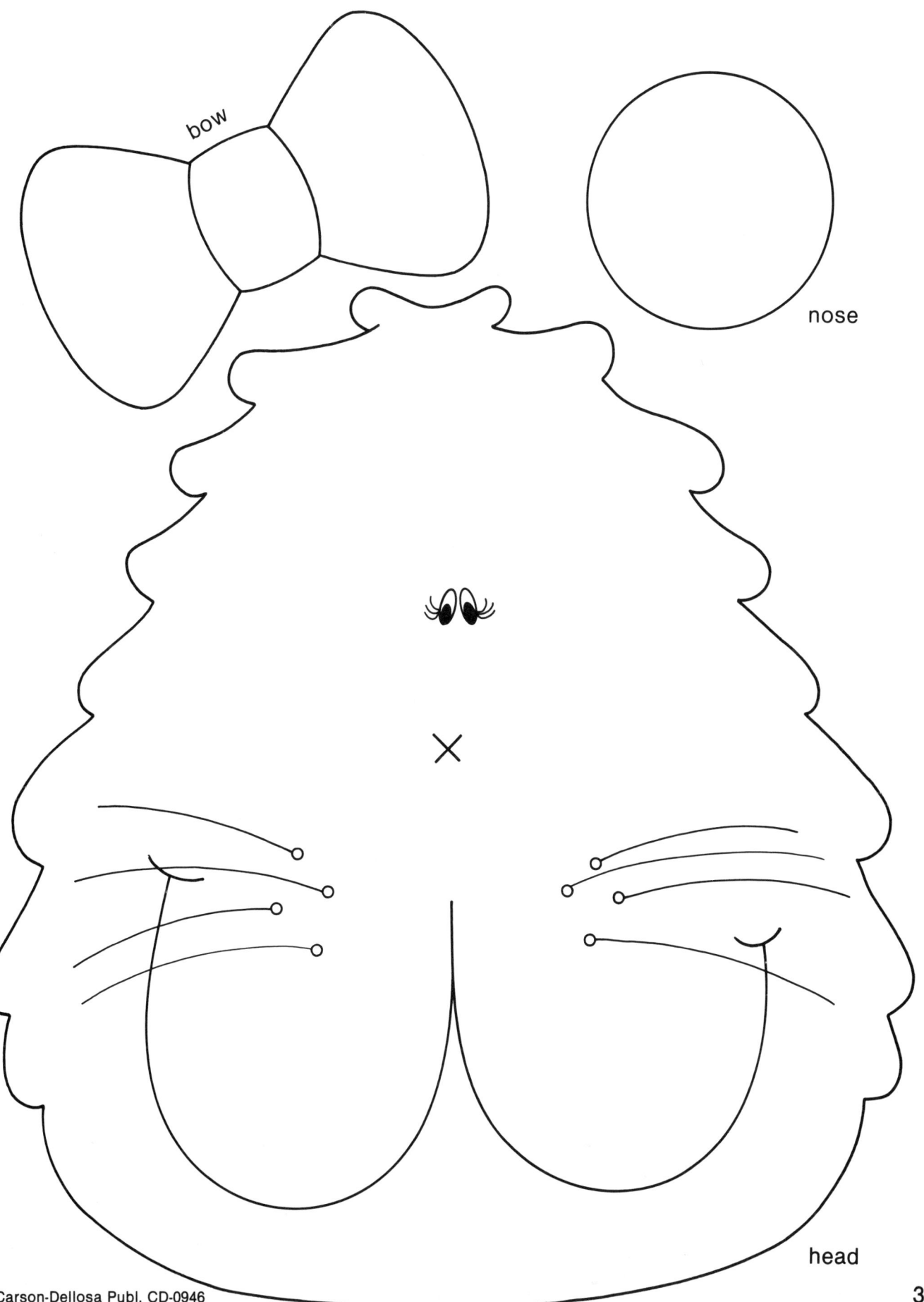

325

Name _____

Match the letters to the numbers below.
Find the message in the secret code.

1-O   3-A   5-D   7-U
2-E   4-G   6-R   8-Y

__ __ __ __ __ __ ,
8   1   7   6   2   3

__ __ __ __ __ __ __ !
4   1   1   5   2   4   4

Name_____
Directions:

Name_____

Directions:

328

© Carson-Dellosa Publ. CD-0946

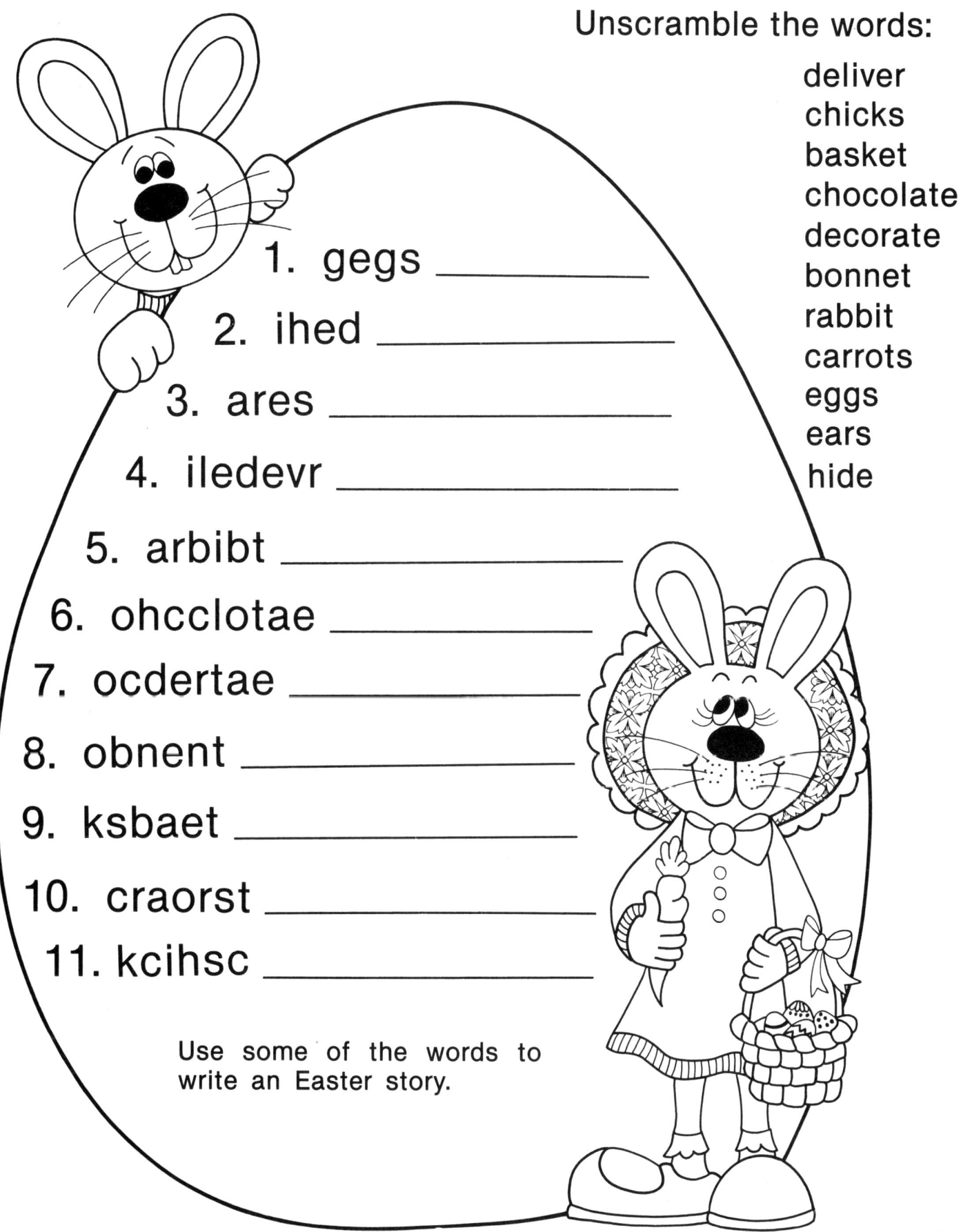

Name_____

Hidden Picture Painters
Name

Find and circle these objects:
candle, ax, baseball bat, traffic light, snail, wooden shoe, chicken's head, teepee, fried egg, crab, canoe, tooth, fishing pole, alligator, shoe

Name _____

Make your own cartoon! Write in each square what you think the character is saying.

Name _____

Easter Story Starter

Use some of the words below to write an Easter story.

decorate
hide   bunny   wait
delivered   package
eggs   cottontail   open
think   basket
egghunt   jelly beans
chocolate   shook   rattle   big
peek   inside   taste
hoped   excited   Easter
ribbon   lifting   carrots
paint   scarf   rabbit

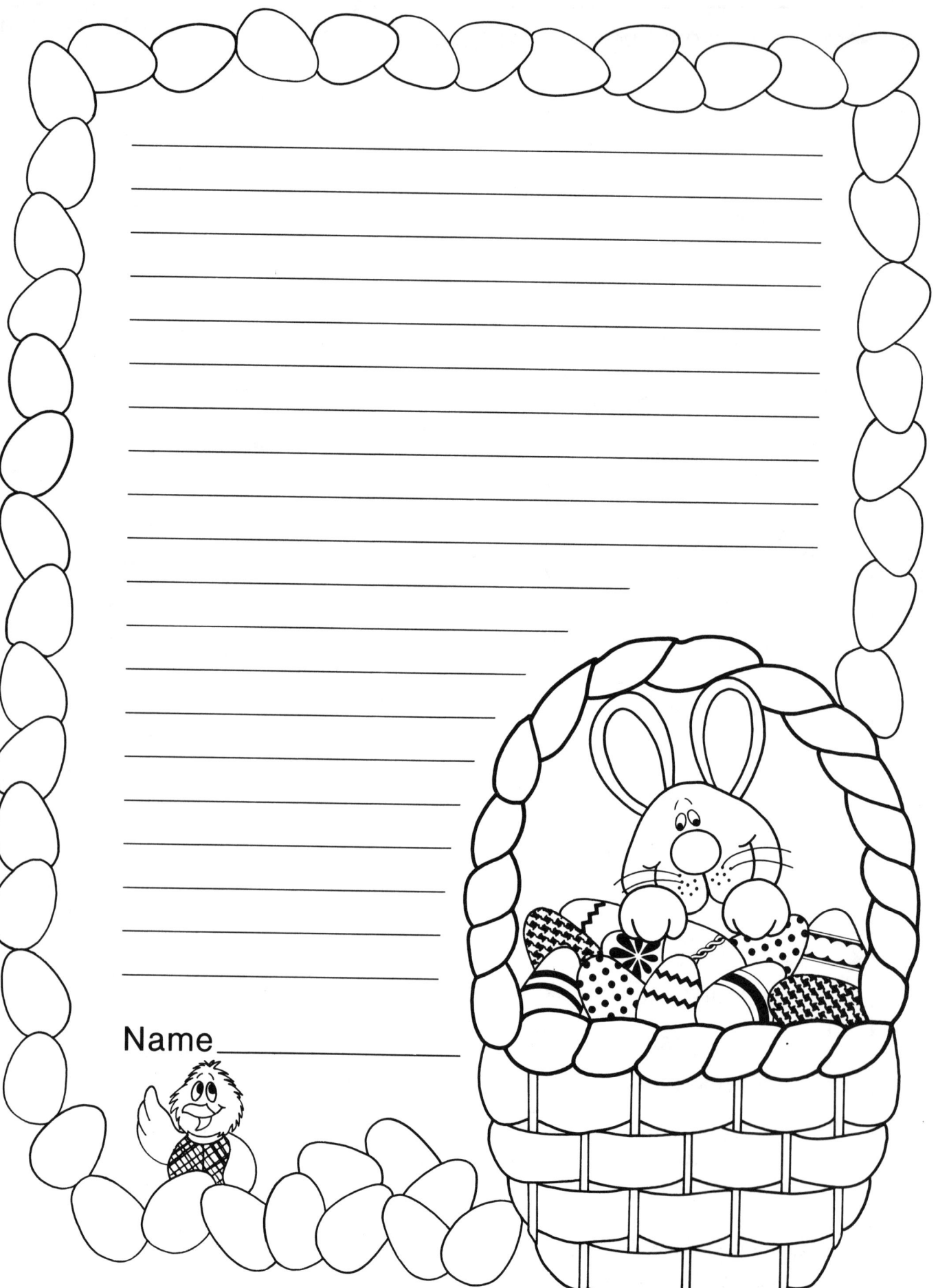

You've earned the **"TOP EGG"** award for outstanding work!

_____

has been doing "Eggs-tra" good work!

_____
Signed

A MOTHER'S AND FATHER'S DAY THANK YOU NOTE

Directions: Use the stationery provided to copy one of the sample notes or write your own message.

A Sample Mother's Day Thank You Note

Dear Mother,
    You are the very best Mom anyone can have. I don't say it every day but I really think it more often than you know. Thank you for being such a good mother.
    Love and kisses,
    Heidi

A FATHER'S DAY THANK YOU NOTE

Dad is great in lots of ways
But has he heard from you?
On Father's Day a little note
Will please him through and through.

A Sample Father's Day Thank You Note

Dear Dad,
    This special day is just for you. I hope you enjoy it.
    Thanks for being a great Dad.
    Your grateful son,
    Jason

The "Sunshine Award" goes to

_____.

Your work really brightens my day!

Signed _____

© Carson-Dellosa Publ. CD-0946

Your work is worth crowing about because

Signed _____

© Carson-Dellosa Publ. CD-0946

338

Name _____
Directions:

Name _____
Directions:

340

Name _____
Directions:

Name _____
Directions:

Name _____
Directions:

343

Name _____   **Seasons - Summer**

Read the clues. Find the correct word in the word list to complete each sentence. Write the word in the crossword puzzle.

Down

1. The last month of summer is _____ .
3. The season that follows spring is _____ .
4. The first month of summer is _____ .
5. We pack our lunches to go on a _____ .
7. My favorite summer food is corn on the _____ .

Across

2. We celebrate our country's birthday on the 4th of _____ .
6. On warm days we cool off by going _____ .
8. We like to play in the sand at the _____ .

Word List

picnic   beach
cob   swimming
summer
June
July
August

344

© Carson-Dellosa Publ. CD-0946

Name_____

Summer Story Starter

Use some of the words below to write a "fish tale."

Name _____

Name _____
Directions:

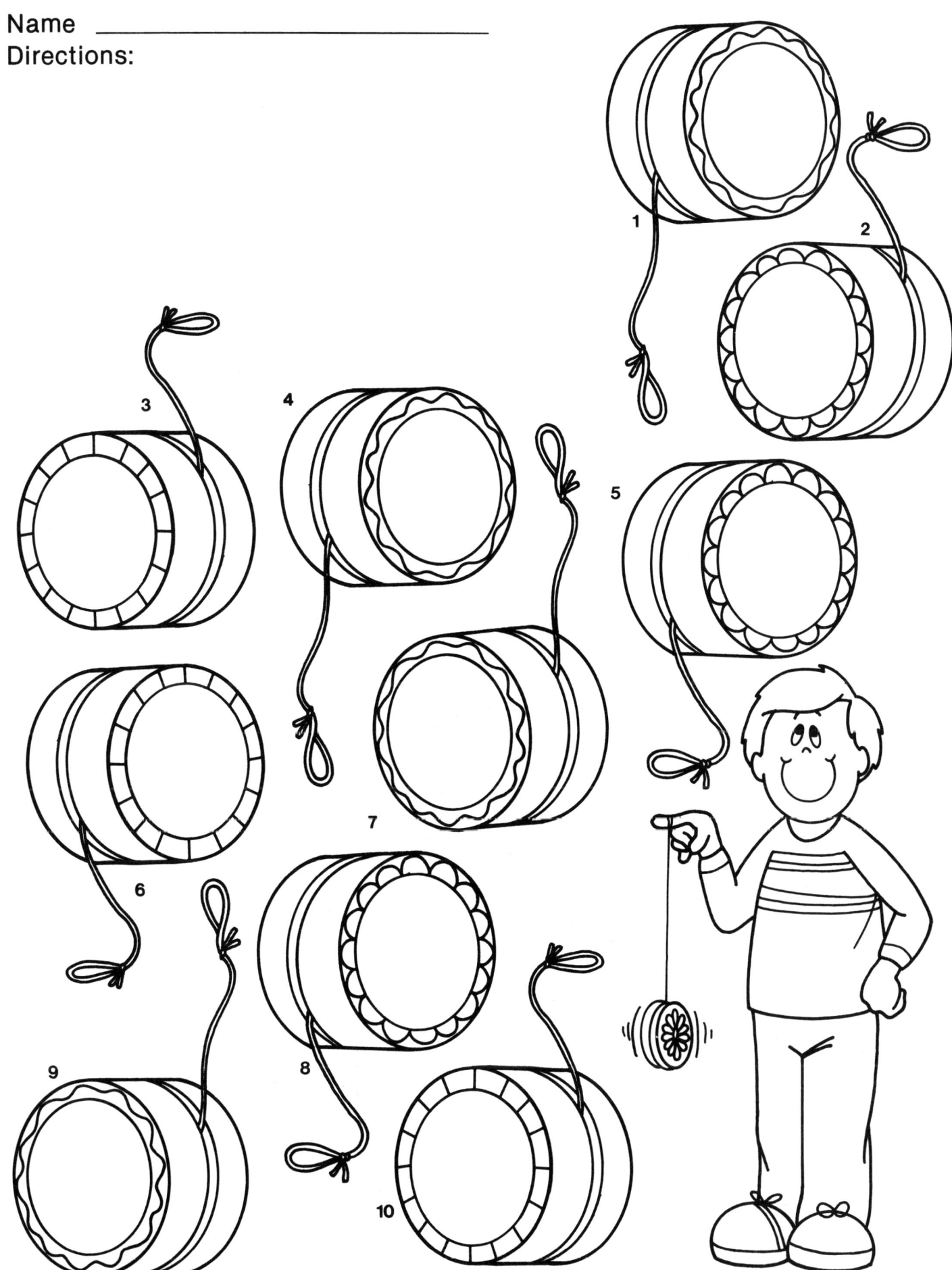

347

Name _____
Directions:

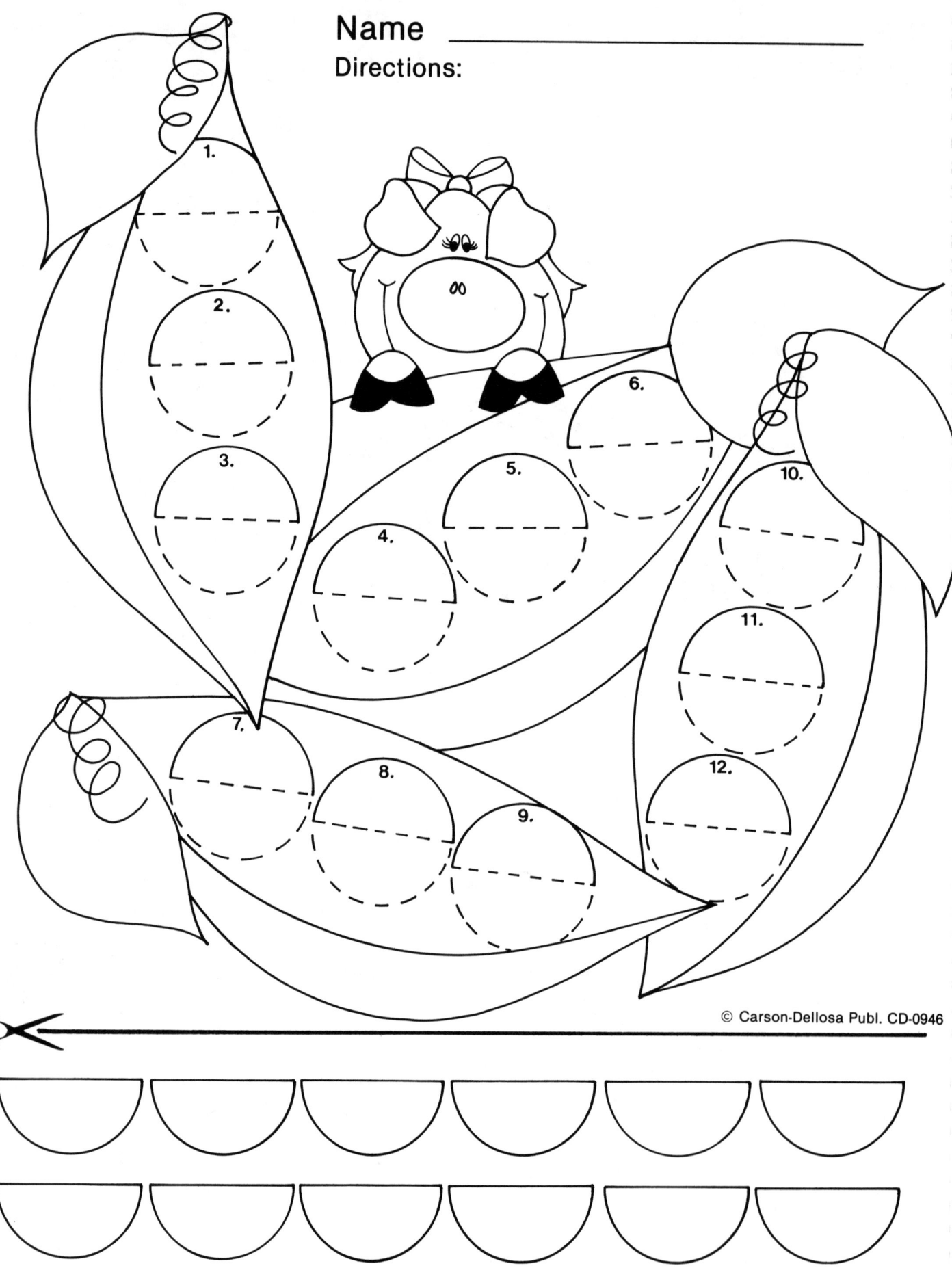

348

Name _____   **Summer Story Starter**

Directions:

Use some of the words below to write a story.

349

Name_____

Count by 2's to connect the dots.

Name_____
Directions:

Name _____
Directions:

Baseball Story Starter

Use some of the words below to write a baseball story. Color the pictures.

baseball, strike, fans, cheer, spring, bleachers, slid, teams, park, hot dogs, ran, scramble, game, peanuts, bases, wave, bat, outfield, score, swing, pitch, positions, outs, home run, players, hero, fun, play, umpire, errors, cheer, foul, single, bunt, double, steal

Name _____

**Baseball Madness—
What's Wrong With This Picture?**

Circle the things that are wrong in this picture.

Name _____

Count by 5's to connect the dots.

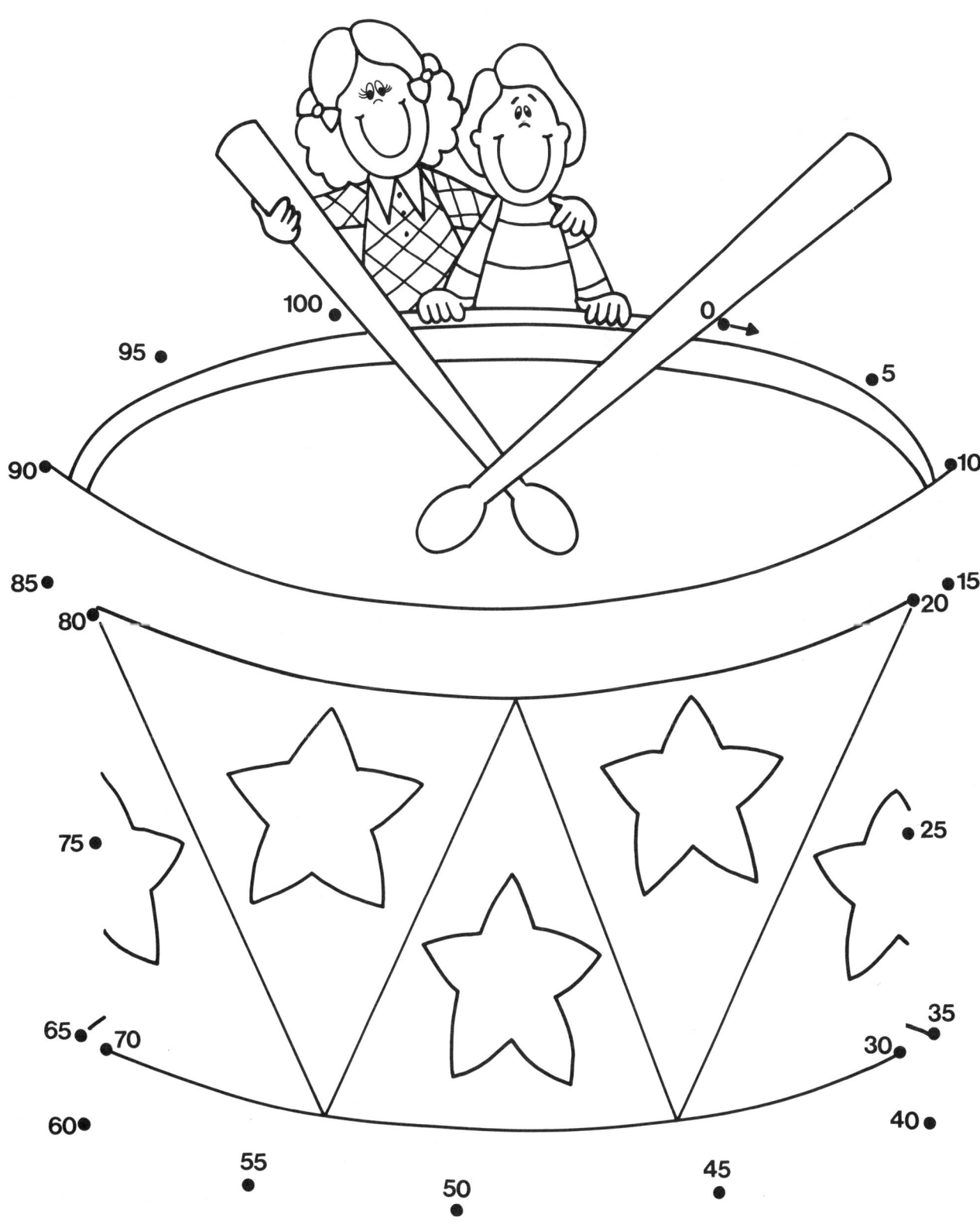

Name_____

Count by 10's to connect the dots.

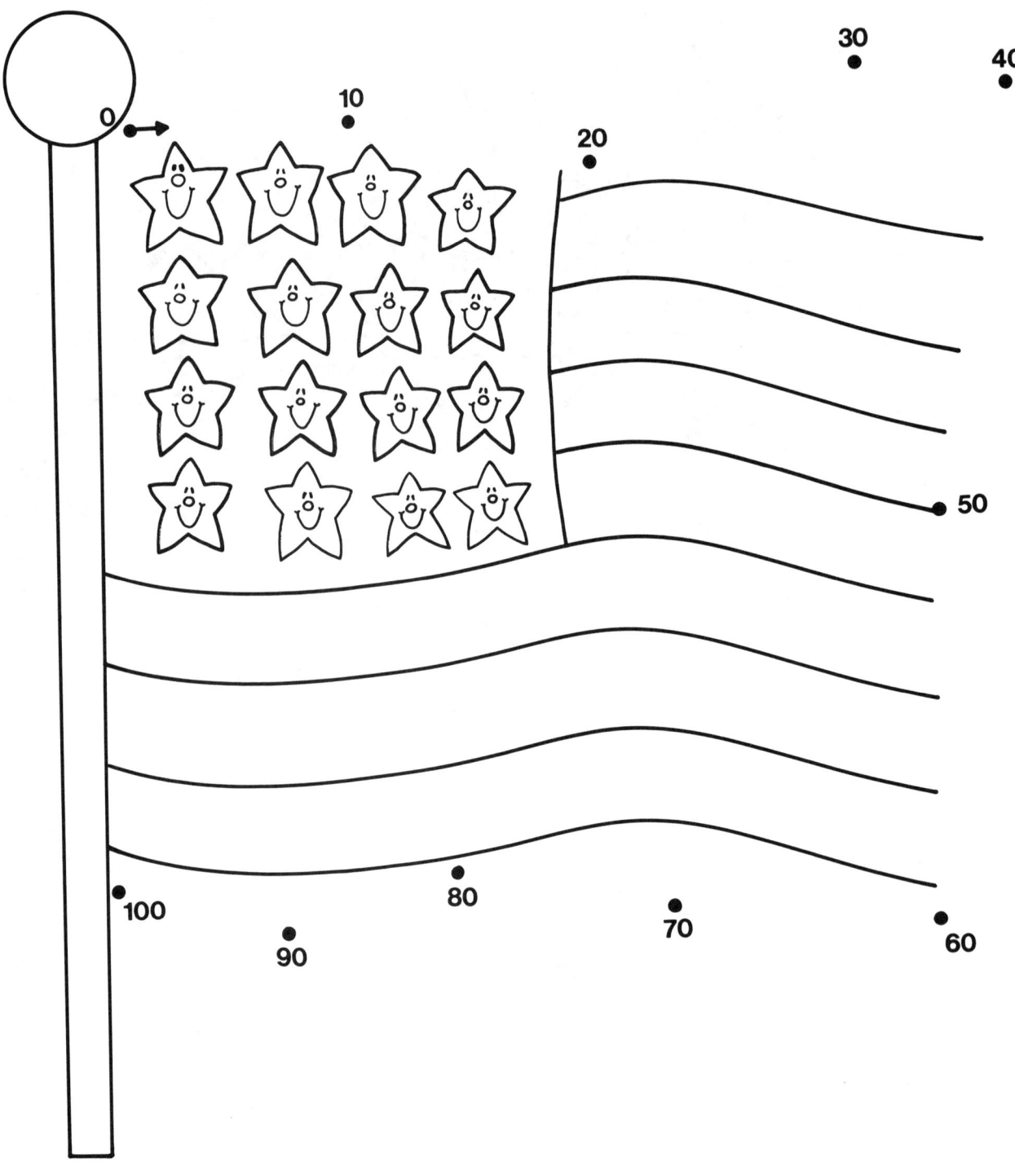

Birthday Story Starter

Name_____

Use some of the words below to write a story.

party
invite   place
friends   receive   time
respond   answer   excited   plan
celebrate   crepe   decorate   hang
streamers   colored   blow   puff
balloons   helium   knot   strings
hats   food   ice cream   cake
frosting   candy   punch   laughing
chase   games   contests   races
prizes   entertainment
cookies   magician   clown
snacks   music   dancing

Name _____

Name _____

Use the word list on the balloon to unscramble these words.

1. tgfi _____
2. yptar _____
3. aiybdrht _____
4. keac _____
5. ecnadl _____
6. oblalon _____
7. tivine _____
8. eci mcear _____
9. wocnl _____
10. egmsa _____

ice cream   birthday
invite   balloon
party   clown
gift   cake
candle   games

Name_____

Use the word list to unscramble the words on the ice cream cone.

Word List
cupcake
candy
present
bows
ribbons
ice cream
party
invite

1. ucapcke _____
2. repsnet _____
3. arpyt _____
4. wobs _____
5. cei mcera _____
6. ibrobns _____
7. niivte _____
8. dacyn _____

Use some of the words to write a story.

364

© Carson-Dellosa Publ. CD-0946

Name_____
Directions:

366

Name_____

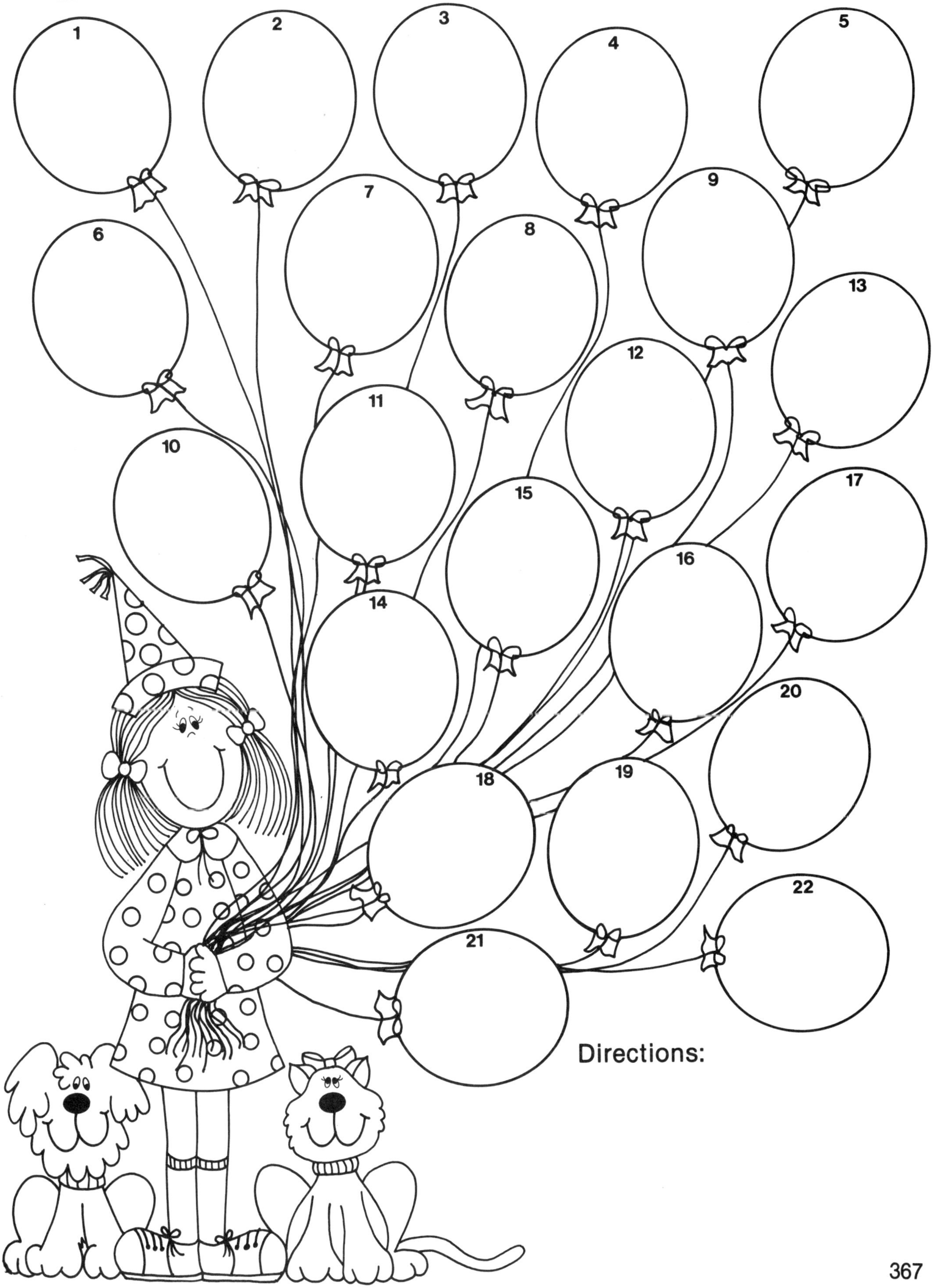

Directions:

367

Name _____   Secret Message

Match the letters to the numbers. Find the message in the secret code.

1-O   5-Y   9-A
2-T   6-F   10-H
3-D   7-S   11-K
4-N   8-R   12-G
       13-E

__,
3 1 4 2   6 1 8 12 13 2

  2 1   7 9 5

  2 10 9 4 11 7!

Name_____
Directions:

Name_____
Directions:

Name _____ Secret Message

Match the letters to the numbers. Find the message in the secret code.

__ __ __ __
11 4 10 2

__ __ __ __
 8 4   6 1

__ __ __
 7 9 2

__ __ __ !
 3 5 1

1 - N
2 - E
3 - F
4 - O
5 - U

6 - I
7 - T
8 - J
9 - H
10 - M
11 - C

Name _____

Circle the hidden words:

invite
fun
friend
cake
dogs
ice cream
music
guests
party

Name _____

Birthday Story Starter

Use some of the words below to write a birthday story.

birthday
planning
party
invitations
guests
decorate
everyone
lunch
stuffed
finally
cake

played   candles
leaving   singing
terrific   wish
thank you   cheer

streamers   balloons
                                        pour

baked   temperature   timer   removed   mix
  cooled   rack   icing   frosted   set
beat   favors   place   arrive   presents
  paper   ribbon   bows   cards   friends
  excitement   games   teams   laughing
      fun   hunt   clues   prizes

Name _____

Name _____
Directions:

1. 2. 3. 4. 5. 6. 7. 8. 9. 10.

© Carson-Dellosa Pbl. CD-0946

375

Name_____
Directions:

Name_____
Directions:

Name _____
Directions:

Name _____

Find the correct path on the maze to find your piece of birthday cake.

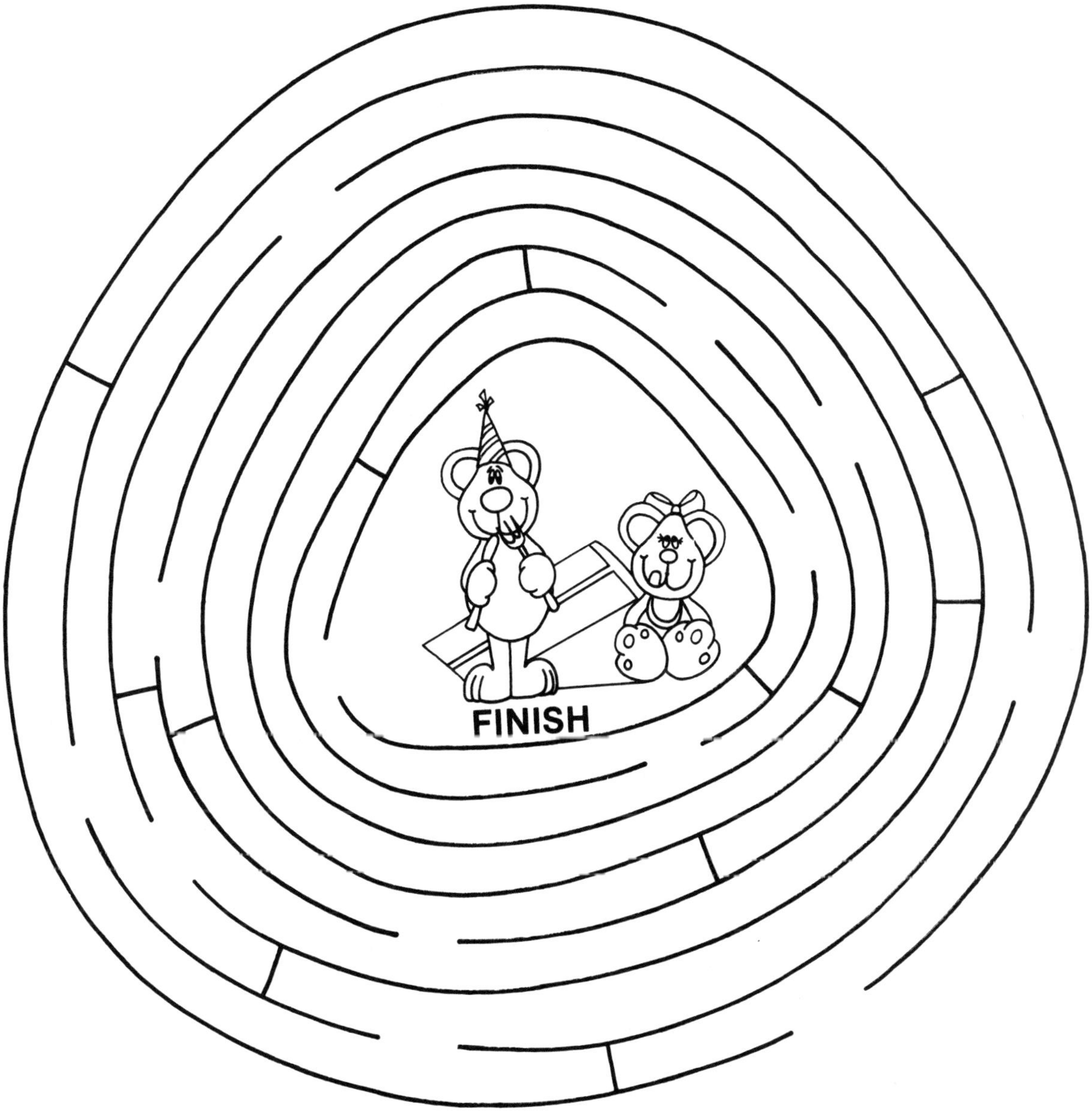

START

Name

Hidden Words

Circle the hidden words:

present
bows
gift
ribbons
games
cake
candy

```
i w v u c p f r v
b p r e s e n t o
l g i f t z x a e
c o m c b o w s k u d h
f i l o b r v c y q t l
n c p d o r c a n d y j
a l j s n l t k b m d m
g a m e s m r e p w c l
```

Name _____

Count the cakes.
There are _____ cakes.

Birthday Girl Award

Happy Birthday to

_____

_____
Date

From your Teacher and Classmates

Birthday Boy Award

Happy Birthday to

_____

_____
Date

From your Teacher and Classmates

A FRIENDSHIP NOTE

Directions: Use the stationery provided to copy one of the friendship notes. If you wish, write your own message. Color the picture and send the letter.

You and your friend
    Make quite a pair.
How about a note
    So your friend knows you care?

A Sample Note of Friendship

Dear Gene,
    It's wonderful knowing someone like you.
    You are really one great friend. I hope we can always be friends.

        Your pal,
        Eric

The school year is over.
    It's come to an end.
You want to tell Janet
    "I'm glad you're my friend."

A Sample Note of Friendship

Dear Janet,
    Even though the school year is over, I hope we can continue to be friends.
    People like you make everything nicer.

        Your friend,
        Sally